THE CHRISTIAN WOMAN'S ULTIMATE LOVE, SEX AND RELATIONSHIPS MANUAL

THE CHRISTIAN WOMAN'S ULTIMATE LOVE, SEX AND RELATIONSHIPS MANUAL

Finally The Truth For Those Married Or Single:
God Wants All Of Us To Know His Secrets

LORI MICHELE

iUniverse, Inc.
Bloomington

The Christian Woman's Ultimate Love, Sex and Relationships Manual
Finally the Truth for those Married or Single: God wants all of us to know his secrets

iUniverse books may be ordered through booksellers or by contacting:

iUniverse
1663 Liberty Drive
Bloomington, IN 47403
www.iuniverse.com
1-800-Authors (1-800-288-4677)

ISBN: 978-1-4759-6677-0 (sc)
ISBN: 978-1-4759-6683-1 (ebk)

Printed in the United States of America

iUniverse rev. date: 12/19/2012

TABLE OF CONTENTS

INTRODUCTION

One of my facebook friends posted the most interesting status: he asked "Why do some women allow themselves to be used and abused by men for years and then try to get a good guy to come to the rescue at the end?" Some of the respondents said that women need to learn to be more independent. Other responded that men should want to help women when they are down. This question really hit home for me and I had to really think about a response. Finally, I said, "*We are not very wise when we are young. We learn through experience what is really important in life. The wisest of us are probably happily married now with three or more children, so you do not meet many of them on the singles scene. I think that women who have made mistakes should be more transparent. They should tell the younger women their story so that there can be more wise young women who do not have to learn everything the hard way. They could learn just by watching and observing. This epidemic of women wearing themselves out with the wrong types of men or trying to be independent and declaring that they do not need men also has something to do with what happened in the 1960's. Prior to the 1960's, it was simply tradition for the younger women to learn from the older women and for cultural norms to be passed down. Then the 1960's came and everybody suddenly wanted to do their own thing and find their own way. Many women are just waking up to the fact that the old way was best all along. The Women's Liberation Movement made so many promises and yet delivered so little. Many of us are just now realizing that we were duped.*" I made the realization that I was duped by the Women's Liberation Movement back in 1998. After spending years feeling empty inside and going from one heartbreaking relationship to another, I finally discovered the missing link: God's wisdom through the Holy Bible. As I read John Gray's **Mars and Venus** series, I began to see the connection between traditional dating practices and the wisdom of the Bible. Once I started approaching men using these principles, I found out that the bible is not just this old outdated book that has nothing to do with our current lives. I discovered that it contains timeless wisdom that millions of young women need right now.

There is a serious issue with dating in the church today. Many Christian youngsters grew up in the age of the book "I Kissed Dating Goodbye". Somehow this book made many singles feel that it is a sin to go on dates. I have met several young Christian women in their thirties who have not been on dates in 2, 5 and sometimes 10 years. They claim that they are waiting for God to send them the right person. One young lady in this category said that there was a nice guy at church who really wanted to take her out, but she turned him down because she does not believe in dating. Later, he married a friend of hers and she is sure that somehow God made a serious mistake on this one. As I listened, I was mortified that she was mistrusting God for the fruits of her following a legalistic rule that was almost guaranteed to leave her with little hope for marriage or even a date. Many of us have forgotten that dating is simply the act of getting to know people. We can use Godly principles in dating just like we can in looking for a job or trying to find a house. "Thou shall not date" is simply not found in the bible. However, "thou shall love and trust the Lord" is the central theme of this book.

Other Christians realize the folly of following legalistic rules; however, they have thrown out the wisdom of the bible along with the unbiblical legalistic rules. I have met many young Christians including members of the clergy who stated that the bible's teachings on sexuality and unselfishness were intended for a previous time in history. They feel that much of the bible has no relevance and its principles do not apply to us today. Many Christians have never taken the biblical rules about sexuality seriously. Their attitude is that "God understands that we have needs and he will forgive us." While it is true that God is merciful and forgiving he is also holy. When we sin sexually, we temporarily lose our peace and fellowship with God. We suffer the penalty of our decision whether we realize it or not. When I was younger, I used to think that God just enjoyed testing us. Now I realize that he has rules for sexuality because he loves us and he knows what is best for us. He gives us his wisdom in the Holy Bible so that we can live the best possible life.

Luckily, Dr. Emerson Eggerichs' book **Love and Respect** and the show "Marriage Today" by Jimmy and Karen Evans have done an amazing job of bringing biblical wisdom about marriage to life for millions of us. The one problem is that there is plenty of great information for those who are married, but little useful information for those who are single. I realized this while attending a singles class at a local church in Katy, Texas. The singles were studying a book designed to make them proud of singlehood while the married couples were studying the biblically inspired book The *Love Dare*, by Steven and Alex Kendrick. The married members of the church were learning how to be more unselfish and loving towards one another while the singles were learning to be more self-focused and proud of singlehood. The single's book emphasized how we should feel perfectly content as singles and should have no desire for marriage. This book made it seem like being single is better than being married and offered no practical advice about how to navigate the world of being single. It seems that the church's message to singles is to be single and satisfied and avoid dating. Many others in the church ignore the traditional church and advocate a more worldly approach that is even less biblical. I will never forget when I went for counseling at the age of 23 because I just could not get any of my relationships with men to work. The pastor of the church that I was attending said that I needed a sex coach to teach me how to make a man never want to leave. I was shocked that a member of the clergy would say such a thing. Many years later, I got a clue about where this pastor was coming from. A young lady was fighting with her husband and she decided to share some of her pain with her facebook friends. She was asking about what qualifies a person to be a counselor in the church. I responded that a counselor should trust the word of God and should counsel from a biblical perspective. Several pastors disagreed with me stating that things have changed since biblical times and we must give advice based on modern times, not biblical times. My final response was that "God's Word is above your human opinions and feelings."

We live in a world that encourages us to live by feelings while God wants us to live by his principles. These principles are outlined in the Holy Bible. The bible is our own personal GPS that guides us to the right direction. Similar to a real GPS, if we ever get off track, God knows how to recalibrate our lives and lead us in the right direction. That direction is always towards him. God has done this time and time again in my life. Even though I have made many mistakes, God used each of my bad experiences for his glory. According to scripture, **"And we know that all things work together for good to them that love God, to them who are the called according to *his* purpose"** (Romans 8:28, KJV). Some of my experiences gave me the wisdom to minister to young women and comfort them with compassion and love. Other experiences have led to great personal growth and development for me. God saw to it that no experience was wasted. His message to his disciples after the miracle of the bread is the same as his message to us. He said, **"Gather up the fragments that remain, that nothing be lost"** (John 6:12, KJV). Regardless of how sordid our past may be, Jesus can cleanse us and make us as if we are as white and pure as snow. If he did this for Mary Magdalene and Rahab who were both prostitutes, he can certainly do this for us.

We live in a culture that idolizes success. Those of us who have not lived perfectly successful lives may feel lost and hopeless. The good news of the gospel is that Jesus came to bring hope to the hopeless and save that in which was lost. Jesus comforts us by the fact that God has always used imperfect women just like you and me to fulfill his purposes. In the genealogy of Jesus, only five women are mentioned and not one of them were perfect: There is Tamar, the woman who posed as a prostitute; there is Rehab the prostitute who gave birth to Ruth's Boaz; there is Ruth who came from the idol-worshipping Moabites; there is Bathsheba, who cheated on her husband and later married David; and then there is Mary, the virtuous woman who got pregnant out of wedlock even though she was a virgin. (Matthew 1: 1-16, KJV) According to worldly wisdom, Jesus should have come through a lineage of perfect virtuous women who never seemed to have a single problem. Worldly wisdom dictates that only perfect women who have "arrived" at some great spiritual plane "deserve" to be used by God. In reality, God turns worldly wisdom upside down; he often uses the weak and the foolish by the world's standards to put the wise to shame.

Jesus Christ himself was perfect; yet, he was rejected by his own family, rejected by the Pharisees and rejected by the people of his own town. The Jews asked that a murderer be returned to them so that Jesus, a perfectly innocent man, could be killed instead. Peter boldly proclaimed to the elders that the power that allowed him to heal a crippled man was from **"Jesus Christ of Nazareth, whom you crucified, but whom God raised from the dead, that this man stands before you healed. He is 'the stone you builders rejected, which has become the [cornerstone]' (Psalm 118:22). Salvation is found in no one else, for there is no other name under heaven given to men by which we must be saved"** (Acts 4: 10-12, NIV). Throughout scripture, God often used those who were despised and rejected in the most profound ways. We serve a God who can make something out of nothing or make something into nothing according to his divine plans and purposes. The one who was despised the most, turned out to be the most important figure in history. According to Isaiah, **"He is despised and rejected of men; a man of sorrows, and acquainted with grief: and we hid as it were our faces from him; he was despised, and we esteemed him not . . . he [bore] the sin of many, and made intercession for the transgressors"** (Isaiah 53: 3-12).

Many of the women that God used the most have had less than perfect lives. The sinful woman who anointed Jesus' feet with perfume before his death was criticized by the Pharisees and Jesus' disciples while Jesus gave her great honor by stating, **"Why are you bothering this woman? She has done a beautiful thing to me . . . When she poured this perfume on my body she did it to prepare me for burial. I tell you the truth, wherever the gospel is preached throughout the world, what she has done will also be told, in memory of her"** (Matthew 26: 10-13, NIV). Jesus pointed out that she showed great love for him and she was even more loving than the Pharisees. He forgave her many sins because of her great love and her great faith. God forgave the many sins of Mary Magdalene who was a prostitute with seven demons inside of her. She became one of Jesus' most devoted followers and she had the honor of being one of the first to discover that Jesus was resurrected. The risen Christ instructed her and the other Mary to **"Go and tell my brothers to go to Galilee; there they will see me"** (Matthew 28: 10, NIV). In a strange twist of fate, Mary Magdalene, a former prostitute, became the first post resurrection evangelist.

Jesus allowed a sinful woman that he met at the well to become Samaria's first unofficial evangelist. This woman had spent years searching for love in all the wrong places. She had five husbands and now she was living with a man. She could not find the love that her heart craved from a man. This woman was too ashamed to go to the well with the other women of the town because the other women did not respect her lifestyle. While the women of the town rejected her, Jesus loved and accepted her and offered her the only water that would fulfill the thirst of her restless soul. Jesus knew that she was looking for love in all the wrong places and the love that she needed was found only in him. Jesus said, **"Whosoever [drinks] of the water that I shall give him shall never thirst: but the water that I shall give him shall be in him a well of water springing up into everlasting life"** (John 4:14, KJV). The Samaritan woman said, **"I know that 'Messiah' (called Christ) is coming. When he comes, he will explain everything**

to us" (John 4: 25, NIV). Jesus directly told her, **"I who speak to you am he"** (John 4:26, NIV). This Samaritan woman, who was despised and rejected by her own people, finally found the love and acceptance that she was looking for. This gave her a boldness and sense of courage to go on with her life. She spread the good news about Jesus Christ to everyone she came in contact with in Samaria. News spread and many became followers of Christ after meeting Jesus for themselves.

Similar to the Samaritan woman, Jesus calmed my restless heart with his love and devotion. He gave me a peace that no earthly man could ever give me. He loved me as I am. He did not wait for me to change to start loving me, he loved me flaws and all because he is love. He quietly whispered to me, **"Come to me you who are weary and burdened, and I will give you rest"** (Matthew 11:28, NIV). As he courted me, he showed me that he was the husband that I had been searching for all of my life. He met me staring in the mirror feeling weary from an intense spiritual battle. My soul became so tired and restless that I finally gave Jesus full authority of my dating life and relationships even though I feared that this would be the end of my social life. In reality, my dating life did not begin until I gave the Lord control of it. I gave up a life chasing heartache for a personal relationship with the **"King of Kings and Lord of Lords"** (Revelation 19:16, KJV). Immediately after my surrender, a peace that is beyond human understanding came over me and the spiritual battle that I was facing was won in an instant.

Since my surrender, the Lord has provided for me, protected me and professed his love for me over and over again. Contrary to my negative expectations, surrendering to Christ made me a male magnet instead of a bitter, lonely dried up prune. Jesus has given me great favor with men and poured his love out to me so that I could share it with others. Jesus is no respecter of persons. Jesus' ultimate promise to all of us is that his grace is sufficient. In His presence we find fullness of joy. We find a happiness that no man can give. We find a peace that no good circumstances could guarantee. We find the strength to forgive and love others. When we delight in Him, he often gives us our heart's desires. Even when he decides not to give us what we thought we wanted, he always provides us with a deeper revelation of him and he allows us to discover that his presence is more than enough. Once we get our relationship with God right, somehow our other relationships begin to fall into place. When we find ourselves disappointed or upset, we are comforted to know that he is with us. His presence is our comfort and his presence is our peace.

CHAPTER 1

Learning to Sit Where Others Sit

Love: Our One Essential Need in Relationships

When it comes to relationships, it is essential to ask questions and get to know the people in our lives rather than just assume that we have them all figured out. We must learn to sit where others sit. As a teacher, there is always the temptation to size my students up prematurely and develop fixed expectations of them. However, experience has taught me that this is a big mistake. When students see us do this, they lose respect for us because they know that we are being unfair and judgmental. Also, we lose the opportunity to inspire and motivate others as well as the opportunity for them to inspire and motivate us. There was a student several years ago who always looked at the floor whenever I began teaching. At first, I assumed that he was being intentionally disrespectful. Luckily, my inner Spirit prompted me to speak with him one-on-one and ask "Why do you always stare at the floor as soon as I start teaching?" To my surprise he said, "Miss, I have been telling my mom and telling my mom that I have ADHD and she will not get me any medicine for it. Even the coaches have noticed that I can't pay attention and they have to call my name three or more times before I answer them." I spoke to him about some things that he could do to focus better and the behavior improved tremendously. By the end of the year, he had taken me to the side and told me that I was his all-time favorite teacher. I thank God for the wisdom to ask what was going on rather than assume. We ended the year on a positive note, but things could have gone badly had I treated him as if he were purposely being rude and disrespectful towards me. This courtesy of asking before assuming and looking for opportunities to help others is a courtesy that is sometimes missing in our churches. Jesus Christ said, **"This is my Commandment, that [you] love one another as I have loved you. [There is no] greater love . . . than this: that a man lay down his life for his friends"** (John 15: 13-14, KJV). Jesus loved us so much that he was willing to die for us. The least that we can do is be willing to die to self for him. We show that we have died to self when we put the needs of others ahead of our own and trust that God will take care of our needs. Many of us have mistakenly concluded that we will be known as Christians by our perfect behavior; in reality, the mark of a true Christian is our love for God and for each other.

We cannot give that in which we have not first received. Our primary source of love is Jesus Christ. He loved us so much that he was willing to die for us so that we may live. John wrote, **"let us love one another, for love comes from God. Everyone who loves has been born of God and knows God, because God is love. This is how God showed his love among us: he sent his one and only Son into the World that we might live through him. This love: not that we loved God, but that he loved us and sent his Son as an atoning sacrifice for our sins. Dear friends, since God so loved us, we also ought to love one another. No one has ever seen God: but if we love one another, God lives in us and his love is made complete in us . . . . God is love. Whoever lives in love lives in God and God in him"** (I John 4: 7-16, NIV). We are bathed in God's love whenever we spend quality time in his presence. We grow closer to him and receive his love by feeding our Spirit. This is done through daily prayer, bible reading and worship. These activities should never become meaningless entries on our "To Do" list. Rather, they should be the first priority for us each time that we wake up in the morning. Many of us start our day running on spiritual empty. We make decision after decision without first consulting God. The only way to stay spiritually full and satisfied is to make being in God's presence our number one priority.

Yesterday's manna is not enough to meet today's challenges. When the Israelites were in the wilderness, they were told that they would be given just enough manna for each day. If they tried to hoard and store extra, it would grow stale. Similar to how the Israelites required fresh physical food daily, we need fresh spiritual food daily. When we fail to feed ourselves spiritually, our lives grow stale. We stop displaying the fruit of the spirit because we fail to feed it. The Apostle Paul described the dilemma that we all face when we try to do good by our own efforts. He said, **"For I know that in me (that is in my flesh) [dwells] no good thing; for to will [to do good] is present with me, but how to perform that which is good I find not"** (Romans 7: 18, KJV). The fruit of the flesh is "**sexual immorality, impurity, idolatry, hatred, discord, jealousy, selfish ambition, dissension, factions and envy . . .**" (Galatians 5:19-20, NIV).

When we spend quality time with God, it shows. We become more patient, kind and humble. When we spend time nourishing the Spirit, we develop the fruit of the Spirit which is **"love, joy, patience, kindness, goodness, faithfulness, gentleness and self-control"** (Galatians 5:22, NIV). God pours out his love to us so that we can share it with others. We become more responsive to the needs of others when we have spent the right amount of time with Him. When we make assumptions about people before asking them about their lives and showing that we care, we show a lack of love and concern for others. This lack of love is due to starving the Spirit while feeding the flesh with too many conversations filled with gossip and envy, too much television, too much time on the computer and too much time focused on ourselves instead of God. The Apostle Paul's warning to the Galatians is his warning to us today: **"You my brothers [and sisters] were called to be free, but do not use your freedom to indulge the sinful nature; rather, serve one another in love. The entire law is summed up in a**

single command: 'Love your neighbor as yourself.' If you keep on biting and devouring each other, watch out or you will be destroyed by each other" (Galatians 5: 13-15, NIV).

Despite popular opinion, Christianity is not about rules and checklists. Rather, it is about relationships. It is about becoming rightly related to Jesus Christ and through this relationship becoming rightly related to God, the Father. In Paul's letter to Timothy, he said **"God our Savior wants all men to be saved and to come to knowledge of the truth . . . There is one God and one mediator between God and men, the man Christ Jesus."** (I Timothy 2: 3-5, NIV) We are not only called to trust Jesus for our salvation, but we are called to become like him. According to Romans 8:29, **"For those God foreknew he also predestined to be conformed to the image of his Son . . ."** (Romans 8:29, NIV). We become like those who we spend time with. If we spend time with ourselves and think about ourselves all the time, we become more selfish. If we spend time with gossiping friends and seek the company of only certain people we become more self-righteous. If we spend time with Jesus, we become more Christ-like. We know that we have spent enough time basking in his love when we genuinely become concerned with the needs of others. We become less concerned with what people do wrong and more concerned with how we can help people make their lives right. This is how Jesus related to the sinners. Rather than condemn sinners, he decided to love them despite their sins and this motivated them to want to change for him. When a sinful woman found out that Jesus would be dining at the home of a Pharisee, **"she bought an alabaster jar of perfume, and as she stood behind him at his feet weeping, she began to wet his feet with her tears. Then she wiped them with her hair, kissed them and poured perfume on them . . . Then Jesus said to her, "Your sins are forgiven . . . Your faith has saved you. Go in peace"** (Luke 7:37-38, 48-50, NIV). While the Pharisees were busily passing judgment on Jesus for letting a sinful woman touch him and passing judgment on the woman for her lifestyle, Jesus' love was healing her and causing her to renounce her life of sin.

Love is the primary tool that we can use to motivate our kids to make positive changes. Our kids are not motivated by the feeling of love, but the act of love. They want to know that we accept them for who they are. They want the freedom to be imperfect and still be loved. A lot of parents try to be perfect around their children. However, this is not what they need most. Good teachers know that kids actually benefit from seeing us make mistakes and handling the mistakes well. It allows them to see that it is alright for them to make mistakes too. Our kids want for us to be honest with them, love them and accept them regardless of their flaws and mistakes. They want for us to discipline them and show them the right way. However, they do not want for us to be fake with them or judgmental towards them. They will accept criticism of their behavior, but they will become angry if we judge them as a person because of their behavior. There is a big difference between saying "you are so stupid" and saying "that was not a smart thing to do." There is a big difference between saying "you are such an awful person "and saying "that was an awful thing to do. "We have to deal with kids like God deals with us: he loves us sinners, but hates our sins.

When kids see that we care, they want to please us and share what is going on in their lives with us. Doing the right thing becomes natural rather than a chore for our kids when they feel that they can count on us for unconditional love. Good teachers have a way of winning the hearts of the most stubborn kids by showing them that we love them and care about them. We show that we care by being honest with them, listening to them and patiently guiding them in the right direction. Kids can tell if someone is speaking to them out of love or patronizing them out of a lack of respect for them. They can smell a phony compliment or an indirect putdown a mile away. For example, one kid greeted me at the door saying, "Ms. M, I am so mad at _____, she came to my game and when I got myself thrown out of the game for a foul, she said, 'You did such a good job, I am so proud of you.' She knows darn well that she was not proud of me at that moment. Does she think I am stupid?" Even though this teacher was nice enough to go and support this student at a game, the kid cared more about the insincerity of her compliment than the teacher's willingness to be there for him.

Over the years, I have taught my share of class clowns. Some of our kids are quite talented as comedians. Some of their best routines have been based on their frustration with adults for not being honest with them and failing to show genuine love and concern. Many of our kids are offended by our pasted on smiles and catchy phrases. They crave to see someone who is real and who really cares. My all-time favorite class clowns did two skits of a principal at my former school. I eventually made him perform the skits in front of the principal and he did not consider it funny at all. Perhaps the principal fully understood the deeper meaning of the skits. In the meantime, the assistant principals, the counselors, and most of the teachers thought that they were the funniest skits ever. The skits reflected this kid's frustration over being patted on the head and patronized all the time. In the first one, the kid says, "Ms. M, can you imagine what would happen if someone came to school with an AK 47?" I answered, "No, and please do not tell me." Of course, in his mind, this was his cue to tell me. He said, "I could see it now. [Our principal] would say smiling the entire time, 'Excuse me sir, we do not allow guns at _____Middle School. Please put the gun down. Sir, sir, sir, you just shot me in the tidy, please put the gun down." Since he caused everyone to erupt with laughter with his first skit, he came back the next day with another one. He said, "Ms. M, can you imagine what would happen if Mr. _____ (our assistant principal) fell down the stairs? I could see it now. He would fall down the stairs saying 'Sir, Sir, Sir, Sir, Sir, Sir.' Then boom, he makes it to the bottom. Then [our principal] would say, 'Excuse me sir, is everything alright? Sir, I will be back to help you as soon as I am finished eating my Quiznos sandwich." The kid actually felt that certain adults in his life would care more about a sandwich than helping someone. Unfortunately, many kids see Christians in the same light. They see lots of smiles and cute and catchy sayings, but they do not always feel the love of Christ in our presence. Instead, they often sense judgment without love and mercy. As Christians, we must work to keep our "love tank" full because people can really tell when we are running on empty no matter how hard we try to hide it.

Today, some kids are going through tragedies that are beyond human imagination and they may lack the ability to even handle a judgmental uncaring attitude. There was once a 13 year old girl in my class who truly struggled in Math. Before I began to speculate about what was wrong and what was needed for this child, something prompted me to ask about her situation. Instead of jumping to conclusions about her, I asked, "Where are you from?" She answered, "I am from Iraq." This was a surprise because I had assumed that she was Hispanic. Then I asked, "How is the education system in Iraq? Is it harder or easier than it is over here?" She answered, "It is much harder over here. The last time that I was in Iraq was in the sixth grade and my teacher did not teach us anything. She just allowed us to color all day. They did not really care if we learned anything." Then I said, "Aren't things getting better in Iraq? I thought that they were rebuilding the place and things were getting better and better." She answered, "No miss, the reason that we are here is because my family found a note at the door of our home stating that they would either have to convert to Islam they would kidnap and murder me within 24 hours." She went on to explain that the family decided to leave and they became one of thousands of homeless Christian refugees in Iraq. Eventually they got the opportunity to move to the United States. She told me that every member of her family that remained in Iraq has been killed. At this point, I became very weak and upset because I could not believe that this sweet young girl had to endure so much tragedy. The next thing that she stated almost made me cry. She said, "Miss, I was so upset last night and I cried while doing my homework because they bombed the entire neighborhood that I used to live in. That means that everyone who I had always known is now dead." I then said, "How were you able to do your homework? You are so positive and sweet. Your strength is amazing." She said, "It is because I am a Christian." It was so inspirational to hear her story and see her coping so well. This young lady who I could have classified as an unmotivated underachiever proved to be a brave champion who has overcome obstacles beyond my wildest imagination. She became a great inspiration to me once I humbled myself enough to discover who she is and what she is all about instead of proudly assuming that I already knew.

The inspirational young girl shows that we should never miss an opportunity to get to know someone and be a positive influence in their life. We never know what someone is going through until we humble ourselves enough to get to know them. People can sense a loving spirit that will accept them instead of judge them. We want to be the type of people that others feel comfortable with. For that to happen, people have to trust us and before they can trust us, they have to feel that we are capable of loving them. One of the tragedies of modern Christian culture has been the rise of the phony smile and parrot-like chatter about everything being great and wonderful when many of us are really dying inside. This lack of genuine emotion does not go unnoticed by those who are watching us. This "I am so perfect, why can't you be perfect like me?" attitude alienates us from each other. We don't feel comfortable sharing our hurts, pains and concerns for fear of being judged and criticized. So we put on this phony façade. We expect ourselves and others to be perfect when Jesus was the only perfect one to ever live. We must learn to be real with God, real with ourselves and real with each other. To walk in love is also to walk in truth.

The Real Reason that So Many People Leave the Church

It has often been said that Christianity is easy until we have to deal with Christians. Many of us have just plain given up on the idea of a loving vibrant church and have tried to find our own way to spiritual nourishment. According to George Barna, *"nearly four out of ten unchurched people in the United States avoid church life because of bad past experiences in a church or in relation to churched people. Whether the issue is judgment rendered against them by churched people, the lack of trust between congregants and church leaders, perceived hypocrisy in the lives of the churched, or outright incivility or meanness suffered at the hands of other church members, some 25 to 30 million adults stay away from Christian churches because of the past treatment they have experienced from the local body of Christ . . . The people who were called by God to represent him as lovers and healers failed"* [1].

For years, I had heard about the alarming number of people leaving the church because of feeling judged or mistreated, but I never took them seriously because I figured that people were just too sensitive and needed to learn how to handle problems without running away from them. My cousin told me that she refused to go back to church and that she knew several others just like her. Instead of empathizing with her and the others, I said, "You have to realize that people in the church are only human. If you feel that they are judgmental, tell them and then go to church to serve Jesus Christ, not people." Even though there was a lot of truth to what I told her, my decision to blow off someone else's pain caused God to divinely arrange for me to experience my own church hurt several months later. God has a way of making us understand people by forcing us to sit where they sit. The Lord supernaturally arranged for me to experience two church hurts within a 2 year time period. I knew that this was a divine arrangement because this had never happened to me before. God orchestrated the opportunity for me to sit where others sit so that I could grow in my own love walk. I finally got the opportunity to feel that desire to run rather than confront. I finally got to feel the pain of being considered unworthy of consideration. It was far more difficult and painful than I ever imagined. At the same time, I am so thankful that I experienced these church hurts. In both instances, the pain that I felt made me vow to never treat anyone the way that I was treated and both experiences humbled me greatly. Now I can relate to those who have experienced a church hurt in a more loving and sympathetic way. This experience also taught me that I must seek my identity in Jesus Christ, not in my church, or my friends or my job. Most important, this experience also gave me the opportunity to discover a serious problem within the body of Christ: the problem of a loveless, self-righteous way of dealing with people.

A lack of love causes us to make the most negative assumptions and statements about people without getting to know them first. It is very tragic when this happens in churches. The individuals that we judge rather than embrace feel this lack of love and often leave the Christian community feeling victimized and unwilling to go back to church. In the book, *The Unchurched Next Door*, over 60% of those surveyed who are not currently attending a church had such experiences. *The Unchurched Next Door* contained dozens of stories about people who left the church because of the lack of love that they found there among Christians. Leda was one such person. She grew up loving both her Heavenly Father and earthly father dearly. She was in awe of her dad as a little girl because he was good to so many people; however, he did not make attending church a priority. According to Leda, "One day after church, this man who was a deacon in the church comes up to me and starts telling me what an awful man my dad was for not coming to church. He then tells me I'd better talk with my dad because he is going to hell. I was so mad! I told deacon _____ that he was the one going to hell and that he better never talk about my dad like that . . . He walked away, the coward. I haven't been back to church ever since" [2]. This deacon as well as many others should study Paul's advice to the Colossians about how Christians should relate to each other: **"As God's chosen people, holy and dearly loved, clothe yourself with compassion, kindness, humility, gentleness and patience. Bear with each other and forgive whatever grievance you may have against one another. Forgive as the Lord forgave you. And over all these virtues, put on love . . ."** (Colossians 3:12-14, NIV).

There are millions of stories just like Leda's out there and the church must address this loveless spirit that is not intentional about building relationships if it wants to fulfill its mission to win the lost to Christ. The deacon that judged Leda's dad just assumed that he knew why the man was not attending church. He did not bother to consider that maybe her father was sick or depressed. Perhaps the father did not attend because of a fear of being judged by the Deacon and others like him. We never know what type of pain someone else is going through. We should never judge anyone before seeking to find out the facts. This story could have had a completely different ending if the deacon would have simply asked Leda "Is everything going alright with your Father? Is there anything that we can do to help you and your family?" If the deacon could have made the father feel welcome and needed in the church, he probably would have been more prone to attend church. Instead the deacon jumped to conclusions without any real information and made a young lady want to run away from the church. The research team for *The Unchurched Next Door* noted that, *"Unfortunately, we heard many horror stories like Leda's. If just some of the stories are accurate, we will be able to write a book, **Christians Say the Dumbest Things** . . . A number of Christians just seem to be rude and insensitive. They may* *be small in number, but their voices are heard loudly. We wonder how many unchurched have been hindered from the Kingdom because of the insensitivity and even stupidity of some Christians"* [3].

Before I was personally confronted with this problem, I got the opportunity to watch a close friend go through a tough time dealing with feeling judged at church. This friend suddenly decided to leave the church and break all contact with all Christians after spending months complaining about how the women at church would always judge her and look down on her and she was tired of it. This friend was suicidal and obsessed with men. Many of the ladies in church realized this. When my friend would complain about these ladies, I would always remind her that Christians have a flesh just like everyone else and they may not even be aware that they are projecting a self-righteous spirit. She was really offended that these ladies never tried to get to know her, but yet, they felt inspired to tell her everything that she was doing wrong. I encouraged her to confront these women and let them know that they are coming across as judgmental and self-righteous. She never gathered enough courage to confront these women. In the end, she left the church very angry and bitter towards all Christians.

There is a big difference between being offended by the truth of the gospel and being offended by the careless and loveless acts of Christians who are supposed to emulate Christ. At my Tuesday night book study, a young lady from our church was frustrated by the passage in the bible showing what a vibrant Christian community looks like. According to the passage, the church should be united with everyone loving one another and meeting the needs of each other. According to the Book of Acts, the early Christians **were of one heart and one soul, neither [did they claim] the things that they possessed was his own; but they had all things in common"** (Acts 4: 32, KJV). In a sigh of frustration, this young lady said, "That is not how it is in my Women's bible class on Sunday. Everything is done according to this agenda and if anyone dares to interrupt the agenda, someone could get hurt. I joined the Women's bible class hoping to bond with some women and develop a sense of community. Instead, it is this impersonal agenda being fulfilled and I feel so alone there." The frustrated young woman went on to tell a story about a girl who was crying about a serious problem and the ladies told her that they must finish the lesson and they would pray for her after class. The women of the study did not understand that the purpose of a bible study is to bring us closer to God and closer to each other. It is not to hurry up and finish a lesson about Jesus Christ and the church; it is about celebrating Jesus Christ by being a vibrant, united and loving church. We must remember to never put an agenda ahead of the needs of people. A crying woman is a legitimate reason to stop the planned lesson. We should meet someone's need right then and there, not tell them to wait until it is more convenient for us. We have to allow God to interrupt our plans so that we can fulfill his. A good motto for any bible class or any Christian life would be "People before Paperwork."

The problem with this particular bible study was that the focus was wrong. My observation was that the women who led this particular bible study gave the appearance of being perfect and never doing anything wrong. It was as if they were saying, "Look at me and how wonderful I am. I am an example of the perfect Christian. Don't you young hussies wish that you could be as wonderful as me?" Rather than point us to Christ, many of the ladies wanted to point us to themselves. They seemed to have assumed that we were living immoral lives without first getting to know us. One woman would constantly make remarks like, "Please don't wear a Jesus bumper sticker on your car if you are speeding. How could you call yourself a Christian and break the speed limit?" She made me feel as if I were in the twilight zone because I could not believe that someone considered speeding to be the greatest sin. Another woman reprimanded me for saying that we should boldly witness for Christ. She said, "If you were living the right lifestyle, you would not have to witness to others, they would just naturally come to you." Aside from this statement being unbiblical because the Great Commission is in every gospel chapter, it was also a direct attack on my character by someone who knew nothing about me or my lifestyle. It is depressing when we are around people who do not know us and do not seem to want to know us or accept us. Rather than inspiring us to move to higher levels, a prideful attitude just makes us want to run.

The situation at the Women's bible study made me curious about why so many young Christians leave the church. Statistics show that 60-80% of younger Christians stop attending church after high school. I began to speculate that it could be due to the fact that they feel judged and unaccepted by the people at church and they would just rather not be around them. This prompted me to interview two of my co-workers who had told me that they refused to attend church anymore because of bad experiences in their teens and early twenties. Wednesday afternoon, I visited both teachers and asked if I could interview them for an article that I was writing regarding the reasons that people leave the church. They both agreed to answer any questions as long as I did not use their names in the interview. The results of the interviews were as follows:

Question: Why did you decide to leave your church?

Teacher 1: "I felt that there were certain beliefs and behaviors that I no longer believed in. The attitude of many of the people in my youth group was 'Well you are not here every Sunday. We have been here all week. Where have you been?' I felt a kind of judgment. I felt that it was an "us" versus "them" mentality and it made me a little uncomfortable. There was a guy that rarely came and they would say, 'What is he doing here? I guess he showed up because the softball game was cancelled.' It was too much like a click and I felt that many of us did not belong in the click."

Teacher 2: "In high school, I enjoyed the community of church. However, I felt that many in the clergy misinterpret the bible and man's hand is all over the bible. Most congregations are being manipulated by power-hungry leaders who care more about appearances than helping others. The church seems to be organized around people's thoughts and opinions rather than bible-based. I want a more personal relationship with God and I don't trust other people's human agendas. There has also been too much bloodshed over religion. All the human weaknesses get tied up in there. A personal agenda is always at play. Too many people have the wrong attitude when they go to church. It is amazing that America is the only country that still has full churches. In Europe all the churches are beautiful and they are empty. I wonder why we are so behind the rest of the world."

Question: Would you be willing to go to church if someone asked you to come?

Teacher 1: "I feel that there are other ways that I can get in touch with my own spirit. Congregating became a forum of comparison and judging each other instead of love. Humans are just naturally competitive. When I go to yoga, it is like church. I found through yoga that I can be in a place with the right energy. Yoga is a spiritual experience for me."

Teacher 2: "I actually enjoy the Universalist churches. I would rather a bible scholar talk to me then to have a contemporary watered-down sermon. Everything is 'do this, do that' with no explanation about why and no scholarship. Sometimes I am forced to go to family events at the Catholic Church with my husband. For Catholics especially, it seems that everyone was unengaged with no real spiritual connection."

During the interview, I was careful to avoid leading the teachers to answer the questions in a certain way. It was just a coincidence that both teachers did mention a judgmental attitude as one of the primary reasons for not wanting to go to church anymore. One teacher seemed to have more of a problem with the people of the church while the other teacher had a problem with the leadership of the church. I told both of the teachers that I interviewed about my recent experience with feeling judged by other Christians and I confided that the only thing that kept me from running away from the church myself was the fact that I have seen Jesus Christ work so many miracles in my own life and the body of believers were often a part of these miracles. I also did major research before becoming a Christian. C.S. Lewis' *Mere Christianity*, Lee Strobel's *The Case for Christ* and Josh McDowell's *Evidence that Demands a Verdict* were instrumental in convincing me that Christianity must be true. God has shown me experientially that every word in his Holy Bible is true and it works in a powerful way when we believe it. One of my favorite verses in Hebrews states, **"Let us draw near to God with a sincere heart in full assurance of faith . . . Let us consider how we may spur one another on toward love and good deeds. Let us not give up meeting together, as some are in the habit of doing, but let us encourage one another-and all the more as you see the**

Day approaching" (Hebrews 10:22-25, NIV). I explained that dealing with a judgmental attitude is hard, but there is power when we assemble together and act on one accord. After joining a church closer to home, I found a Christian community that made me feel valued and accepted. I realized in my own church hurt that we simply don't fit in every environment. Just like there is no one man that is for every woman, there is no church for every person. If we keep searching, we can find the church community that fits our personality and meets our needs. One of the teachers responded, "I would really like to see some of this evidence that you speak about and I definitely want a copy of the article that you are writing from this interview." The other teacher said that she may have given up too quickly and that she may return to church after all. This really excited me because I realized that God was using our interview as an opportunity for me to connect with others and share the love of Christ. It always amazes me how God uses negative experiences and situations to bring about good results.

The trap of the "look at me spirit" is one that any of us can fall into. It is normal to start out with a "Look at me" attitude when we first develop our spiritual gifts and grow in knowledge about Christ. However, we are not fit to be used in ministry until we develop a "Look at Him" spirit. Powerful people in ministry point others to Jesus Christ, not to themselves. We want to make sure that we do not become a stumbling block for others; yet, we do ourselves and others a disservice when we pretend to be perfect and try to base someone's Christian walk on our lives. We were never meant to play the role of God. When others think that we are, it is just a matter of time before we disappoint them. There has only been one perfect person in the history of the world and his name is Jesus Christ. We also put people on the defensive when we approach them with the "Look at me" spirit. The first question that people start asking is "What makes you so much better than me?" When I first started sharing my testimony, I ran into a lot of opposition partially because I seemed to be pointing them towards me and not God. Once I admitted my faults and started pointing others to Christ, I have had many more positive responses. Sometimes we inspire others the most when we let them know that they are not alone in experiencing a certain hurt or pain. In fact, one of the interviewed teachers was inspired to possibly go back to church again after I shared my experience about feeling judged at a Women's bible study. She said, "This whole thing may have just been a test for me. I just might eventually return to church again. Thanks for sharing your story." When we approach people with a "Look at Him (Jesus)" Spirit, we motivate others to change and lives are transformed. They begin to find the missing part of the puzzle in their lives. That missing part is a deeper relationship with Jesus Christ.

The Greatest Threat to the Christian Church: The Spirit of the Pharisee

The judgmental "look at me" attitude is the result of spiritual pride. Spiritual pride is far more subtle and deadly than other sins because those who are eaten up with it usually do not even realize that it is there. It is also the complete anti-God state of mind because a proud heart depends on itself for salvation rather than the blood of Jesus Christ. Self-righteousness is being righteous based on one's own efforts rather than depending on the righteousness of Christ. This was the central issue with the Pharisees of Jesus' day and it was the primary reason that he warned the people to avoid the practices of these leaders. Jesus said, "**Watch out for the yeast of the Pharisees and that of Herod**" (Mark 8: 14, NIV). The yeast was the yeast of pride in one's own ability to be "holy" instead of a humble dependence on God and love for God. In *Mere Christianity*, C.S. Lewis explains, "*All the worst pleasures are purely spiritual: the pleasure of putting others in the wrong, of bossing and patronizing and spoiling sport, and back-biting; the pleasure of power and hatred. For there are two things inside me competing . . . They are the Animal self and the diabolical self. The Diabolical self is the worst of the two. That is why a cold self-righteous prig who goes to church regularly is nearer to hell than a prostitute. But of course, it is better to be neither*" [4]. Spiritual pride is born of Satan himself and it typically eats at the souls of people with leadership positions in churches. In fact, most of the people that I have encountered who were eaten up with this problem had major positions in ministry. Some people who serve God become proud of their position and lose sight of the God who gave them their position. They start looking at their accomplishments and think of what a great job they did and how other people are not as good as them. We are always on dangerous ground when we forget where we came from and forget the one who really made us who and what we are.

Jesus spent much of his ministry warning those suffering from the "look at me" spirit about the dangers that they are facing. According to the bible, "**To some who were confident in their own righteousness and looked down on everybody else, Jesus told the parable: Two men went up to the temple to pray, one was a Pharisee and the other a tax collector. The Pharisee stood up and prayed about himself: 'God thank you that I am not like other men' . . . But the tax collector . . . beat his breast and said, 'God have mercy on me, a sinner.' I tell you that [the tax collector] rather than the [Pharisee] went home justified before God. For everyone who exalts himself will be humbled and everyone who humbles himself will be exalted**" (Luke 18:9-14, NIV). God is not pleased with a proud heart that looks down on others. We are all sinners who deserve punishment before a holy God. In God's mercy, he allowed his only begotten Son, Jesus, Christ to take the punishment that each of us truly deserve. When we forget the magnitude of each of our sins, we begin to get the "look at me and I am so great" Pharisee—like spirit. This is one of the most loveless spirits in the church. Modern Pharisees, similar to their biblical counterparts, look good on the outside, but their hearts are filled with anger, hatred, greed and arrogance. Jesus warned the Pharisees of his day, "**Now then you Pharisees clean the outside of the cup and dish, but inside you are full of greed and wickedness**" (Luke 11: 39, NIV). Unfortunately for the Pharisees, God judges the heart, not the outside.

We know that we have the spirit of the Pharisees when we care more about whether a person tithes than if the person loves. Jesus said, **"Woe to you Pharisees, because you give a tenth of your mint, rue and all other kinds of garden herbs, but you neglect justice and the love of God"** (Luke 11:42, NIV). This statement by Christ reminded me of how several of us were treated at a Women's Bible class and at a Bible class on racism. There was constant talk about the importance of tithing, being on time, and having perfect behavior. However, there was almost no mention of the love of God or being good to others that are different than us. Whenever some of us would mention these points, we were immediately cut off and were not allowed to finish our points. These teachers failed to realize that God cares more about us loving him and loving others than any of that other stuff. Jesus said that you will know them by their love for one another, not by their ability to fill out paperwork on time, ability to give money or ability to dress to impress. What is important to us as men is of very little significance to God.

We know that we have a Pharisee spirit when we show favoritism to the rich and powerful while devaluing others. Jesus said, **"Woe to you Pharisees because you love the most important seats in synagogues and greetings in marketplaces"** (Luke 11: 43, NIV). One of the things that I noticed about some of the bible teachers was that they would never speak to several of us. We could be standing right there and say hello; yet, they would turn the other way. We were not important enough for them bother with. At the same time, they would go out of the way to speak to those who they deemed important. These teachers would express how they felt very uncomfortable around the homeless and people of different races in the church. When there was an incident of vandalism inside the men's restroom, the automatic assumption was that it was the homeless men. Church leadership and the building owners demanded that the bible study that attracted the homeless men be cancelled and that the homeless would have to show their ID to get into church. Several off-duty police officers were hired and everyone had to have their bags checked before entering church. This disturbed me and several others, so we decided to leave. Rather than serving as a beacon of hope and a place for rest and refuge, this church suddenly became our greatest source of stress and we knew that it was time to go.

The Spirit of the Pharisee is a close cousin to the racist spirit. It is the idea that some people are better than others and deserve more respect because of their race, social status or even gender. Instead of looking at everyone as fellow members in the body of Christ there to serve the Lord, those eaten up with this spirit classify people based on their own prejudices and experiences. During the time of slavery, racist slave owners justified their treatment of those that they enslaved by declaring that the slaves were not fully human or of a lesser group. They used this excuse to rationalize their brutality. It allowed them to treat others poorly and still look at themselves in the mirror and think of themselves as good people. The treatment of the homeless was the result of a similar rationalization. Since they were supposedly a lesser group, it became OK to treat them as if they were less than human. In reality, we are all made in the image of God and God wants for us to love each other and not be a respecter of persons.

Paul's warning to Timothy is also his warning to us: he said, **"Do nothing out of favoritism"** (I Timothy 5:21, NIV). James went even further when he said, **"If you really keep the royal law found in scripture, 'Love your neighbor as yourself,' you are doing right. But if you show favoritism, you sin and are convicted by the law . . . Speak and act as those who are going to be judged by the law that gives freedom, because judgment without mercy will be shown to anyone who has not been merciful. Mercy triumphs over judgment"** (James 2: 8-13, NIV).

We know that we have a Pharisee spirit when we judge others before lifting a hand to help them or minister to them. Jesus said, **"Woe to you because you load people down with burdens that they can hardly carry, and you yourselves do not lift one finger to help them"** (Luke 11:46, NIV). This lies at the heart of the criticism of Christians who carry picket signs for Christ instead of the cross of Christ. It is good to be against abortion. However, it is not right to protest against abortions before offering the gospel to those who go into clinics. It is good to be against sexual sin; however, it not right to tell people what not to do if we do not offer them something better to do. We were called to do the Great Commission: Jesus said, **"Go and make disciples of all nations, baptizing them in the name of the Father and of the Son and of the Holy Spirit, and teaching them to obey everything that I have commanded you. And surely I will be with you always, to the very end of the age"** (Matthew 28: 19-20, NIV). Statistics show that the Great Commission is the Great Omission for the average Christian. Many of us have avoided engaging with the culture and telling others the good news about Jesus Christ; yet, we become upset when we see the culture moving in the wrong direction. Prayerfulness and a commitment to being a light in a dark world could transform the lives of many people. We are called to be messengers carrying the good news of love and salvation through Jesus Christ. Most sin is due to people trying to meet their real needs in a way that is not pleasing to God. Drugs and sex are often false gods that people use to satisfy the longings of the human heart. As we introduce others to the living water that is guaranteed to satisfy the deepest needs of the soul, the appeal for false idols diminishes.

While we must avoid offending others with a loveless attitude, there are certain issues that make offense inevitable as a true disciple of Jesus Christ. We must remember that the gospel of Jesus Christ is offensive to some and we cannot apologize for it. We live in a pluralistic society in which all views are acceptable except the view that there is an absolute truth found in the bible. People will often become offended when they hear the statement, **"I am the way, the truth and the life; no man comes to the father but by me"** (John 14:6, KJV). We cannot apologize for the truth according to Jesus Christ himself as many Christians are in the habit of doing. If the statement is true and Jesus knew it to be true, then Jesus is the Son of God and he holds the only key to eternal life. This means that failure to take him seriously has serious eternal consequences regardless of how we feel about it. Jesus warned that some would become offended because of him and he gave us the instruction to persevere through the trials. Jesus offers us this promise during this postmodern age of tolerance: He said, **"You will be hated by all nations because of me. At that time, many will turn away from the faith and will betray and hate each other . . . the love of most will grow cold, but he who stands firm to the end will be saved. And the gospel of the kingdom will be preached in the whole world as a testimony to all nations . . ."** (Matthew 24: 9-14, NIV).

Even when we follow Jesus' teachings on love, there will be occasions when people reject the gospel. I got to experience this at an interfaith meet and greet at a friend's house. Each person got an opportunity to share their faith. The guy from the African Spirituality camp stated that "you Christian black women are confused. Don't you know that you are Gods?" I answered, "This is what Lucifer said in Isaiah 14. He claimed to be God and he wanted to exalt himself above God and got kicked out of heaven." Next, the friend that I rode in the car with became angry because I said that Jesus is the only way to salvation according to biblical Christianity. She said that her sister is a member of the Nation of Islam and she knows that her sister is going to heaven. She said that her sister lives a much more moral life than any Christian she knows. I responded, "Your sister is probably a much better person than I will ever be. Unfortunately, unless she is perfect and has never sinned before, she stands before God guilty just like the rest of us. Jesus was the only perfect man to ever live because he was both God and man. Since none of us have ever been able to keep the law and the wages of sin are death, Jesus took our place on the cross. This allows us the opportunity to have a relationship with a Holy God who is also just and merciful. Unfortunately, the truth is the truth and we cannot back down from it just to make others feel better and like us. The only thing that I could tell her in the end was that "When Jesus claimed that he was the only way to salvation, his statement is either true or false. We will all know the answer exactly one second after we die." She simply refused to accept that Christianity is exclusive and we Christians cannot be made to feel guilty about our fundamental beliefs.

Even though the gospel does offend some, we must make sure that we do not offend others with a loveless self-centered spirit. As Christians we must guard against developing this spirit that seeks mainly to judge and criticize instead to love. We must think more like the Father than the older brother in the story of the Prodigal Son. When the Prodigal son came back home, the Father rejoiced and celebrated while the older brother became angry and offended. The Father had to explain to the brother that **"we had to celebrate because this brother of yours was dead and is alive again; he was lost and is found"** (Luke 15:32, NIV). The church is a place of healing for those who are spiritually sick. It is not a place for well people to pat each other on the back and glorify themselves while looking down on others. Our goal should be to glorify God by loving one another. According to the bible, **"Put on therefore . . . [mercy], kindness, humbleness of mind, meekness, longsuffering; Forbearing one another, and forgiving one another . . . as Christ forgave you . . . And above all these things put on charity [or love], which is the bond of perfectness. And let the peace of God rule in your hearts . . . Let the** words of Christ dwell in you richly in all wisdom; teaching and admonishing one another in psalms and hymns . . . singing with grace in your heart to the Lord. And whatsoever [you] do in word or deed, do all in the name of the Lord Jesus, giving thanks to God and the Father by him "(Colossians 3: 12-17, KJV). The only way to remove the Pharisee spirit is to embrace the love of Christ. We must repent from the sin of pride and embrace humility in order to grow closer to God and to each other.

CHAPTER 2

Moving from Pride towards Humility

A Painful Personal Journey
from Wanting to be God to Learning to Depend on God

My journey to understanding the importance of humility began twelve years ago. It is tough to grow up having everything and still be depressed. Similar to countless other parents, my mother would try to cheer me up by buying more and more, but the unhappiness would continue. She would take me shopping every weekend and I always had the latest toys, gadgets and clothes. None of this satisfied the emptiness that I felt inside though. Starting at age 15, I became fascinated by psychology and sociology. While other kids were reading about the latest celebrities, I was reading about Freud, Jung, Maslow and Rogers. During that time, my favorite talk show was Oprah. Every time she would feature a new psychologist or New Age guru, I headed to the bookstore to buy the latest book to end my unhappiness. Psychologists and New Age gurus successfully convinced me that the greatest problem facing the human race was low self-esteem and negative thinking. My central goal became to get rid of low self-esteem and think positive all the time. I just knew that this was the root of all my problems and disappointments. Unfortunately, no psychology book in the world was able to keep me in a peaceful state of mind. Every few months, my moods would go up and down depending on my circumstances. It was not until the age of 25 that I finally had a breakthrough. After spending years and years reading countless psychology books on how to raise my self-esteem, it was like manna from heaven to finally discover that my real problems were arrogance, self-absorption and self-centeredness. This realization occurred after reading chapter 8 of C.S. Lewis' *Mere Christianity.* Lewis noted that "*There is one vice of which no man in the world is free; which everyone in the world loathes when they see it in someone else, and which any people, except Christians, ever imagine that they are guilty of themselves . . . And the more we have it, the more we dislike it in others . . . . According to Christian teachers, the essential vice, the utmost evil, is pride. Pride leads to every other vice: it is the complete anti-God state of mind . . . Nearly all those evils in the world which people put down to greed or selfishness is really far more the result of Pride*" [1]. Even though this statement by Mr. Lewis was the opposite of everything that I had read or seen on TV, somehow I knew that he was right. An interesting series of events showed me that the solution to our collective unhappiness and depression is to avoid pride and embrace humility.

The C.S. Lewis discovery changed the course of my entire life. Suddenly, I realized how pride was ruining my relationships. It became clear that I was shy because I was completely self-absorbed and was thinking about myself instead of the other person when speaking. Instead of focusing on another person's needs or point of view, I would let my mind race trying to figure out what I would say next. I focused on my need to be liked and heard rather than attentively listen to what the other person was saying. This made my answers to their comments seem illogical because I never really heard what they said in the first place. I realized that I stuttered partly because I was so focused on what I would say next that I would actually confuse my words. It is hard to think about how you sound to another person and talk at the same time. Once I learned to take a real interest in what other people said, talking became easy and natural. My real issue was that I was a hopeless people-pleaser who had to learn how to be a God pleaser instead. Every word had to be monitored and ironically it was never good enough. I was constantly walking on egg-shells with every social interaction. After reading C.S. Lewis' famous chapter 8, I changed the whole way that I approached people and situations. I realized that I needed to relax and be myself. I realized that everyone would not like me and that is fine. It became more important to please God more than pleasing others. I also learned the appeal of focusing on others more than myself as I trusted that God would take care of me. Instead of wanting to tell my whole life story, I attentively listened to the life story of others. The results were amazing once I started doing this. My shyness simply disappeared along with my stuttering. People suddenly found themselves magnetically drawn to me instead of recoiled. I suddenly became a natural communicator who truly enjoyed speaking to others and learning about their lives. After months of unsuccessful job hunting, I finally got 2 job offers because my interviews were so much better now that I was no longer in a self-absorbed stupor.

It became equally as clear that pride was the root of my problems with men. Before age 25, no one had worst luck with men than me. From 13 to 16 my experiences were traumatic. Starting at 17 and continuing to age 24, I had a series of boyfriends who broke my heart. I was hopelessly obsessed with men and always wondered why I had such little success with them. I considered myself a strong, independent woman who always tried to take the lead in relationships. It was not until I reached age 25 that I realized that this was the problem. Instead of humbly submitting to God's way by letting the man take the lead, I felt that my way was better. My desire to manipulate men into doing what I wanted them to do instead of accepting them as they were was what drove men away from me. Yet, my prideful heart believed that the problem was that I was too nice and men were intimidated by my beauty. I can only imagine how many friends wanted to scream as I wasted hours of their time talking about the latest guy who victimized me. Instead of trusting that God would eventually send the right guy along, I trusted in myself to make the "guy of the month" like me by any means necessary.

Instead of using my relationships with men to glorify God, I used God to help me get the men that I wanted and then I would forget about God once he came through for me. In each "relationship" my idolized guy would dump me and I would suddenly remember God again. I would cry out to God and ask for him to remove the pain and he would faithfully restore my joy each time. Then I would meet the next guy and forget about God. Instead of worshiping God, I was worshiping men as my idol. Without realizing it, I was in serious violation of the most important commandment to love God with all my heart, soul and mind. This pattern of worshipping men as my idol continued until I took a year off from dating and read the Mars and Venus series of books by John Gray. I discovered that I was doing everything backwards.

In **Mars and Venus on a Date**, John Gray noted that strong, independent women rarely have success with men because men need to feel needed and respected [2]. Strong independent women have an "I don't need a man attitude" and these women usually refuse to submit to any man. Once I lost some of my independence, I became more feminine and attractive to men. For the first time, I understood Ephesians Chapter 5 as a good bargain for women instead of a negative sexist chapter of the outdated bible. I found that submitting to God and submitting to men could bring about wonderful results. As I became more feminine, men became more protective of me and they expressed their desire to provide for me as well. I had wonderful dates whereby men would bring me gifts and treat me like a queen. This happened without me compromising my morals. It happened as a result of me changing my morals to God's morals by simply treating men with love and respect. Dating became fun and exciting as men started seeing me as good wife material for the first time.

It was during this time that I realized that God is far more superior to me. This discovery led me to start focusing on what God wants instead of what I want. For the first time, I realized that God is far more intelligent than I am, so I need to trust his wisdom more than my own. This is the true meaning of Proverb 3:5-7 which states, **"Trust in the Lord with all thine heart; and lean not unto thine own understanding. In all thine ways acknowledge him and he shall direct thine paths. Be not wise in thine own eyes; fear the Lord and depart from evil" (KJV).** Before my revelation, I honestly thought that I was capable of being equal to God or above God. The New Age Movement taught me that my ultimate goal in life was the attainment of Godhood. C.S. Lewis' **Mere Christianity** and the Holy Bible explained to me that my ultimate goal in life was to be in proper relationship with a God who is far wiser and powerful than I could ever hope to be. Once I stopped trying to attain Godhood and humbly submitted my plans and my will to God, the creator of the universe, I felt truly at peace for the first time in my life. My New Age friends claimed that my aura had changed and there was a bright white light surrounding me. My career counselor noticed that my confidence had increased significantly and both of us realized that I would no longer need her services. I told her that the only thing that has changed is that I am now focused on others more than myself and I have decided to trust God instead of trust myself. I was embracing Christianity and Jesus

Christ instead of the New Age teachings that encouraged me to focus on myself and exalt myself. I exchanged self-confidence for God-confidence and, surprisingly, it really worked.

Lessons about Humility from Unlikely Sources

My first experience teaching was slightly traumatic to say the least. It was at an inner city school and I was the fourth teacher that year for the class. The kids literally ran the other teachers away. However, it was not all bad because there were at least five amazingly wonderful students in each class. Many of these students showed up for after-school tutoring with me, did all their homework and had a very respectful attitude. Many even showed up when I agreed to meet them at the library before a big test. These kids had a secret weapon that guaranteed success: humility and obedience. They would just go to class with a good attitude, follow directions and do what they were supposed to do. By simply doing the best they could with what they had, the results took care of themselves. Without realizing it, these kids were imitating Christ's humility. According to scripture, **"Your attitude should be the same as that of Jesus Christ: Who being in the very nature of God, did not consider equality with God something to be grasped, but made himself nothing, taking the very nature of a servant . . . he humbled himself and became obedient to death . . . Therefore, God exalted him to the highest place and gave him the name that is above every name"** (Philippians 2:5-9, NIV). These students never wasted time asking "Why we got to do this?" They just did what they were told and they learned what they needed to learn and made great progress. They were great teachers for me: I needed to learn that obedience quickens the desired results. Asking "Why?" all the time just slows down any blessing from arriving.

Humility and obedience win over pride and talent every single time. A person of little talent who is obedient to God is always going to be more successful than a person of great talent who is determined to do whatever he wants to do. This principle was illustrated in the movie "Forest Gump." Forest was of very low intelligence, but he succeeded more than all of his friends who were much smarter than him. Forest was humble and wise enough to listen to what his mom told him and follow the biblical principles of honesty, courage and obedience to authority. He just went about life doing what he was supposed to do and things would always go favorably for him in the end. He did the best he could with whatever gifts and talents that he was given and he left the results up to God. The results of his wise approach to life were amazing to say the least: he got to meet the President several times and became very rich and famous. On the other hand, his smart childhood friend Jenny tried to obtain fame and fortune by any means necessary and wound up used, abused and empty-handed with AIDS. Jenny's life was an illustration of Solomon's warning that **"There is a way that seems right to a man but the end [is] the way of death"** (Proverbs 14: 12, KJV). Similarly, Forest's friend, Kernel Dane was determined to die in war just like all of his other ancestors in the military. When his plan did not work, he decided to waste his life on cheap booze and cheap women. Forest had to get him out of this rut. Once Kernel Dane began to follow in Forest Gump's footsteps by trusting God, his life began to change. The Kernel had to take the lemons that life left him and turn them into lemonade. He too became successful and found a good wife once he made the choice to humbly accept the hand that God dealt him and do things God's way.

Humbly doing things God's way is one of the great secrets to a happy, successful life. C.S. Lewis correctly predicted that discovering humility would be a great relief. He noted that if you really get in touch with God, "*you will, in fact, be humble-delightedly humble, feeling the infinite relief of having for once gotten rid of all the silly nonsense about your own dignity which has made you restless and unhappy all your life . . . [A humble person will seem] a cheerful intelligent chap who [takes] a real interest in what you said to him. If you do dislike him it will be because you feel a little envious of anyone who seems to enjoy life so easily. He will not be thinking about humility: he will not be thinking of himself at all*" [3]. Once we embrace humility, we discover that it was never about us in the first place. It was always about God. True joy emerges because we become rightly related to God and to each other. We exchange the insecurity of being self-confident for the security of being God-confident. Deep down, we knew all along that we could never depend on ourselves. The reality is that we each have a flesh that is imperfect and flawed and feeling insecure is only natural if we are depending on this flesh. Once we take our mind off of ourselves, we can discover a perfect God who has created all things, can do all things and can fix any situation. We know that anything is possible through him. We are limited in what we can do in our own strength, but God is limitless in what he can do. Once we exchange faith in our limited abilities for faith in God's limitless possibilities, we develop true confidence and stability. We know that God is capable of supplying our every need or he can give us the grace to wait for something better. Either way, we know that we have a win-win situation with him.

The Real Truth about Pride and Self-Esteem

Today, even Oprah has realized that pride and self-esteem are not nearly as valuable as humility and self-control. In the January 2008 edition of The Oprah Magazine, Amy Lee Ball wrote an article called "Groundbreaking Research on Self-Esteem". In the article, Roy Baumeister, a professor of psychology at Florida State University, showed that of 15,000 studies on self-esteem, only 200 were done using scientific standards. Of these 200 studies, it was concluded that self-esteem does not improve relationships, career success, grades in school, violent behavior or anything else that we would have expected. If anything, high self-esteem increased problems in several of these areas. Baumeister had previously proven that high self-esteem and a lack of self-control are key ingredients for violent behavior and aggression towards others. His latest research expands the list of things that self-esteem cannot do. The implications of this research are profound, especially in the area of education. Many kids in school have been patted on the head and told good job for every little thing. Roy Baumeister said that we actually *get the best results when praising exactly what [they] did right and criticizing exactly what [they] did wrong. Just praising kids regardless of what they do contains very little useful information. Self-control [and] self-regulation give more bang for the buck [and] deliver a lot more in practical results* [(4)]. Today, social scientists are learning what the bible always taught: we should put no confidence in the flesh and put all confidence in God. We should replace the goal of self-esteem with the goal of God-esteem.

On Facebook, a world-famous actor and author had shared "The Greatest Love of All" with his fans. He and his fans discussed the need for people to have more self-love and self-esteem. As I read his post, I thought about Ephesians 5:29 (KJV) which clearly tells us that "**no man has ever hated his own flesh.**" The bible just assumes that we are all naturally selfish and self-centered which means that we probably love and respect ourselves too. Yet, pop culture tells us that we are not selfish and self-centered enough. Two opposite views cannot be true at the same time. Luckily, real researchers conducting scientific studies have shown that we actually have an epidemic of narcissism in our society, not an epidemic of low self-esteem. Dr. Jeane Twenge, author of **Generation Me**, noted that youngsters are becoming more and more depressed even though they have higher self-esteem and self-confidence than previous generations. She noted that these higher rates of depression may be due to disappointment when the overconfident personality does not get what he or she feels she deserves [(5)]. It was actually Nietzsche that popularized the idea that we should love and respect ourselves more. He was deeply anti-Christian. He advocated a values revolution in which we no longer think in terms of good and evil, but think in terms of power versus weakness. Nietzsche considered selfishness, greed and manipulation to be good because they make us more powerful. At the same time, he considered traditional virtues such as love, humility, forgiveness and kindness bad because they signal weakness. He advocated a value system very similar to the "laws of the street." Gang members have to mark their territory because respect or power is their greatest virtue. The worst thing that could happen is to be considered weak by running away from a fight. This is why there is so much violence associated with gangs. In gangster rap songs, the rappers have to prove their strength by threatening other lives for the slightest offense. We also see this in the modern laws of the corporate jungle. Often it is the most manipulative rather than the hardest working that rise to the top. Everyday folks get indoctrinated to Nietzsche's ideas when they watch shows like "Survivor" and "Big Brother". These shows usually portray the most cunning and manipulative person as the winner. The nicest or most honest person is often the first to go.

Nietzsche's ideas are the heart of the writings of Hitler, Freud, Jung, and a host of other famous writers. Even more frightening is the fact that he heavily influenced the Humanist Manifesto as well as most New Age and Satanic writings. According to the **Satanic Bible**, "*Only if a* *person's ego is sufficiently fulfilled can he afford to be kind and complementary to others without robbing himself of self-respect. We generally think of the braggart as a person with a large ego; in reality, his bragging results from a need to satisfy an impoverished ego"* [6]. This is very similar to Nietzsche. Satanic Priest Anton LaVey basically wrote that a person who brags all the time is not suffering from being too arrogant, but from low self-esteem. This the same view adopted by many psychologists who tell us that aggressive criminals just do not love themselves enough. Nietzsche and his followers completely contradict the Holy Bible and basic common sense.

The Christian bible has always warned us about the dangers of pride and self-esteem. If we studied every verse in the bible on the subject of pride, it could be summarized in the following statement: God sets himself against the proud and honors the humble. For example, David spoke these words to the Lord, **"And you save an afflicted people; But your eyes are on the haughty (prideful) whom you abase."** (II Samuel 22:28, NASB) David also wrote, **"Though the Lord is on high, he looks upon the lowly, but the proud he knows from afar"** (Psalm 138:6, NIV). We cannot truly know God when we are proud. This is what makes pride such a spiritual sin. Pride keeps us from fulfilling our true purpose for being here: to know God and be conformed to the image of his Son Jesus Christ. Solomon, the son of David and the wisest king to ever live wrote, **"I wisdom dwell together with prudence: I possess knowledge and discretion. To fear the Lord is to hate evil; I hate pride and arrogance, evil behavior and perverse speech. Counsel and sound judgment are mine. I love those who love me and those who seek me find me. With me are riches and honor, enduring wealth and prosperity. My fruit is better than fine gold; what I yield surpasses choice silver"** (Proverbs 8:12-19, NIV). Solomon went on to note that **"pride [goes] before destruction and a haughty spirit before a great fall. Better it is to be humble of spirit with the lowly than to divide the spoils with the proud"** (Proverbs 16:18-19, KJV). In the New Testament, James, the brother of Jesus noted that **"God [resists] the proud and gives grace to the humble"** (James 4:6, KJV). Peter the Apostle told the people to **"be subject to one another, and be clothed in humility; for God [resists] the proud and [gives] grace to the humble. Humble yourself therefore under the mighty hand of God that he may exalt you in due time: Casting all your care upon him: for he [cares] for you . . . To [God] be the glory and dominion forever and ever. Amen"** (1 Peter 5: 5-11, KJV).

The opposite of the Holy Bible is the Satanic Bible. There are only two pure belief systems: Christianity and Satanism. Everything else is a mixture of both of them. Two opposite ideas cannot be true at the same time. We have to pick which we choose to believe and live with the consequences of that choice. While the bible warns about pride, the Satanic Bible states that pride is good. Christians and New Agers who preach the importance of pride and self-esteem should learn where these teachings actually come from. Satanism encourages us to honor ourselves and give ourselves the credit and glory instead of God. According to the Satanic Bible, *"Then all thy bones shall say pridefully, 'Who is like unto me? Have I not been too strong for mine adversaries? Have I not delivered myself by mine own brain and body?"* [7]. The Satanic endorsement of pride is almost identical to what King Nebuchadnezzar said before God removed his kingdom from him. According to Daniel, King Nebuchadnezzar said, **"Is not this great Babylon that I have built . . . by the might of my power and the honor of my majesty?"** (Daniel 4:30, KJV). While most self-help gurus would assume that this statement of high self-esteem and display of a positive self-image would guarantee good results for the king, the bible shows something quite different. According to the bible, **"While the word was in the King's mouth, there fell a voice from heaven, saying, 'Oh King Nebuchadnezzar, to [you] it is spoken: the Kingdom is departed from [you]. And they shall drive thee from among men and [your] dwelling place will be with the beast of the field: they shall make [you] eat grass like oxen . . . until [you] know that the most high [rules] the kingdom of men, and [gives] it to whomsoever he will.' . . . At that same hour the thing was fulfilled . . . [until Nebuchadnezzar realized that] those that walk in pride, [God] is able to abase (make them humble)"** (Daniel 4:31-37, KJV). King Nebuchadnezzar did not get his kingdom back until he was humble enough to admit that it was not his great talent and mental capabilities that allowed Babylon to prosper. Rather, it was the favor of God so that God could accomplish his purposes. God will not share his glory with a prideful man.

Pride puts us in a selfish state of mind and ruins our relationships with others. We are so busy thinking about ourselves, we forget to focus on the needs of others. Modern humanistic teachings about the importance of self-esteem and self-love have caused many to interact with others with a complete "what's in-it-for me" attitude. Similar to Satanists, modern self-help gurus have preached the idea that we must love ourselves before we can be kind to others. New Age guru, Neale Walsch puts it like this: *"Let each person in a relationship worry not about the other, but only, only about self . . . The most loving person in the world is self-centered . . . There is an extraordinary principle in making relationships work: self-centeredness"* [8]. The modern rise of self-centeredness as a virtue was noted in Professor Allan Bloom's ***The Closing of the American Mind***. Bloom noted that *"Modern psychology has this in common with what was always a popular opinion, that selfishness is somehow good. Man is self and the self must be selfish. What is new is that we are told to look more deeply into the self . . . The great change is that a good man used to be the one who cared for others, as opposed to the man that cared exclusively for self. Now the good man is the one that knows how to care for himself, as opposed to the man who does not . . . Psychology has distinctions only between good and bad forms of selfishness . . . The psychology of self has succeeded so well that it is now the instinct of most of us to turn for a cure for our ills back to ourselves"* [9]. Today, we continue to hear many psychologists describe unselfishness as "being codependent" or "failing to love ourselves enough." Today, friends and family will often say, "don't let her or him use you like that" whenever you do something nice for someone else without expecting anything in return. These well-meaning people do not understand that the greatest joy in life is to give and the happiest people in the world are also some of the most generous. People who keep a mental log of everything they have done for others are often quite miserable. There is a freedom that comes once we give our lives away instead of always trying to get something back from everyone around us.

We need interactions with others and a purpose for living that is not about "me, myself and I." A young lady named Barbara illustrated this well. She was the most self-absorbed person that I had ever met. She walked around for most of the day taking her own pictures. She had little regard for the property of others as she would do this. She would pose at the bottom of hotel stairs. She would get on top of people's cars never thinking about how this would impact others. Her entire conversation revolved around her need to be the center of attention. She would say things like, "Why don't we stand in the middle of the parking lot so that all the guys will stare at me because I look so much better than their fat old-looking wives." She would constantly talk about herself and how she plans find a rich man to take care of her. This self-absorption would often lead to depression because she would feel bad when it appeared that she may not get what she wants. She was also angry at most women for judging her attitude. She was completely oblivious to how her self-absorbed attitude impacted others. She could not figure out why none of her relationships with men would work. She failed to realize that few people are attracted to a person who is completely self-absorbed. Most important, she failed to realize that self-absorption would never lead to the happiness that she craved. Barbara, like so many others, desperately needs a revelation about the emptiness that results from selfishness and self-centeredness. Selfishness and self-centeredness is the cause rather than the cure for our depression anxieties.

The Danger of Pride and Self-Centeredness in the Church

Similar to the idea of self-esteem, the idea of selfishness and self-centeredness being good is not found anywhere in the Holy Bible and defies basic common sense. How can a selfish person be more loving, kind or happy than an unselfish person? How can a person who seeks his own interest be nicer than a person who seeks the good of others? According to scripture we should, **"Do nothing out of selfish ambition or vain conceit, but in humility, consider others better than ourselves." Each of you should look not only to your own interest, but also to the interest of others. Your attitude should be the same as that of Jesus"** (Philippians 2:3-5, NIV). Jesus approached people with a servant-like attitude. He was not "looking out for number one." He was constantly doing things for others. It is in doing for others that we become truly fulfilled. Despite the bible's many warnings against selfishness, many Christians honestly believe that selfishness and self-centeredness is good. This concept is even being preached by some pastors.

A Christian minister who wrote a book a few years ago said the following in his press release for the book titled ***The Way of Prosperity***: *"Yes, I tell people that God wants for them to be selfish* *[and rich]. While that may shock many people, it comes straight from the bible"* [(10)]. My question to this pastor is *"Where does it say this in the bible?"* In the bible, we are told to be humble and seek the interest of others. According to Romans 15:1-3 (KJV), **"We that are strong ought to bear the infirmities of the weak, and [we should do this] not to please ourselves. Let every one of us please his neighbor . . . For even Christ pleased not himself."** The bible warns us that proud self-centered people will not seek God's wisdom or consult God about his plans. Proud, self-centered people just go about doing what they want. David said, **"For the wicked [boasts] of his heart's desire, and blesses the [greedy] which the Lord [hates]. The wicked, through the pride of his countenance, will not seek after God: God is not in all his thoughts"** (Psalm 10:3-4, KJV). God is not pleased until we trade in what we want for what he wants. In the bible, Jesus said, **"If anyone comes after me, he must deny himself and take up his cross and follow me. For whoever wants to save his life will lose it, but whoever loses his life for me will find it. What good will it be for a man to gain the whole world and yet forfeit his soul?"** (Matthew 16:24-25, NIV). Ministers like Mr. Duke are trying to make Christianity more appealing to the public by telling Christians what they want to hear. They combine humanism with its "all about me teachings" and Christianity with its "all about Jesus teachings" in an effort to appeal to a wider audience.

Two opposite statements cannot be true at the same time. The bible says, **"What communion hath light with darkness?"** (II Corinthians 6: 14, KJV). Ministers who mix humanism with Christianity do not realize that humanism is a close cousin of Satanism. The feel good approach to Christianity results in satanic teachings entering the Christian church itself. Many churches have become so concerned about meeting the needs of men that they have left out the teachings of God. The Satanic Bible dedicates an entire chapter to ways in which Satanism has infiltrated the Christian Church itself. Satanist Anton LaVey wrote, *"In recent years there has been an attempt to humanize the spiritual concept of Christianity. This has manifested itself in the most non-spiritual means . . . The religionists wail 'we must keep up with the times', forgetting that there could never be sufficient changes in Christianity to meet the needs of man . . . the only way that Christianity could ever completely serve the needs of man is to become as Satanism is now . . . Just look at how liberal the churches have become. Why they're practicing all that the Satanists preach . . . If many religions are denying their own scriptures because they are out of date, and are preaching the philosophies of Satanism, why not call it by its rightful name—Satanism? Certainly, it would be far less hypocritical"* [(11)]. Satanist Anton LaVey realized something that even many in the clergy still do not understand: Christianity is about self-forgetfulness and focusing on Jesus Christ while Satanism is about self-worship and man taking the place of Jesus Christ. It was through pride that the devil became the devil, so pride could not possibly be something for Christians to promote as good. Jesus Christ told his followers, **"Whoever humbles himself like this little child is the greatest in the kingdom of heaven"** (Matthew 18:4, NIV).

Some Christian teachers take the "pride is good" philosophy so far that they claim that we can actually control God by our thoughts and words. Colossians 2:8 (KJV) tells us to "**Beware lest any man spoil you through philosophy and vain deceit, after the traditions of men, after the rudiments of the world, and not after Christ**." Whenever we hear someone say that we can control God by correctly following certain spiritual laws, we are hearing the false teachings that Paul warned us about in Colossians. Far too many Christians look at God as a personal servant who must give them what they want as long as they follow the rules of positive thinking and positive action. This sense of entitlement causes them to become angry at God when he fails to give them what they want.

A young, beautiful Asian girl named Marianne was truly hurt by false teachings that God is pure love and his main purpose is to be our cosmic servant. She saw God as pure love rather than the almighty creator of both heaven and earth who is the source of all love and all that is good. In reality, God is love, but he is so much more. She was constantly telling God what he should be doing for her and viewed God as the cosmic Santa Claus that would give her whatever she wanted. In her mind, all she had to do was be positive. Without realizing it, she had formed a habit of using God to get the things instead of using things to glorify God. She thought that God's job was to serve her instead of her job to serve and glorify God. She was unemployed at the time we met. Whenever someone would mention great jobs for her to be pursuing, she would refuse to check it out. She would respond, "Oh, I am running away from God about that one. I don't want to do that and I have already told God no to that idea." Eventually, it became clear to me that she wanted to do what she wanted to do and she was not willing to submit to a God who actually told her what to do. She truly thought that she was in control of her own destiny as well as the actions of God. Happiness was very elusive for her during this time because the world simply did not work the way that she imagined. She finally found the happiness that she was looking for once she surrendered to God and allowed him to take the lead in her life. She replaced her entitlement mentality with a thankful heart and discovered true joy for the first time. God even blessed her with the man of her dreams. She told me, "I just did not want to give up control. I had always controlled everything and I thought that it was working for me. Now that I trust God to lead me, I am so happy and content. Men respond to me with so much more respect. My man is actually happy to see me every single day now. Most of my boyfriends from the past would try to avoid me."

True Christianity is about developing a personal relationship with Jesus Christ. We cannot develop this relationship unless we understand who he is. It is not about finding ways to get Him to give us what we want. In reality, God does as he pleases. He is all-powerful, all-mighty and he does not exist to be our cosmic Santa Claus. We were created for him and not the other way around. Those who think that they can control God by using positive thinking or some other technique should heed the warning of James, the brother of Jesus: "**Now listen you who say, "Today or tomorrow we will go to this or that city . . . and make money. Why you do** not even know what will happen tomorrow. **What is your life? You are a mist that appears for a little while and then vanishes. Instead you ought to say, "If it is the Lord's will, we will live to do this or that. As it is you boast and brag. All such boasting is evil"** (James 4:13-16, KJV). Imagine a five year old telling a 40 year old man what to do. That is exactly what we sound like when we live according to spiritual laws that tell God what to do. When modern pastors try to serve both God and man, God always loses. Today many ministers are repenting for teaching the false doctrine that we control our own destiny through positive thinking and positive action. Too many people have been led astray by this false teaching; in fact, some have even left the church assuming that Christianity is false rather than realizing that this teaching is what is really false.

As we attempt to humble ourselves, we must be careful to avoid trading pride for insecurity. Insecurity is false humility that is really born out of pride. When I first decided to go into ministry, I was so afraid and felt so inadequate and undeserving. It was during that time that I was dealing with some very unsupportive women in a bible study and the fact that I lacked their support made me even more insecure. Finally, I realized that it is not about me; rather, it is about Him, the great I AM, Jesus Christ. Suddenly, my feelings of nervousness disappeared. My insecurity and feelings of inferiority were born out of being focused on myself instead of being focused on God. Isaiah 26:3 says, that God **"will keep him in perfect peace, whose mind is stayed on thee because he [trusts] thee"** (KJV). I had good reason to feel insecure when I was planning for my ministry in my own strength. I had good reason to feel insecure when I was pointing others towards me. I have too many flaws to count even on my best days. However, there is nothing to fear and no basis for insecurity when we depend on Christ and point others to Him. Jesus Christ was the only perfect human being to ever live because he was fully God and fully man at the same time. Jesus has been through everything that we are going through. He is our permanent High Priest who intercedes for us continually in the presence of God the Father. According to Hebrews we have a High Priest who, **"is holy, harmless, undefiled, separate from sinners, and made higher than the heavens; Who need not daily as those high priests [of the past], to offer up sacrifice, first for [their] own sins, and then for the people's; for this [High Priest Jesus] did once, when he offered up himself . . . For Christ [has] not entered into the holy places made with hands . . . but into heaven itself, now to appear in the presence of God for us"** (Hebrews 7: 26-27and 9:24, KJV). We may not know what to do or how to do it. However, if we know Christ, we know the one who knows. Low self-esteem and insecurity are the opposite side of the proud "Look at me" coin. In both cases we are focusing on ourselves instead of the all-powerful, all-mighty, God who controls everything.

The bible teaches us that confidence in God is far better than confidence in ourselves or any technique that we may use. Having confidence in God leads to humility and favor from God. Self-confidence leads to pride. Pride always leads to conflict and disappointment. Since our knowledge is less than a millionth of God's knowledge, the wisest thing for us to do is to take God's advice. Our lives do not change until we realize that God is far wiser than we will ever be. True humility is resting in God and knowing that he knows what he is doing in our lives. It is trusting his rules for living instead of trying to follow our own. Our human wisdom is foolishness to God and God's wisdom is foolishness to us until he has humbled us. The bible states that the **"message of the cross is foolishness to those who are perishing, but to us being saved it is the power of God . . . the world did not come to know God through wisdom . . . . Christ is the power of God and the wisdom of God. For the foolishness of God is wiser than human wisdom and the weakness of God is stronger than human strength . . . God chose the foolish of this world to confound the wise, and God chose the weak of this world to shame the strong, and God chose the lowly and despised of this world, those who count for nothing, to make nothing of those who count for something, so that no human being may boast before God . . . It is due him that you are in Jesus Christ, who became for us wisdom from God, as well as righteousness, sanctification, and redemption, so that as it is written, 'Whoever boasts should boast in the Lord' "**(1 Corinthians 1: 18-31, NAB). Humbly following God gives us a win-win scenario. If we are successful, then all glory must go to God. If we are a failure, we can trust that God will use our trials and mistakes for his glory to bring us closer to him and to make us more like him. Our trials allow us to better relate to those in need. They equip us to humbly minister to others. In other words, God can take our messes and turn them into messages. He can take our tests and turn them into testimonies. He can pick up the broken pieces of our lives and put together a beautiful mosaic.

CHAPTER 3

Sex-My Way or God's Way?-Which One Works?

A Personal Testimony of the Blessing of Obedience

When I first became a Christian, I proudly thought that God's rules about sex were just plain dumb. I could not understand why God would give us such powerful desires for sex and then say abstain until marriage. At age 25, I was dating a relatively nice guy and having the best sex of my life. During this period, God called me to stop engaging in pre-marital sex. I was confused and began polling my male friends. I asked each of them, "Would you date a woman who did not engage in pre-marital sex?" Each of them answered a loud and clear "no!?!" After months of confusion, I reluctantly gave in to the Holy Spirit's promptings. I knew that as long as I was being disobedient, there would be no peace in my heart. It took a long time for me to realize that I could never understand the mind of God and I needed to do his will whether I felt like it or not. Eventually, it became apparent to me that if Jesus could die on the cross for my sins, then the least I could do is surrender my life, including my sex life, to him. One sunny day in August of 1999, I stared in the mirror and said, "Lord, I surrender my life to you. You died for me, so I will surrender my entire life, including my sex life, to you even if it means that no one will ever want to date or marry me, ever." I was scared to death that this would be the end of my dating life and I would die a bitter old religious prude. However, God is full of pleasant surprises, especially when we walk in obedience to him.

The day after I surrendered my entire life, including my love life, to Christ an old boyfriend from Detroit called. This was one of the many men that had broken my heart over the years. I met him in Puerto Rico and we were hooked on each other for the next few months-writing and calling every single day. He even visited me after 3 months at my parent's house in Louisiana. He convinced me to apply to Wayne State so that I could be with him during graduate school. As soon as I got accepted and made plans to move to Detroit to be with him, he told me that he had met someone else. At that point, it was too late to apply to other schools and I had already accepted a $25,000.00 a year scholarship. This caused me to attend Wayne State University as a heartbroken and angry woman who foolishly moved to another state for a man who no longer wanted her. Now, four years later he called out of the blue and I was actually happy to hear from him. He was still in Detroit and I was in New Orleans. He informed me that he had gotten his PhD in psychology and was working as a psychologist at a major corporation. He told me that he had given up pre-marital sex because he had become a youth leader at his church. I informed him that I too had given up pre-marital sex and he was shocked. He said, "Does this mean that we were meant to marry each other and be together?" I told him "no, but I do think that this is a sign from God that we are both on the right track." The thought of moving to a cold place like Detroit was out of the question for me at this point. In fact, I left graduate school early with my Master's degree instead of the intended PhD because I simply could not handle the cold weather of Detroit. Even though, I knew we were not destined for marriage, I was definitely flattered by the conversation discussing the possibility. I was thankful that God was showing me such great favor with men despite the fact that I expected for the opposite to happen.

About three weeks later, God allowed me to get closure with the guy that I was dating when the Holy Spirit prompted me to stop engaging in pre-marital sex. He had dumped me as soon as I told him that we could no longer have pre-marital sex. After many months of not hearing from him, he called and asked to see me. We talked and laughed about old times. Then suddenly, he said, "You know, I have had more fun with you than with any other woman. I took your advice to start respecting my boss and I have made a lot more money in the past few months. You know, I think that you would be a positive addition to my life. Why don't we get married?" I was shocked and flattered, but the answer was no. The Lord reminded me that marriage is forever and I could not imagine marrying a man who made me so angry and passionate all the time. We had fun together, but we also had lots of fights. I also remembered that he dumped me as soon as I told him that I could no longer have pre-marital sex with him and this still bothered me. At the same time I knew that God was showing me that submitting to His will did not mean the end of my love life. It turned out to actually be a brand new beginning.

Over the next few months, I felt as if I were in the heavenly inspired twilight zone. Men who had previously broken my heart were talking about their desire to marry me. I also noticed that dozens of guys would often casually mention that I would make a good wife in conversation all the time. This was strange because prior to devoting my life fully to Jesus Christ, no one had ever mentioned my name and marriage in the same sentence. Most of my college friends knew me as the dumb girl with no common sense that walked around with a broken heart. I would force them to stay up for hours listening to sob story after sob story about how this or that guy mistreated me. There was the story about the cute guy who turned out to be a pimp. There was the story of the guy who took me out and had no money. My friends even set me up with guys who turned out to be 2 feet shorter and hated black people. There were two men who turned out to be drug dealers-one was shot in the head and the other went to jail. Any normal guy would always break my heart within 3 weeks or if they were really good, I would break their heart. My teen years and early twenties were a real life never-ending horror movie when it came to dating and relationships. It was like an endless Lifetime movie. Now, without even trying to impress anyone, nearly every guy that I would come in contact with stated that they would love to marry a woman like me. God rewarded my obedience to him with favor from men. It was nothing short of a miracle and I was not even expecting it.

God blessed me with magical dates before I married my first husband. The guys that I dated after my commitment to the Lord treated me like a queen and gave me gifts even though I made it clear that there would be no pre-marital sex. There were a few rejections along the way, but God gave me the wisdom to understand that if a guy did not want to be with me, God would send someone better along anyway. Once I committed to fully obeying God, men found me to be more interesting than ever. Before marrying my first husband, I received three other full proposals. This happened in spite of the fact that I was expecting the exact opposite to occur. Once I started using God's rules and standards, dating became more fun and exciting than ever. I would have never predicted this in a million years. My confession that giving up pre-marital sex would end my dating life was completely wrong. This proved that we do not always get what we confess. We get what God our heavenly father has in store for us. Those who claim that words contain lots of power must realize that God's will is even more powerful than our words. His will triumphs over our thoughts and expectations. I failed to realize that God invented relationships, so following the principles of his word and following the promptings of the Holy Spirit should make relationships better, not worst.

A Generation Bombarded with Bad Information

Following God's rules regarding sex was difficult for me to accept because the people of our generation have been raised on a constant diet of secular humanism. The Humanist Manifesto states, "*In the area of sexuality, we believe that the intolerant attitudes, often cultivated by orthodox religions and puritanical cultures, unduly repress sexual conduct. The right to birth control, abortion and divorce should be recognized . . . The many varieties of sexual exploration should not in themselves be considered 'evil' . . . . individuals should be permitted to express their sexual [needs] and pursue their life-styles as they desire*" [1]. This statement is almost identical to the Satanic Bible's statement, "*Satanism encourages any form of sexual expression that you may desire, so long as it hurts no one else*" [2]. Both humanism and Satanism are the major philosophies promoted when we go to the movies, watch TV, read most popular novels or listen to the radio. The theme is to enjoy ourselves sexually with whomever and however we want. In movies the good sex is between people who are not married and the boring sex is between married couples. This distorted view of sex and relationships has kept many of us from even wanting to get married. Since we have so many people willing to have sex without commitment these days, today's man could easily live by the philosophy "why buy the cow when we can get the milk free from so many places?"

The minority of us who state that sex is sacred are often referred to as "intolerant" and "narrow-minded." However, we would not call Jesus Christ intolerant even though he said, **"You have heard that it was said, 'Do not commit adultery.' But I tell you that anyone who has looked at a woman lustfully has already committed adultery with her in his heart. If your right eye causes you to sin, gouge it out and throw it away. It is better to lose one part of your body than for your whole body to be thrown into hell"** (Matthew 5:27-29, NIV). Jesus' statement completely goes against everything that we hear in this culture about sex and sexuality. The fact that Jesus said that even thinking lustful thoughts are wrong implies that sex and sexuality has a spiritual component to it. Few of us have heard sermons or heard discussions on TV explaining the biblical view of sex as a spiritual union between two souls. Pastor John Bisagno explains, *"A sexual relationship outside the bond of marriage is not simply wrong because God forbids it, though that [should] be sufficient. God forbids it because it is wrong, and it is wrong because it cheats and robs people of the best . . . Where there is no permanent commitment, there is no satisfaction. There is only trauma, guilt and frustration. This sort of guilt and frustration is not induced by some [outdated moral code as the Humanist would have us believe.] It is produced because [sex outside of marriage] can produce nothing else. Spirit, mind, soul, emotions, security, need-everything that makes us divinely human—is expressed sexually. That is not simply the message of the church. It is a fact of life, the plan of the divine. Sex for the woman demands security . . . and sex for the man demands responsibility . . . Sex outside marriage demands security it cannot provide and pretends responsibility it does not accept"* [3]. In other words, sex is exactly what God intended for sex to be-a divine union of two souls. In this divine union, the man gives himself to the woman and the woman freely accepts him and trusts that he will take care of her afterwards. When we join together before a commitment has been made, there is a certain emptiness felt afterwards. The woman often wonders, "Is he going to call me again?" or "Was I good enough for him to stay?" Her insecurity increases afterwards. The man often wonders, "Does she do that with every guy that she meets?" Or "I hope that she is not pregnant because I do not want to see her again." We suffer great consequences when we try to cheapen sex or make it less than God intended it to be.

Fornication, or sex outside of marriage, is the only sin that we actually commit against ourselves. A sexually active single is not going to enjoy the peace and joy that God wants for us to experience in the sexual union. Sex brings married people closer together as it is a physical expression of the oneness that God intends for the marriage union, but sex often tears singles apart from each other. Many psychologists are beginning to find that married people have better, more frequent sex and more satisfying sex than singles. ***The Case for Marriage: Why Married People are Happier, Healthier and Better Off Financially***, by Linda Waite and Maggie Gallagher, was reviewed by Richard Niolon on PsychePage. According to findings in the book, *"About 40% of married people have sex twice a week, compared to 20-25% of single and cohabiting men and women. Over 40% of married women said their sex life was emotionally and physically satisfying, compared to about 30% of single women. For men, it's 50% of married men* *are physically and emotionally contents versus 38% of cohabitating men"* [(4)]. It is wonderful to see that modern psychologists are beginning to find that sex God's way is really the best way.

We can pretend that sex is only the animalistic meeting of body parts, but we only fool ourselves when we do this. This lesson was learned the hard way by the famous video vixen, Karrine Steffans. Steffans had affairs with many of the music industry's leading men and wrote a tell-all about her escapades. She had an epiphany about the cheapness and futility of casual sex years later. Steffans wrote, *"I began to think about everything that comes with sex without commitment. I pondered how things have changed between the sexes. How not only can today's liberated woman supposedly do anything boys can do, but do it better and with just as much emotional disconnect. I thought about it long and hard—and came to the conclusion that the theory of us having sex as casually as men is all a bunch of crap . . . Being a woman who has had more than my share of casual sex and all the subsequent pitfalls, headaches and ridiculously negative consequences, I am a believer that casual sex requires too much energy for so little return"* [(5)]. Karrine, like me and many other modern ladies, assumed that the bible is outdated and the bible's advice about sex and relationships only applies to the people of the past. This has been our modern brand of wishful thinking. In reality, the bible is a timeless relationship manual. It gives us God's advice on how to be rightly related to him and to each other. God should be able to give the best relationship advice because he invented relationships.

Even though I gave up pre-marital sex kicking and screaming, "God, why are you doing this to me?," it has now become clear that God has rules regarding sex to protect us and allow us to enjoy it more at the proper time. These rules are not mere "tests" and ways for God to torment us. These rules keep us from allowing sex to destroy our lives. In old episodes of the Maury Povich Show, we see example after example of how pre-marital sex can lead to problems. Many of the women have slept with multiple men and have become pregnant. Some women have to do eight or more paternity tests before identifying the father of the baby. Each woman that goes on the show starts out angry and upset. Towards the end of each episode, they seem sad and full of regret for the decisions that they made. Instead of leading to fun and excitement, their decision to "do whatever they want with their own body" led to poverty, shame and broken relationships. There was even one woman who became homeless as a result of being unable to care for her child. Many others would have 3, 4 or 5 men tested and still not be able to identify the baby's father. Many of the women would be called "slut" and worthless by the very men that had declared that they loved them months earlier. Men on the dating scene will say many things and make many promises, but there is no guarantee that they are telling the truth. Women are more protected when they engage in sex during marriage. A man may still abandon us and declare us as a slut after walking down the aisle, but it is far less likely. Sex in marriage is beautiful and leads to deeper intimacy between the husband and wife. Sex outside of marriage often leads to guilt, shame and complications that few are prepared to face. When a baby is produced in marriage, the couple is often happy and excited about the child. A baby produced outside of marriage usually causes fear and financial strain. Instead of bringing the couple together, it often tears the couple apart because the guy often wonders if it is really his baby and the woman feels insecure because the guy has not fully committed to her yet. We cannot help but to be thankful for God's wisdom and guidance as we watch what happens when left to our own devices. If I continued to do things my way instead of God's way, I easily could have been on that show. God declared that we should not have premarital sex for our protection, not to deny us one of life's great pleasures. God wants for us to have sex, but he just wants for it to be with the right person and at the right time.

Sex God's Way

God has a certain order to things. God declares marriage should be first then sex is second in a similar way to how he declares salvation is first then an intimate relationship with Christ second. Marriage is a profession of love and devotion to a spouse forever similar to the way that being born again and baptized is a profession of love and devotion towards Christ forever. Sex is the most intimate act that we can engage in with another human being. We are getting as close to another human being as possible during the sex act. The intimacy that we share with our sexual partner is a physical manifestation of the intimacy that we share with God. Throughout the bible, God's relationship with his people is illustrated using the imagery of man and wife. The sensual Song of Solomon is an example of the use of the sex act between man and woman being used to illustrate the intimacy that God wants to share with his people. According to amplified bible, allegorically "Solomon is identified with God and the [woman] with Israel or [God's people]. Thus, in this view the Song of Solomon is an allegory of the love relationship between God and Israel. In the literal perspective, the experience of Solomon is the basis of the poem and provides God's teaching on marriage and sexual relationships. The typical interpretation takes the poem as a reflection of Solomon's actual experience and stresses the major theme of the warm human emotions of love and devotion. In the Old Testament, it typifies God's love of Israel and in the New Testament; it represents Jesus' relationship with the church" [6]. Whether one looks at the Song of Solomon allegorically or literally, one is left with the impression that the devotion of Solomon to his lover and the feelings of wanting to be closer to that person than anyone else in the world is far greater than any cheap thrill with multiple lovers.

Sex is an act of worship. When a woman lays down and allows a man to enter inside of her she is surrendering her entire being to him similar to how a Christian surrenders his entire life to Jesus at the moment of salvation. The man acts as the giver while the woman acts as the receiver. Since the woman is the receiver, she is impacted the most by the sex act. The two souls automatically meet in ecstatic pleasure becoming one soul. It is one of God's greatest gifts to mankind when done in marriage. Singles who must wait to have sex should spend their extra time worshiping and praising God when they find themselves sexually tempted. Using the flesh to fight the sexual urge is rarely successful, but submitting the flesh to the spirit always works. The single person has the Lord as a husband. As we fill ourselves up with thanksgiving and praise towards him, we not only become closer to the Lord, but we become much more attractive to the opposite sex. Our goal as singles is not to repress our sexuality. Our goal is to fulfill these urges by engaging in higher pursuits. There is no higher pursuit than praising and worshiping God. Praise and worship is the one thing that we can give God. It allows us to surrender to God completely and meditate on how much we love and trust him. This is what makes it so special to him. In the same way, sex and devotion is the one thing that a woman can give to a man. Most real men are not interested in a woman's money or her status. They want sex and devotion.

Throughout the Old Testament, God would refer to his people as adulterous as they would seek after other Gods. Seeking after other Gods is like a wife seeking other men. Sex before marriage is preemptively cheating on our husband. The intimacy that was only to be shared with him is now shared with others and we bring soul ties into the marriage when it finally occurs. The apostle Paul explains the importance of sexual purity in 1 Corinthians 6:12-20, NIV:" **Everything is permissible for me-but not everything is beneficial . . . . The body is not meant for sexual immorality, but for the Lord and the Lord for the body. Do you not know that your bodies are members of Christ himself? Shall I then take the members of Christ and unite them with a prostitute? Never! Do you not know that he who unites himself with a prostitute is one with her in body? For it is said, "The two will become one flesh. But he who unites himself with the Lord is one spirit. Flee from sexual immorality. All other sins a man commits are outside his body, but he who sins sexually sins against his own body. Do you not know that you are the temple of the Holy Spirit who is in you, whom you have received from God? You are not your own: you were bought by God for a price. Therefore honor God with your body."**

A few months ago, I was thinking about the fact that three gorgeous guys had rejected me over the past few years, but I was not very disturbed about it. God reminded me that I never formed soul ties with these individuals, so when they left, my spirit was not torn apart. In other words, I was still in possession of my soul. God prompted me to remember my horrible college years which were just the opposite. I would find a guy that I really adored and give my body to him, and then he would usually dump me and leave me depressed and upset for months or even years. During those years, I had the legs of Tina Turner and a face like Halle Berry. Even though many men were interested in me, I would walk around in a depressed stupor for months and sometimes years over the same guy. I would call and call. Sometimes I would even sit in the car in front of a guys' house and cry. Getting dumped was the worst tragedy in the world to me because I had developed soul ties with these men. These men carried little pieces of my soul with them and I did not even realize it. The creation of soul ties is the major reason why premarital sex is so unsatisfying. The sex act merges two souls together whether we realize it or not. Untangling two souls is a job that only God can do. Only he can heal the broken parts of our souls that result from multiple sexual partners. This is why repentance and prayer are essential.

The bible clearly outlines that sex outside of marriage has spiritual consequences and should be avoided. According to Paul, **"If you cannot control yourself, [you] should marry. For it is better to marry than to burn"** (1 Corinthians 7:9, NIV). It is only in marriage that we can freely enjoy our mate without fear of being abandoned or feeling guilty after the sex act. To modern ears, this standard seems harsh and unattainable. For those of us who decide to seek sexual purity, we can be comforted by the words of the famous author C.S. Lewis: *Perfect chastity-like perfect charity will not be attained by any merely human efforts. You must ask God for help. Even when you have done so, it may seem to you for a long time that no help or less help than you need, is being given. Never mind. After each failure, ask forgiveness, pick yourself up, and try again. For however important chastity may be, this process trains us in habits of the soul which are more important still. It cures our illusions about ourselves and teaches us to depend on God. We learn on the one hand that we cannot trust ourselves in our best moments and on the other hand, that we need not despair in our worst, for our failures are forgiven. The only fatal thing is to sit down content with anything less than perfection* [7].

The Real Choice: Sex God's Way or Sex Satan's Way

Many argue that they do not seek sexual purity because nothing really bad ever happens to them when they do whatever they want sexually. Others swear that their whorish friends found the best husbands while they unfairly remain single because they did the right thing. These arguments would be valid if we had no soul and were created to do whatever we want and be whoever we want to be as stated in Satanism and Humanism. Christianity teaches that we are here to glorify and serve God as we are conformed to the image of his Son Jesus Christ. Sexual sin takes us off our true path and derails God's purpose for our lives. God is holy and we have trouble being in proper relationship with him when we sin sexually. We may not lose our salvation when we sin sexually, but we certainly lose our peace, joy and happiness when we do. We become like Eve who felt the need to hide from God instead of running towards him. We are not our own, God bought us for a price. He sent his only Son Jesus Christ to die for our sins and the least that we could do is die to our fleshly desires. Whenever we do Godly things, it seems difficult at first but then you feel so much better afterwards. For example, when we go on a diet, it is so hard to get started. However, we are glad that we decided to do it once we see how good we look and feel. Sexual sin is like eating two dozen donuts at once. We have so much fun as we lick our lips and enjoy that sweet taste in our mouth. The problem is that afterwards we have to deal with a five pound weight gain, a headache and a sick feeling in the stomach. Sin promises so much, but delivers so little in the end.

Sin is no big deal to both Humanists and Satanists, but it should be a big deal to Christians. Both Humanism and Satanism declare us as our own God who gets to make up our own rules. While this may sound like a dream come true, the end of this dream is death. James, the brother of Jesus explains that "**every man is tempted, when he is drawn away in his own lust, and enticed. The when lust hath conceived, it [brings] forth sin: and sin, when it is finished, [it brings] forth death**" (James 1:14-15, KJV). The breakdown of the family, the epidemic of sexually transmitted diseases, the hurt feelings as lovers part company are all clues to the fact that making our own rules and ignoring God is not such a good idea. The Satanist and Humanistic idea to get rid of the guilt instead of the sin still leaves us feeling empty after everything is said and done. Both Humanism and Satanism erroneously teach that we are our own God, so we make up our own rules. While this may sound like fun, we endanger ourselves because we are drawn away from God and towards Satan himself. When we compare the Humanistic manifestos to the basic beliefs mentioned in the Satanic Bible, we will find almost identical philosophies that promote the notion of human Godhood. The 2nd Humanist Manifesto claims, "*We believe . . . that traditional dogmatic or authoritarian religion that places revelation, God, ritual or creed above human needs and experience do a disservice to the human species . . . We find insufficient evidence for the belief in the supernatural . . . as non-theists, we begin with humans, not God, nature, not deity . . . . No deity will save us; we must save ourselves*" [8]. This is almost identical to the statement in the Satanic Bible: "*The Satanist feels, why not really be honest . . . if you are going to create a god in your image, why not create that god as yourself*" [9]. The Satanic Bible further states that we should "*say unto [our] own heart, I am mine own redeemer*" [10]. Both of these philosophies place man above God and make the claim that man essentially save himself. Even the author of the Satanic Bible recognized this common bond between his philosophy and the universally accepted philosophy of humanism when he said, "*But why call it Satanism? Why not call it humanism?*" [11]. When we embrace humanistic values, we are really embracing Satanic values and most of us don't even know it. Both philosophies take God and his rules out of the equation. When we hear people say, "Let me do my thing and you do your thing" or "you do you and let me do me" they are repeating the modern version of famous Satanist's Aleister Crowley's summary of how Satanism: "Do what thou wilt shall be the whole of the law"[12]. We only fool ourselves when we think that we have things figured out better than God.

This Satanic philosophy that allows its members to do whatever they want with their bodies has the ultimate goal of self-worship. Satan fell from heaven because of his desire to be God and be worshiped as God. According to Isaiah 14, "**How art thou fallen O Lucifer, son of the morning! . . . For [you] said in [your] heart, I will exalt my throne above the stars of God . . . I will be like the Most High [God]. Yet [you] shall be bought down to hell,** to the sides of the pit" (Isaiah 14: 12-14, KJV). Satan is pleased whether we worship him directly by engaging in satanic rituals or indirectly by worshiping ourselves. When we worship ourselves, we are following in Satan's footsteps and imitation is the ultimate form of flattery. Thinking that we can determine what is good or evil without any regard for God's standards is the ultimate form of self-worship. When we do this we are telling God that he can be replaced because our thoughts are above his thoughts. We are allowing the serpent to trick us like he tricked Eve in the Garden of Eden. Satan told Eve, "**Did God really tell you to not eat from the tree? . . . God knows that the moment that you eat of it, your eyes will be opened and you will be like gods who know what is good and what is bad**" (Genesis 3:1-5, NASB). Eve displeased God by deciding to follow Satan's advice to "do as she pleased." We do the same thing when we have sex with whomever we please because it feels good even though we know that God said that it is not right. One of my older friends who never got married would sometimes say, "If God does not send me a husband soon, I am going to sin like crazy and have sex with whomever I want." One day I had to share with her the fact that this is exactly what Satan said. He made this declaration before he fell from heaven. Similar to many of us, he planned to do whatever he wanted without any regard for God's standards.

Sex is one of those issues that few of us can ever fully agree with God about. However, we must trust that God is wiser than us and knows when sex will be most satisfying both spiritually and physically. Psychologists have found that God's word is right: sex is most satisfying in the context of marriage. Most older folks who are honest with themselves have to admit that premarital sex demanded so much for such a little return. Married people do not usually have to worry about abandonment, unwanted pregnancy, sexually transmitted diseases and getting a bad reputation after sex with their spouse. However, all single people have to worry about one or more of these issues. Even if those issues are not a problem, we should wait because God says to wait. If Jesus could die on the cross for us, the least that we could do is die to our own lustful desires for him. Mostly everyone wants to have sex. The million dollar question is "Are we humble enough to wait and do it God's way?" We must remember that Jesus said, "**If you love me, you will obey what I command**" (John 14:15, NIV).

CHAPTER 4

Dating in the Age of Bad Information

Dating and relationships are hot topics these days and everyone seems to have a strong opinion about them. I got some major insight into some of these opinions and why they make dating so difficult at my friend Allegra's single mixer. At the event, there were two Christian couples with their live-in lover, two Afro-centric Spiritualists, two Atheistic Buddhist, two bible believing Christians and about fifteen others who were a mixture of all of the above. One atheist declared, "I only have sex twice a year and it had better be good or I will curse the guy out." She stated that she was not interested in a relationship because it was too much responsibility and sex twice a year was enough to keep her satisfied. Everyone laughed at her comment and told her that she was being cruel to men. Next, one of the younger women who was a mixture of religions said, "all I know is that a guy had better have his finances right or he can't be taking me out because I have my stuff together. His equipment better not be small either." Next, one of the bible-believing Christians spoke and said, "A man should love a woman like Christ loved the Church." This statement excited me and I added that God had been showing me some interesting things in the bible about love and relationships. I told the group that Ephesians 5 is so beautiful and represents a good deal for both men and women. Before I could even say another word, a guy who was living with a Christian woman said, "You cannot cast stones at anyone when your life is not perfect either." Confused, I asked, "Who is casting stones?" One of the Afro-centric Spiritualists then asked me, "What does God have to do with relationships anyway?" I responded, "Didn't God create relationships?" Next, the other atheist who was clearly wounded by his last girlfriend shouted "We can never let God or religion enter a discussion about relationships because it is simply not fair." He began crying as he talked about the last woman who broke his heart. It was so tragic to see so many hurt and wounded people searching for the answers to their relationship woes when the answer was right before them in the Holy Bible: yet, they seemed antagonistic to it. It seemed that all views were allowable except for the Biblical view which happened to be the only view that could heal all the wounds and broken places in the lives of these young singles.

This was a wake-up call for me because I never expected for people in an age of tolerance to be so intolerant of the biblical view. My heart was grieved because it became clear why dating and relationships are so disappointing these days. As I looked around the room, it became apparent that the majority of the singles at the mixer were simply confused by all of the mixed messages that they see on TV and hear in music. The ideology of both the Christians and non-Christians in the room could have been taken right off of the pages of famous Satanist Aleister Crowley's Book of the Law: "Do what thou wilt shall be the whole of the Law"[1]. Today, there are so many people with so many different opinions and there is usually no basis, other than feelings, for any particular view. Once we have elevated our changeable opinions over the eternal Word of God, we have crossed a very dangerous line.

The men at the single's mixer reminded me of the countless men that I dated when I was younger. I would spend hours by the phone waiting for a guy to call when he was probably not relationship material in the first place. As women, we often find a guy, develop feelings for a guy, and then get serious about a guy before really knowing his values and habits. Many men do the same thing. There were two women at the seminar that would leave any man wounded for the rest of his life. There was one thing that everyone, except me and the other bible-believing Christian seemed to agree about even though each person had a slightly different opinion about everything else: God has no place in a discussion about relationships and each person should do what he wants to do as long as they hurt no one else.

The comment that disturbed me most of all, was the comment "What does God have to do with relationships?" It was not until the next day that I got the perfect answer for that question. Pastor Terence Johnson of Higher Dimension Church in Houston preached a sermon called, "Whose Fries are These Anyway?" The minister told the story of a trip to McDonald's with his two sons. He ordered each son some fries and even supersized the order for the oldest one, hoping to get a few for himself. When he asked the son with the supersized fry for just one fry, the boy answered, "no, these are my fries daddy." Pastor Johnson said that he was in shock. He said to himself, "does this boy know who bought him these fries?" Does he know that I am the one who drove him here and paid for this food? Does he not know that I could take them away at any time?"[2]. The actions of this preacher's son reminded me of how many of us treat God our Father. Even though God gave us everything that we have, we still have the nerve to tell him, "this is mine and you cannot have this back." We forget that God is powerful enough to bring King Nebuchadnezzar to his knees when he bragged about his Kingdom without acknowledging God. He struck Herod down as soon as he started thinking that he was God and could do as he pleased. How could anyone ask "What does God have to do with relationships?"? Does he not know that God is the one who gave him his relationships and gives him the gift of speech to ask such a question? Does he not know that God invented relationships and has all wisdom about relationships and everything else? Does he not know that if we ask the question, "What does God have to do with relationships?" the only correct answer is "Everything!"

My heart was broken by what I saw at the event and I decide to do some research to see how serious the problem is in this culture. Research confirmed that the people at the singles mixer were not alone in having a deep aversion to any mention of God or the bible when it comes to relationships. I should not have been surprised that most of the Christians in the room were as determined to leave God and the bible out of relationships as the non-Christians. Gallop poll results show that 85% of nonbelievers see no difference between their lifestyle and that of their Christian peers [3]. Current data suggest that 60% of younger Christians and one-third of older Christians think that living together, gambling and sexual fantasies are OK. Roughly 44% of younger Christians and 23% of older Christians feel that pre-marital sex is morally acceptable. Roughly a third of youngsters also believe that using profanity, getting drunk, having an abortion or homosexual activity is OK [4]. Several studies also show that over half of Christians are involved with pornography. It is clear that the bible is no longer the guidebook for proper behavior for many Christians. In today's world of value relativism, if a Christian or non-Christian falls short of an established moral standard, he can just create a new moral standard for himself.

On a positive note, more and more men and women seem to be willing to find out what the bible has to say about relationships these days. Just recently, several of the people from the mixer that was held two years ago told Allegra that they would like to schedule another mixer to allow me to discuss what the bible says about relationships. I also found hope at the 2012 Essence Festival which was one of the best ever. This was the first year that most of the black leaders spoke about accountability and the need for the Fathers to return home to their families. After the Saturday seminars were over, I visited the Hilton Hotel and enjoyed a lively discussion with several young adults about love and relationships. In the Hilton lobby and restaurant area, one young lady told a young single guy that he was selfish because he always put his needs ahead of the woman's needs. He started bragging about his many sexual escapades and said that this is just the society that we live in. When they observed me laughing at them as I ate my salad, they wanted to know my opinion. I told they guy the following: "We are taught selfishness in our culture, but true happiness comes from giving rather than receiving. The happiest people are those who share what they have with others. When it comes to sex, we have to remember that two souls become one during the sex act. When we separate from someone that we shared our souls with, we are still connected to that person by soul ties. This may be why you see ex-girlfriends hiding out behind dumpsters looking for you after you have left them. They are carrying little pieces of your soul with them and they are deeply wounded that you have left. Sex is harder for women than for men because we are the receivers while you are the giver. Sex is an act of worship. It is the most intimate act between two people. This is why God tells us to wait until marriage. He is not trying to be a cosmic killjoy. He loves us and wants what is best for us." The guy was absolutely intrigued by my statements and he insisted that we exchange numbers and become facebook friends. He said that I have definitely spoken the truth on this issue and he wants to hear more. Later, in two different situations at the festival, several other guys had a similar reaction to my statements. This successful experience with sharing the biblical perspective on dating and sex shows that there are people willing to listen, but the church must start spreading the message. After speaking with these guys, I realized that I was the first person to ever clearly share the biblical perspective about dating and sex with them. It troubled me that no other Christian guy had shared this with them when God's plan is so beautiful. It would be wonderful if men would intentionally share the biblical view of sex with other men and women would do the same with other women. We Christians must seize every opportunity to be a positive impact on our culture or else we lose our right to complain.

Nothing is as fulfilling as being a positive impact on younger Christians. It was wonderful to mentor two young ladies this summer as they tried to make sense of their dating relationships. I was able to share with them my experiences to encourage them. One young lady was complaining that she was so afraid that she would never get married. She began to cry as I shared my testimony with her about dating and relationships. I told her that "We do not know what will happen tomorrow, but it is wonderful to know the one who knows. We are God's children and God loves us as a doting Father. He wants what is best for us. If someone has left your life, they were not meant to be there. If God wants them back in your life, they will come back. God is in complete control. He will give you the right relationship at the right time. To be honest, I have had many marriage proposals and one marriage that had to end. After my divorce, I got at least 10 marriage proposals using the secret that the Lord shared with me: The Lord shared the following: *Men want the same things as God wants from us. All that we have to offer God is the same thing that we have to offer a real man: respect, loyalty and trust. We come to God bankrupt the same way we come to a real man. God does not need our money because he already owns everything. We tithe just to show that we trust him. We respect God by obeying him-just like with a man. We show loyalty to a man by being faithful to him-just like with a man. We show that we trust God by laying our hearts, souls and bodies naked before him in surrender. This is what sex is for a man. Sex is an act of worship. Worship is to God as sex is to a man. God causes us to be male magnets when we spend time worshipping him. Just like we surrender our bodies, concerns and soul to a man during the sex act, we surrender everything to God during worship. God pours out his blessings to us when we delight in him. He wants for us to enjoy sex, just at the right time and with the person that promises to be there when it is all over-our husband. As singles, God wants for us to enjoy spending time with him give ourselves fully to him in reckless abandon. Worship God whenever those sexual feelings start getting overwhelming,"* The last time I spoke with the young ladies, several of her past boyfriends are suddenly extremely interested. She was very confident that she would one day find a husband. However, I was careful to remind her that even if she does not get married, Jesus Christ can keep us in perfect peace as long as we keep our minds on him. As more and more of us learn God's secrets for awesome relationships, we can share this wisdom with the next generation and be a force for positive change. The next generation is hungry for the truth and they are so tired of falsehood.

The Problem of Unbiblical Advice from Well-Meaning Christians Inside of the Church

The lack of established dating standards and conflicting messages in the media and popular culture makes dating hard for all of us, both Christians and non-Christians. However, it is even harder for Christians since we are in a constant battle between the world that says, "Do whatever you want to do" and a bible that says, "Be Holy and honor your body as the Temple of the Holy Spirit." The problem is further complicated by many well-meaning, yet, misguided people in the church drowning out the clear teachings of Jesus Christ in the bible with false unbiblical ideas. Jesus introduced us to the law of love throughout scripture. In fact, he summed up all the rules of the bible as one simple rule: he said for us to love God with all our heart and love our neighbor as ourselves. Jesus was not pleased with the religious leaders of his day who added to the Word of God or took things away from it. He was frustrated that the Pharisees were very rule oriented, but lacked the love and compassion that comes from a clean heart. They added hundreds of extra rules for the people to follow that had nothing to do with God. Their hearts were filled with anger, hatred, and pride rather than love, righteousness, peace and joy. Jesus warned these men by saying **"Isaiah was right when he prophesied about you hypocrites: as it is written, 'These people honor me with their lips but their hearts are far from me. They worship me in vain: their teachings are but rules taught by men.' (Isaiah 29:13) You have let go of the commands of God and are holding on to the traditions of men"** (Mark 7:6-8, NIV). The Sadducees were very worldly religious leaders who cared very little about the rules. They talked about love all the time, but they were unable to show it because they were too busy looking out for their own self-interest and doing whatever they wanted to do.

While there are many biblical voices rising up, today's Christian dating and relationship scene is still dominated by the modern-day version of these two groups. We are told to either deny our sexuality altogether by religious zealots or to live freely and enjoy every pleasure by liberal theologians. One group asks us to do that which is not humanly possible while the other asks that we become "tolerant" cultural conformists. With such bad advice dominating the airwaves, we really should not be surprised that the dating and marriage patterns of Christians are often the same as, if not worse than that of non-Christians. Luckily, there is an easy solution to this problem: returning to the teachings of Jesus Christ and using the bible as the timeless relationship manual that it was designed to be. The bible clearly shows us how to properly relate to God and to each other.

Many young Christians are rejecting Christianity altogether because they are burdened by the extreme rules and regulations given by the modern day Pharisees. These young people have been bombarded by advice and catchy sayings like, "Wait for God to send someone", "Dating is wrong", or "Sex is evil". We have a natural tendency to want to rebel rather than repent when faced with strict rules. Often these rules have nothing to do with anything that God expects or even cares about. In the *Screwtape Letters*, the demon Screwtape celebrated the Pharisee as a delightful creature of hell. He noted that "different types of Pharisee have been harvested, trodden and fermented together to produce subtle flavor . . . Some were all rules and relics and rosaries; others were all drab clothes, long faces and petty traditional abstinences from wine or cards or the theatre. Both [types] had in common their self-righteousness and the almost infinite distance between their actual outlook and anything [God] actually is or commands" [5]. C.S. Lewis characterized the problem well. Pharisees spend endless hours making and monitoring rules that do nothing but increase their own pride and self-righteousness. The truth is that if we sit at home bored because we refuse to date out of self-righteousness, we are no closer to God than those who do date and enjoy themselves. If we claim that "dating on-line is for desperate people who don't know God", we are no more Godly than those who date online or meet people all the time. If we think that sex is evil, we fail to appreciate the fact that sex is a gift from God used to glorify God. God wants for all of us to enjoy this gift at the proper time and in the context of the only union that makes it most fulfilling: that union is marriage. The center of being a Christian is not found in these man-made rules. Christianity is a religion based on a personal relationship with Jesus Christ. This relationship is based on adoration of God, mutual love and forgiveness. Following man-made rules brings us no closer to Christ, but could easily keep us from finding him. When we excessively focus on rules without a balance of love, we increase our pride and experience religious burn out. This excessive focus on rules does not bring us any closer to God or anyone else.

Some of us have embraced the rules of the Pharisees and have essentially given up on dating and finding a mate altogether. Some of us self-righteously proclaim "I don't need a mate because Jesus is all I need." Many of us who have embraced this idea are turning to food, career obsession, ministry obsession and a host of other things to fill in this absent part of our life. We have all heard Christian friends say "God wants me to be without a mate" or "I am waiting on the Lord to send my Prince." This is fine if God did in fact call us to singleness. However, there is no need to sit at home forever eating bon bons on Saturday night if this pronouncement stems from a refusal to try anymore because of disappointment and lots of bad advice. Some of us go out and interact with people so infrequently that we may not get practice in one of the most essential relationship skills: acting lovingly even when we don't feel like it. Christianity is about following the teachings of Jesus Christ. This includes loving your neighbor as yourself and doing good to even those who treat you poorly. Christianity is also about selfless giving and having a life that glorifies God. These are skills that are best practiced in the context of relationships. We develop relationship skills by having relationships. Avoiding relationships only leads to loneliness and pain. Timothy Keller noted that "Even people who completely avoid romantic relationships out of bitterness or fear are actually being controlled by its power . . . [If] you are so afraid of love that you cannot have it, you are just as enslaved as if you must have it . . . If you are too afraid of love or too enamored by it, it has assumed godlike power, distorting your perception and life" [6].

Many of the youngsters who ran from the church have fallen for the doctrine of the Sadducees and the voice of our own pop culture. The "tolerant" and worldly Sadducees say things like "Do whatever feels right for you. Who am I to judge?" Their only rule is "It is OK to sin because God is forgiving." One of my facebook associates placed a status on her wall that stated, "Sin away because the more we sin, the more God gives his grace." This person would also often say, "If God does not send me a husband quickly, I am going to sin like crazy." There are many Sadducees in the pulpit. One pastor once told me that he counsels from the bible at first, but then he gives his personal opinion based on the times we live in. He told me, "The bible was written so long ago and its principles just don't apply to what we are seeing today." Another Sadducee in the pulpit could have destroyed any hopes of me becoming a serious Christian when he suggested that he could be my sexual coach who would teach me how to have sex with a man and never make him want to leave. We constantly hear Christian men say, "It is OK to have sex, God understands and he will forgive you." Others will say, "You have to try it before you buy it." Modern Sadducees have fooled themselves into believing that we can have one foot in the world and one foot in God's Kingdom at the same time. The truth is that there is no safe spot where we are free from God's rules and safe from Satan's enslavement at the same time. The further we run from God, the closer we get to Satan himself. The neutral option that many of us were hoping for does not even exist. Without knowing it, modern Sadducees have the same doctrine of the Satanists and secular humanists. The message of the Sadducees is the message of the world: Do what you want to do with your own body as long as you hurt no one else. It is impossible to tell these Christians from non-Christians. Many of our church scandals are due to pastors and other individuals who have embraced this way of thinking. Modern Sadducees not only hurt themselves, but they hurt others and damage the entire body of Christ. Muslims and atheists continually site the actions of these individuals as the reason for believing that Christianity must not be true. One former Muslim who is still undecided about becoming a Christian confided that the loose lives of Christians are the reason why he knows Christianity must be false.

The situation is not hopeless because God is rising up an army of Christians who understand the beauty of his plan for love and sex. As I was writing this book, I ran into two other women who were divorced and clearly had the prophetic gift. Both of these women were writing a book very similar to mine. I think that God is so loving and caring for his church that it grieves his heart that the body of Christ does not have a clear understanding of his most precious gifts: sex and marriage. He is calling divorced women because we can share our mistakes. People who are in great marriages have no desire to figure out what makes a marriage work: however, people who are broken must spend hours putting themselves back together again and figuring out what caused the brokenness in the first place. God has been faithful in revealing it to us and giving us the courage to reveal it to others. Within 5 years, I am certain that the tides will have changed.

Many pastors in the body of Christ have excellent books that drown out the voices of the Pharisees and Sadducees who make dating and relationships so much harder for Christians. Dr. Henry Cloud wrote the best dating manual for Christians that I have ever read and it is called *How to Get a Date worth Keeping*. This book goes into detail about getting rid of the attitudes and ideas that keep many Christians single and lonely on the dating scene. Pastor Gregg Matte wrote an excellent bible study called *Birds and Bees*. This bible study goes into detail about the beauty of God's plan for relationships, especially marriage. Dr. John Bisagno has an excellent book called *Love is Something You Do*. This book has a wealth of wisdom and it contains the best antidote for couples who are falling out of love. The book series that changed my entire dating life when I was 25 was *Mars and Venus on a Date* by John Gray. He teaches us the wisdom of our ancestors that many have forgotten in this generation. Steve Harvey's books and movies are similar to the Mars and Venus books. Mr. Harvey wrote *Think Like a Man* as a manual to help his daughters find better dates. He never expected to find a nation of daughters who needed his help. His book is awesome and offers a wealth of wisdom about what to look for in a man. Many others rave about the book *Love and Respect*. In recent years, there have been numerous pastors who have been holding seminars for single Christians with excellent advice. Things are definitely improving, but each one of us has to get the word out about what works and hold each other accountable.

The Secret to Joyful Victory over Sexual Sin

In addition to the false voices from the outside, we Christians have a serious conflict going on inside his body between the flesh and the spirit. In the bible, Paul instructs us that every Christian has a flesh that screams, "I want___, I think_____ and I feel____." The flesh wants what it wants when it wants it and it thinks that it can do whatever it feels like doing. At the same time, we Christians have a spirit that has the mind of God. Paul wrote, **"For we know that the law is spiritual; but I am carnal, sold under sin . . . what I hate, that I do . . . For I delight in the law of God after the inward man: But I see another law in my members, warring against the law in my mind, and bringing me to captivity to the law of sin which is in my members. O wretched man that I am! Who shall deliver me from the body of this death? I thank God through Jesus Christ our Lord. So with the mind, I serve the law of God; but with the flesh the law of sin. There is no condemnation to them which are in Christ Jesus, who walk not after the flesh, but after the Spirit. For the law of the Spirit of** life in Christ Jesus has made me free from the law of sin and death . . . **For to be carnally minded is death; but to be spiritually minded is life and peace . . . For if ye live after the flesh, ye shall die: but if ye through the Spirit should mortify the deeds of the body, ye shall live. For as many are led by the Spirit of God, they are the Sons of God"** (Romans 8:1-14, KJV). As Christians, we are instructed to place the flesh, with all of its selfish and self-centered desires, in submission to the spirit. The secret of being victorious is to starve the flesh and feed the Spirit.

The Spirit of God is powerful enough to handle our weaknesses when we put our feelings on the backburner and let the wisdom of God guide our choices. For singles, this means that when lust thoughts enter our minds we need to quicken our thoughts to something more beneficial or read God's word. If we need to get out the house, we could go for a prayer walk. We could also call a friend or an accountability partner. Another great thing to do is to spend time worshipping God. Sex is an act of worship so sexual thoughts about someone to whom we are not married are thoughts of worship towards the physical aspect of sex devoid of its spiritual significance. It is impossible to worship God and something else at the same time. Those who are married can do the same thing when they have thoughts about someone other than their spouse. Rather than fight wrong thoughts, we can replace them with better thoughts. It is so important to stop the sin of lust at the thought level. We often wonder how a pastor of 20 years could lose it all after just one affair. It always starts with a failure to guard one's thoughts which contaminate the heart. When our hearts are filled with lust instead of the wisdom of God, sexual sin is just around the corner. Those of us who have given our lives to Christ will always have our flesh warring against the Spirit of God. It is natural for us to desire sex because God gave us this awesome desire. He just wants for singles to channel this desire towards him and married people to keep this desire channeled towards their spouse. God wants this because the greatest pleasure comes from purity. Pain, guilt and shame are the fruit of lust and God wants something better for us. The best weapon that we have at our disposal is the Word of God. Lustful thoughts and desires will come to all of us, but the Word of God supplies us with tools to defeat these enemies of our souls.

The Problem of Misunderstanding the Flesh and Spirit

There are two errors in thinking about the flesh and the Spirit that are extremely common in Christian circles today:

• Error 1: This is the liberal doctrine of cheap grace. Some of us think that the flesh is so powerful that we have to give in to it until the Holy Spirit heals us in that area. Since we are waiting for the Holy Spirit to cure us, we constantly mess up in certain areas because of uncontrollable impulses.

- Error 2: Some think that we are perfected at the time of salvation and we have to act perfectly at all times. According to this doctrine, perfection is maintained by strict rules of conduct and being careful to never be tempted. This lies at the heart of the legalism of the Pharisees.

Christians who adhere to the doctrine of cheap grace give the flesh too much power while ignoring the Spirit. They mistakenly emphasize God's mercy while ignoring the fact that he is also holy and just. They also mistakenly emphasize our freedom in Christ without acknowledging that we must also submit to him. These individuals assume that the flesh can one day be satisfied once it has gotten enough of what it wants and Christ heals it. This is only partially true. Jesus Christ is the one who heals our flesh, but he does it in the midst of us submitting to him, not as we give into the flesh. The more satisfaction that we give the flesh, the more satisfaction the flesh wants. We see this clearly with alcoholics and drug addicts. They start off as social drinkers and smokers, then the next thing you know, they wind up losing everything for their addictions. This is the slippery slope of sin. Sin starts out with a wrong thought. If we fail to hurry and think about something else, we begin to meditate on it. Then we commit the act of sin. We can either turn away from sin through repentance or we can do it regularly and form a habit. Eventually, the habit becomes a compulsion. At this point, we lose control and either seek help from other Christians or a counselor or continue as the sin leads to death. Many of us fail to realize that the flesh stops its cravings as we starve it. Each time that we submit the flesh to the Spirit, the flesh gets weaker and weaker. We must use our will to avoid sin. Our feelings do not cooperate at first, so we have to do the right thing in spite of feelings.

There are no happy, carefree, peaceful Christians who sin as much as they did before conversion. With this in mind, modern day Sadducees must make sure that they are born again. Being born again means that a person's heart has changed and the Spirit of God now indwells in them. A person who is not born again cannot submit their flesh to their Spirit because the Spirit is not in them. Paul noted, **"Now if any man [does not have] the Spirit of Christ, he is none of his"** (Romans 8:9, KJV). Modern day Sadducees must make sure that he is in Christ's family. This means that he has surrendered all areas of life to Jesus Christ and now trusts Jesus' death on the cross as full payment for all sins—past, present and future. When the Holy Spirit comes, sin will lose its appeal because the Holy Spirit is grieved by it. The secret to victory is to learn how to ignore feelings and follow the promptings of the Spirit. At first, it will be difficult because the flesh is going to rebel when it is not getting what it wants. However, eventually the feeling of peace and joy that comes from being obedient will feel so much better than the momentary pleasure of sin. Sin promises so much, but delivers so little. In the book, Sex and the Soul, Donna Freitas describes how one woman felt after a casual sexual encounter. The student wrote, "*Most of the time my stomach is in a knot and I try to suppress memories of the night before, misplaced guilt wells up and I am somewhat miserable. But I think it's a good thing: I* *think that is life: the night of beauty, wonder and arousal, the morning of destructive thought and regretful recollection"* [7].

Guilt is a Christian's friend because it tells us when we are going in the wrong direction. It tells us to turn around and do things differently. This is not what we usually hear on television or on the radio: pop culture tells us to keep the sin and get rid of the guilt. We unwittingly embrace this philosophy not realizing that it is a major principle of Satanism. According to the Satanic Bible we should *"accept man as he is, and promote turning a bad thing into a good thing rather than bending over backwards to eliminate the bad thing. Therefore, after intellectually evaluating your problem through common sense and drawing on what psychiatry has taught us, [we should] emotionally release ourselves from unwarranted guilt"* [8]. God's way is quite different. God uses guilt to remind us that we need to deal with a particular sin in our life. If we feel guilty about something, then we probably need to avoid the cause of the guilt. Guilt is the voice of our conscious correcting a certain behavior. Once we admit our sin by confessing it to Jesus Christ, he promises to forgive us. According to scripture, **"If we acknowledge our sins, he who is just can be trusted to forgive our sins and cleanse us from all unrighteousness. If we say that we have never sinned, we are a liar and the truth is not in us"** (1 John 1:8-10, NAB). Guilt is only unwarranted if we continue to feel it after we have repented. Guilt does not need to be permanent, but we must listen to it as a warning that we are going in the wrong direction and need to ask for forgiveness. The sad truth about today's culture is that many of us do not even know what the right direction looks like because the truth has been drowned out by so many conflicting voices.

Pharisees are guilty of placing unneeded guilt on themselves and others. The modern day Pharisees lead more productive lives than the Sadducees; however, their behavior is still born of the flesh instead of the Spirit of God. Even if we do all the right things, God is not pleased if they are done for the wrong reasons and in the wrong spirit. God wants us to have a pure heart towards him. He is not pleased when we do the right thing outwardly for the carnal purposes of pride and greed and other selfish motives. In Romans Paul warns, **"Because the carnal mind is enmity against God: for it is not subject to the law of God, neither can it be. So they that are in the flesh cannot please God"** (Romans 8:7-8, KJV). Doing good just to be able to proudly pat ourselves on the back does not drive us closer to God. It in fact leads us further away from him. If we think of ourselves as already perfect, then we certainly do not need a savior. If we do not need a savior, then we do not need Jesus and if we do not need Jesus we do not need God. If we do not need God, then we will not seek him and we may find ourselves eternally separated from him in the end while actually behaving better than the average Christian. To do righteous acts for the purpose of glorifying ourselves is being "self-righteous." Paul called self-righteousness "filthy rags" because it is born out of pride and independence from God. This is why Jesus warned that the tax collectors and prostitutes were closer to heaven than the actual Jewish teachers. Paul wrote, **"For they being ignorant** of God's righteousness, and going about to establish their own righteousness, have not submitted themselves unto the righteousness of God . . . For whosoever shall call upon the name of the Lord shall be saved" (Romans 10:3, 11, KJV). The Jewish teachers had hearts that were proud and loved places of honor. They were constantly patting themselves on the back for doing such a good job while looking down on other people. They thought that it was more important to tithe 10% than to save someone's life. They did not glorify God because they were too busy glorifying themselves. Their pride kept them from actually knowing God and being in relationship with him. They fell for the satanic lie: "I don't need a savior because I can save myself." Jesus warned them that hell awaits all those who have hearts that do not need a savior. Jesus said, "That except your righteousness exceed the righteousness of the Scribes and Pharisees, [you] shall in no case enter the kingdom of Heaven" (Matthew 5:20, KJV). We have to be mindful of Christ's warning that those who do not have a righteousness based on their relationship with him will not go into the kingdom of Heaven. We must be careful that we are not in the group that Jesus was speaking of when he said, "Not everyone who [says] unto me 'Lord, Lord,' shall enter the kingdom of heaven; but he that doeth the will of my Father which is in heaven" (Matthew 7: 21, KJV).

What is the clear will of God the Father? Rather than being like the Pharisees or Sadducees, God desires that we become disciples of his Son, Jesus Christ. Jesus Christ told us to love one another. According to scripture, "And this is his commandment, That we should believe on the name of his Son Jesus Christ, and love one another . . . Beloved, let us love one another: for love is of God and every one that [loves] is born of God and [knows] God. He that [loves] not [knows] not God: for God is love. In this was manifested the love of God toward us, because God sent his only begotten Son into the world that we might live through him. Herein is love, not that we loved God, but that he loved us, and sent his Son to be the propitiation for our sins. Beloved, if God so loved us, we ought also love one another"(I John 3:23; 4:7-11, KJV). When we put God first and get our love from him, we will have plenty of love to share with others. We cannot claim to belong to Jesus Christ if we are without love for him and love for each other. If we are Modern Pharisees, we understand God's rules but we do not have love and compassion for others because our ability to follow rules comes from the flesh and not the Spirit of God. If we are modern Sadducees, we so concerned with our own personal interest that we seek God's hand instead of his face. When we approach God from the flesh, asking what he can do for us, we rarely find him. Sadducees forget that Jesus said that if we love him, we will obey him. If we truly love others, we will put their interest ahead of our own just as Christ laid down his interest for us. Jesus told his followers, "If [you] keep my commandments, [you] shall abide in love; even as I have kept my Father's commandments, and abide in his love. These things have I spoken unto you, that my joy might remain in you, and that your joy might be full. This is my commandment: [You must] love one another, as I have loved you. Greater love hath no man than this, that a man lay down his life for his friends" (John 15: 10-13, KJV). We move from selfishness to selflessness as we follow God's law of love. Scripture tells us to treat everyone that we come into contact with love and concern. This includes both men and women. This includes the people that we date. We please God when we approach dating and relationships asking the right questions: "Do my actions and heart attitude show love towards God?" and "Do my actions and heart attitude show love towards this person and to myself?" God wants for us to stop getting bogged down by man-made rules and stop trying to make up our own rules and simply live by his "law of love."

CHAPTER 5

Facing the Problem:
Christian Dating and Relationships Gone Wild

How Did We Get Here?

Teaching eighth graders is interesting to say the least. One day one of my students entered the classroom saying, "Miss, did you know that a lot of your students don't believe in God." I answered "No, I did not know that." The student responded, "You know your student _____, she actually believes that she is God. If you were to sneeze right now and someone said God bless you, she would say 'No problem'." It was hard for me not to burst into hysterical laughter at this point, but what happened next was quite disturbing. One student after another told me that they never go to church and are unsure as to what religion they are. One student said, "I have not been to church in years. Well I know that I am not Catholic because I have never bent over." Another student said, "My mom has a Buddha statue and I pray to Buddha. I just love rubbing his belly." Then two other students said, "I don't really believe in God." So out of a class of six students, only one student went to church. If we were to poll their parents, at least 75% of them would probably say that they are Christian. We live in a very unique period in history. Many Americans claim to be Christian; however, studies show that less than half of those claiming to be Christian actually believe in the essential Christian doctrine that would make that claim true. There is also a trend to mix many different religions together and call it Christianity. Many people criticize the actions of Christians, but many claiming to be Christians are probably not real Christians in the first place. Even those who are Christian have been bombarded by lots of bad information on television and in the media. Surveys show that less than 10% of the general population and less than 20% of those claiming to be born again actually believe all of the essential doctrine of the Christian faith [1]. Most of us pick and choose bits and pieces from several faiths and mix it with what we hear in popular culture. Both Christians and Non-Christians alike have embraced the humanistic idea that we control our own destinies. If we are honest, most of us have also embraced the satanic idea that we do whatever we feel like doing, when we want to do it and how we want to do it. Humanism and Satanism have infiltrated our thinking to the point in which most studies show that Christians often have the same opinions as everyone else on sex, marriage and relationships. It is no wonder that the divorce rate in the church is similar to that in the culture. It should not be shocking that Christians are known to be the worst ones to date on the dating scene and in marriages when they really should be the best.

Just How Bad is the Problem?

My favorite biblical story from the book of Judges illustrates what we are seeing today. Chapter 19 of the book of Judges begins with the following phrase: **"In those days, Israel had no King"** (Judges 19:1, NIV). To have no king, means to have no final authority ruling over us. When we pick and choose which parts of the bible to believe and pick and choose which parts of various faiths to accept, we have basically decided that we have no King or final authority. PEW Researchers have found that this is exactly what significant numbers of Christians are doing. According to the researchers, "large numbers of Americans engage in multiple religious practices mixing elements of diverse traditions. Many say they attend religious services of more than one faith . . . Many also blend Christianity with Eastern or New Age beliefs [2]. They are essentially creating their own religion based on their personal opinion. Some mix a little yoga, with a little reincarnation, with a little Christianity and a little Islam and presto, we have created our very own religion out of thin air with no bible or religious organization to hold us accountable. While this sounds like a childhood fantasy come true, the following story shows us what can happen to us when we exercise the freedom to do whatever we want to do, when we want to do it, and how we want to do it:

"A Levite . . . took a concubine. And his concubine played the whore against him and went away from him unto her father's house . . . and was there for four months. And her husband arose, and went after her, to speak friendly unto her, and to bring her [back] again. When the father of the damsel saw him, he rejoiced to meet him. And his father in law . . . retained him [for] three days. And it came to pass on the fourth day, when they arose early in the morning . . . to depart: the damsel's father said [to] his son in law 'Comfort [your] heart with a morsel of bread, and afterward go your way. And they sat down and did eat and drink both of them together: for the damsel's father had said unto the man, 'Be content, I pray thee, and tarry all night and let thy heart be merry. And with the man rose up to depart, his father in law urged him [to stay]: therefore he lodged there again. And he arose early in the morning on the fifth day to depart: and the damsel's father said, 'Comfort thine heart I pray thee. And the tarried until afternoon, and they did eat both of them . . . the [Levite] would not tarry that night, but he rose up and departed . . . . [The Levite and his concubine lodged at an older man's home in Gibeah] . . . Now as they were making their hearts merry, behold, the men of the city . . . beat at the door and [spoke] to the master of the house, the old man, saying, 'Bring forth

the man that came into [your] house that we may [have sex with] him. And the [old man] said, 'Nay, do not this folly. Behold here is my daughter . . . and his concubine, I will bring them out now' . . . The man took his concubine, and brought her forth to them; and they [raped] her and abused her all night until morning; and when the day began to spring they let her go. Then came the [raped and abused concubine in the morning], and fell down at the door of the man's house where her lord was, till it was light" (Judges 19: 1-26, KJV).

This story only gets worst. After the Levite priest found his concubine dead at the door, he carried her home and cut her into 12 pieces. He then sent the body parts to all of the tribes of Israel demanding justice for her murder. Israel went to war and killed over 25,000 members of the tribe of Benjamin over the murder of this concubine. This story has a tragic ending; but the beginning explains the ending: "**In those days, there was no King in Israel: every man did that which was right in his own eyes**" (Judges 21: 25, KJV). If there was no one in authority over these people and they did not consider themselves under the authority of God, then everybody did whatever they wanted to do. Contrary to popular belief, we do not have a natural goodness that will keep us from doing wrong when we have no ruling authority and feel the freedom to do as we please. History has shown us this fact over and over again; yet, we never seem to learn the lesson. From the German Nazis to the school shooters, the most awful crimes have always been the result of a group of people who decided that they could be their own final authority or their own God. A lot of people mistakenly think that Hitler was a Christian. In reality, Hitler was an occultist who studied Nietzsche and Madame Blavatsky the same way that a real Christian studies the bible. Hitler's murderous rage was produced after he declared himself no longer under God's rule, but able to make up his own rules. He was just like the people in the book of Judges who had no king and did whatever they saw fit.

The story of the concubine being raped and murdered and the Levite sending the body parts everywhere is so far-fetched until most of us think that it has no significance for each our lives today. However, the Lord showed me that any area that we have failed to submit to God is subject to the same degree of turmoil. For example, the Lord has been showing me that my failure to surrender my use of time to him would eventually lead me to the same situation if I do not change. How, you may ask? The problem began when the concubine ran away from her master's house. If she would have never ran away, she would have never been raped and murdered on the trip back. This situation reminded me of all the times that I had difficult jobs or problems at a particular church. I would often just run away from it without praying and asking, "God do you want me to leave this place or is there something that you want me to do here?" We often fail to realize that the safest place to be is in the perfect will of God. God does not always lead us to places that are comfortable, but he always leads us to where we need to go to fulfill his perfect plan for our lives. When we step outside of his plan, we invite trouble.

The second problem was the fact that the Levite Priest seemed to have no particular plans for his journey. He kept allowing the bait of pleasure to lead him to stay longer than he should have stayed with the Father-in-law. When he finally did leave, it was at the least safe hour the Levite was forced to depend on the hospitality of strangers. If he would have left early in the morning after he obtained his concubine, they would have made it safely home. Similar to the Priest, when I am not working, I just get up and do what I want to do without acknowledging that God may want me to do something important for him on any particular day. Instead of praying about what I should do and planning my trips, I just get in the car and drive to the destination. When my mom begs me to stay one more day at her home in Louisiana even though I have things to do in Houston, I usually agree. Without God's directions, we live haphazardly and unproductively. That small favor for a friend that we could not do because we stayed out late partying on Saturday night may have had great eternal significance. We will not know how our plans without God impacted the world around us until we get on the other side of heaven. Only those things of eternal significance will remain, everything else will wither and fall away. The days of Israel having no king is a wake—up call for us to live lives that please God instead lives of mindless activities that bear no fruit.

The men of that town did not start out as drunken homosexuals that would rape and kill a woman just for the pleasure of it. One bad choice after another bad choice led them down the wrong road to a destination that they never imagined for themselves. The process by which the men of the town turned from normal Jewish men, to brutes that would rape and kill a woman just for the fun of it is a process that is going on every day in each of our lives. These men, who did the unthinkable, just made it to the end of that process when most of us are still at steps one, two or three. Today, it is so common for us to say things like, "you do you and I will do me" or sing songs like Bobby Brown's "It's my prerogative, I do what a want to do." We like to think of ourselves as "good" and we would like to think that we would never do such horrific things. This is not how God sees us. He knows what the human heart is capable of when left to its own devices. According to the Bible, **"The heart is deceitful above all things and desperately wicked: who can know it?"** (Jeremiah 17:9, KJV). This verse does not refer to the bad people of the world; this verse refers to all people of the world. This natural goodness is found only in our imagination. Jesus would not even allow others to call him good while he was still a man. The man who called him "good teacher" was corrected by Jesus for calling a human being good: Jesus said, **"Why do you call me good? No one is good except God alone"** (Mark 10:18, NASB). All of our so-called goodness comes from God. When we lose touch with God, we also lose touch with our only source of goodness. Once any of us no longer consider ourselves under God's rule, we compromise a little here and then a little there. When we disregard the bible as a standard by picking and choosing which verses we like, we move further and further from God's point of view and begin to live by feelings. If we get to pick which verse is true, then we are doing "what is right in our own eyes." We fall away so slowly that before we know it, without any warning, we wake up just like the men of who were depraved enough to rape women for fun.

God brings order to our lives. Chaos is our natural state. A garden just naturally becomes eaten up with weeds if we leave it to itself. We have to work hard to pull the weeds, turn the soil and cut the shrubs to keep things in order. The same thing happens to our hearts when left up to ourselves. God is the gardener who pulls the weeds from our hearts. Without his gardening, our hearts become more and more wicked. We have to live intentionally with a focus on his plans and his wishes. When we get off track, we need to ask God for forgiveness and turn back to him as quickly as possible. When we allow ourselves to just drift with the tide of the culture, we wind up where the people of this story found themselves. Sin starts with a thought, then the thought becomes an act, then we develop a habit. Once the habit becomes a compulsion, we begin to lose control and find ourselves in bondage. The bondage of sin ultimately leads to either spiritual or physical death. James wrote, **"Let no man say when he is tempted, 'I am tempted by God.' For God cannot be tempted with evil, neither he tempts any man, but every man is tempted, when he is drawn away of his own lust, and enticed. Then when lust hath conceived, it brings forth sin; and sin when it is finished brings forth death"** (James 1: 13-15, KJV). If we can capture sin at the thought level and surrender our thoughts to God, we will not have to go down the slippery slope that eventually leads to the spiritual condition of the men in the Book of Judges.

In the days that Israel had no King, the people had lost the fear of God. Similarly, today we have been incorrectly taught that all fear is bad and God is our buddy. In reality, we can either fear God or fear the consequences of failing to fear God. Proverbs tells us that **"the fear of the Lord is the beginning of knowledge, but fools despise wisdom and instruction"** (Proverbs 1:7, KJV). When we do not fear God, we get the feeling that we can do whatever we like to do without having to worry about anything. We begin to feel that we don't need to consult the bible about sex and relationships because our feelings and opinions are what counts and they alone will lead us to make good decisions. The fruit of this great experiment of doing whatever we feel like doing has been broken relationships, broken marriages, increased venereal diseases, increased single-parent families and rebellion among kids. When we fail to fear the Lord, we set ourselves up to fear our circumstances and fear man instead. Solomon wrote, **"Because [wisdom] has called and [you] refused: I have stretched out my hand and no man regarded . . . When your fear cometh and desolation and your destruction cometh as a whirlwind; when distress and anguish cometh upon you . . . For they hated knowledge and did not choose fear of the Lord . . . they despised all my reproof. Therefore they shall eat the fruit of their own way, and be filled with their own devices . . . [The] turning away of the simple shall slay them, and the prosperity of fools shall destroy them. [Whosoever] hearkens unto me shall dwell safely, and shall be quiet from fear of evil"** (Proverbs 1:24-33, KJV). In other words, when we do whatever we want with our own bodies, we have substituted the fear of God with the fear of AIDS, venereal disease, a bad reputation, abandonment, and a host of other things that God never intended for us to be plagued with.

The failure to take sexual sin seriously has had a negative impact on our lives. Since we have been trained that all opinions are the same, including religious ones, many have chosen our culture's opinion about sex and relationships. Many of us have failed to acknowledge an all-powerful, loving God who is holy, just and merciful at the same time knows what is best for us. We forgot that this loving Father loves us so much and wants to be in relationship with us so much that he sent his only begotten Son to die for us and save us from our sins. When we reject Christ and his wisdom, we reject the very words that bring us life and truth. We forgot John's point that **"In the beginning was the Word, and the Word was with God and the Word was God . . . . All things were made by him . . . In him was life; and the life was the light of men. And the light [shines] in darkness: and the darkness comprehended it not . . . And the Word was made flesh and dwelt among us, (and we beheld his glory as of the only begotten of the Father,) full of grace and truth"** (John 1: 1-14, KJV). We have made the error of elevating our opinions above the Word of God. Nothing is as great as God's word. Peter reminds us, **"For all flesh is as grass and all the glory of man as the flower of grass. The grass [withers], and flower [falls] away: But the word of God endures forever. And this is the word which by the gospel is preached unto you"** (I Peter 1:24-25, KJV). Today, the church stands at the crossroads. We can continue to do business as usual or we can seek God's wisdom and counsel to change the current tide. God is merciful and forgiving when we return to him with a humble and sorrowful heart. According to scripture, **"If my people which are called by my name, shall humble themselves, and pray, and seek my face, and turn from their wicked ways; then I will hear from heaven, and will forgive their sins, and will hear their land. Now mine eyes shall be open and mine ears [attentive] unto the prayer that is made in this place"** (II Chronicles 7: 14-15, KJV).

What Does Repentance Look Like?

As a person who has had trouble keeping their home organized, the Lord revealed the most profound secret to me: Start with the closets. At first, this did not make any sense to me. I said, "How can cleaning the closets make the rest of the house look better?" God showed me that in order to clean something up, it has to be an inside out job. When we clean the outside and the inside is still filthy, it is only a matter of time before the outside looks like the inside. However, if we start from the inside, the outside can easily be kept spotless. The inside determines the outside and not the other way around. We can put make up over our acne to cover the outside, but the same problem that caused the acne remains. A better way is for us to eat the right foods, cleanse our bodies and take the right medicines and clear up the acne so no make-up is needed. In the same way, true repentance is a change on the inside that produces fruit on the outside. It is a change in heart. When we try to act friendly with pasted on smiles and phony compliments, it is only a matter of time before the truth comes out. A hateful vengeful heart is very difficult to hide.

Rotten roots will ultimately lead to rotten fruit. Jesus tried to explain this principle to the Pharisees of his day. He said, **"You brood of vipers, how can you who are evil say anything good? For out of the overflow of the heart, the mouth speaks. The good man brings good things out of the good stored in him, and the evil man brings evil out of the evil stored in him"** (Matthew 12:34-35, NIV). The Pharisees were masters at making their outside appear clean; however, Jesus told them that their hearts were full of dead men's bones. While they were able to act righteous for brief periods in the public, the fact that they were filled with hatred, anger, jealousy and murder was impossible to hide from God because God judged their hearts. God knew that their heart condition kept them out of true relationship with him.

Until we have given our hearts to Jesus Christ in the process of repentance, we cannot truly know God nor have any promise of eternal life. Jesus explained to Nicodemus that the only way to completely cleanse the heart is to be born again. Even when we are born again, we sometimes let the world get into our hearts. When we are dating, it is easy to put on a show for a few hours. However, once we get married, we cannot hide our heart condition for very long. This is what makes marriage so hard: we have spent a lifetime being loving and forgiving on the surface as singles only to be forced into being loving and forgiving for real in marriage. God knows that once the heart changes, the fruits from the heart will change. Repentance means turning around and asking God to cleanse our hearts from iniquity to that we can serve him with a pure heart. Most of us, including me, are always looking for change on the outside. Every single person must lay down his problems and issues at the foot of Jesus. Only Jesus Christ has the answer that leads to our individual healing. In my own dating life, I had to repent for entering relationships with the idols of respect and success.

My Personal Repentance from the Idol of Respect

Pastor Greg Matte did an amazing sermon on parenting and mentioned that many parents have an idol of respect. As soon as he said that, I was immediately convicted that this was my particular idol in dating and relationships. This idol causes us to overcorrect someone when they offend us. Instead of lovingly correcting someone so that they could learn and grow, we try to make that person pay for failing to treat us with the dignity that we think we deserve. The idol of respect is born out of pride and selfishness rather than a genuine love for others. This idol would cause me to behave in the most unloving ways without even realizing it. This habit was developed after my divorce. I had developed the habit of saying extremely cruel things to any man that showed the slightest disrespect towards me. My threshold for disrespect was very low. Any man who mentioned sex within the first few dates would get the phone hung up in his face or he would get the pleasure of seeing me walk away calling him a jerk. Any guy who would try to get me to go to his house too soon would get an earful of nasty demeaning sarcasm. For example, a pro football player who broke a date with me got the pleasure of hearing me say, "Do you know what you need to do with all your money? You need to go buy yourself some character because you certainly don't have any. How dare you treat anyone with such disrespect, I do not ever want to speak to you again." Then I hung up in his face. He tried to call me back about 20 times and even said that if I were a Christian, I would forgive him. However, I never returned his calls. Looking back, my goal was to hurt these men to make them feel as bad as they made me feel. I was not acting in love towards these men because I was too busy thinking about myself.

Sometimes we need other Christians to help us see areas that we need to work on to become all that God wants us to be. A lady at church named Ms. Juanita told me that this habit of being purposely disrespectful to men that I considered arrogant and rude did not make me look good and it was not what God wanted me to do. At first, I resented her insight, but a few weeks later, another older Christian told me what ending dating relationships in a Godly way actually looked like. She said that she would use bad experiences as teachable moments for herself and men. She said that there was a guy who told her that his baby's momma would not let him see his kids. She told him, "No real man would allow a woman to keep him away from his children. You need to go to court and demand to see your kids or you will regret this decision for the rest of your life. I refuse to date a man who is not taking care of his kids." She said that they parted for several years and they saw each other at the store just recently. She said, "He told me, 'Thank you so much for telling me to keep my kids in my life. I did what you said to do and it was the best decision of my life. I really appreciate your honesty. It is so wonderful to have my kids in my life right now.' See, I always level with a guy about what I expect and use different experiences as teachable moments." When she finished speaking, I thought about the fact the God was convicting me to do the same thing. God was telling me to use each date as an opportunity to glorify Jesus Christ and bring others closer to him. God convicted me to ask, "Does my conversation with this person glorify myself or does it glorify God?" God also prompted me to ask, "Am I saying this to this person out of love or am I just trying to make myself feel better?"

God is faithful as he teaches us our life lessons. I got the opportunity to put this insight into practice twice after painful dating situations. One was with a boyfriend who I was supposed to marry and the other was with a rich, handsome stranger. Both of these men were disrespectful as they tried to demand premarital sex from me. Instead of finding ways to hurt them back, I blessed both of them and both relationships ended on a positive note. With my boyfriend, I told him that God loves him and I gave him a leather bound copy of the bible with a sympathy card for the death of his mother. I never sent him a card when his mother died and the Lord prompted me undo this wrong on my part as we parted. His last words to me were, "Thanks baby, I love you." A few weeks later, I met a handsome wealthy man who I thought would be Prince Charming. Unfortunately, he turned out to be a frog and really disappointed me. We fought after I refused to have sex with him. Even though I was angry and wanted to tell him about himself, I resisted the urge and prayed for guidance about a way for God to get glory out of this situation. I remembered that the handsome stranger mentioned that it is good to write a letter of forgiveness to those who have hurt you and I wound up taking his advice to deal with him. I decided to write the handsome stranger a thank you note for bringing me such great insights and launching me into ministry. Once he saw the note, he called me and angrily stated "just, lose my number and stop wasting my time." To my surprise, I responded, "I forgive you and God loves you. You just need to watch how you treat women in the future. You never know where your blessing is coming from." Eventually, he wound up apologizing and saying, "I love you for being so forgiving and understanding; I don't know why I was treating you that way." It was wonderful to see God change my heart and the hearts of these men. For the first time, I got to see God being glorified at the end of relationships. God is so awesome and amazing. His ways are so perfect and healing to the soul.

We are all works in progress and our transparency about mistakes and issues can be used to help others. At first, I did not want to share the mistakes that I made in these relationships. Then I realized that it is not about me; it is about me using my life and problems as well as successes to glorify God. Satan wants for us to put on a phony face and pretend that everything is OK when we are really dying inside, but God wants to bring light to those dark places of the heart. As we bring the dark places in our hearts to the surface, we can help others do the same. God is honored when we use our messes to form a message that points others to him. It was through this experience that I realized my need to stop looking for a Prince when I am a daughter of the Most High King. This lesson launched me into my ministry. I have helped so many young ladies with this message and I plan to continue to help others as well. It is so strange, yet, amazing that God uses our failures to bring about our greatest successes. He uses these failures to humble us and give us a heart to help others going through the same pain.

This spirit of repentance is the only way that we can come to revival. God is not interested in our appearances. He wants for each of us to return our hearts towards him. Any phony cleaning up the outside of the cup will not do right now. Rather than covering up our problems, the church needs to address them head on. The only way to remove darkness is to bring it to light. We must expose these deeds that are done in darkness and repent of them. When we try to hide these things, we only fool ourselves. Everyone knows anyway. Things just get worst when darkness is hidden and not exposed.

The Christian Dating Hall of Shame Can Turn into God's Hall of Fame

We must stop grieving the heart of God and return to his loving arms. The first step in repentance is to look at where we are and admit our problem. We are all sinners in need of grace. At the same time, there is no sin that is too much for the blood of Christ to heal. We must return to God with humility and respect for our loving Father. We must repent from the sin of idol worship. Some of us have made getting a man or making money our primary focus. The Lord warns us over and over throughout scripture that we cannot serve two Gods at the same time. Some have made our primary focus seeking pleasure for ourselves at the expense of others. Others have made pornography and sex their primary source of fulfillment. Stories of scandals among pastors and leaders are found in the newspapers all the time as a result of men of God seeking the pleasures of the flesh rather than trying to build God's Kingdom. For example, Joyce Myers mentioned a pastor who was cheating on his wife by having sex with his mistress inside the church itself. There was another woman who met a pastor on a popular online dating site and the first time they met, he asked her to perform oral sex on him. In Houston, a pastor had premarital sex with a very poor woman at her home. This lady was so broke that she could not afford her light bill. Rather than offering to pay her electricity bill for the month, he simply slept with the woman in the dark. This scorned woman eventually showed up at his church complaining about his treatment of her in front of the entire congregation. The list of stories can go on and on. Christians should be the most kind, loving and self-controlled individuals on the dating scene. They should be the best dates and not the worst. Unfortunately, in the age of bad information we have a lot to work on. However, we are blessed to have Jesus standing at our side ready to work with us.

The Woman Who Gave Up

Katie is a beautiful 35 year old woman living in New York. New York is a fun place, but Katie had read many of the books that made dating seem like a worldly activity and she spent most weekends alone. Katie found that most of the guys that she met at church seemed to only be interested in sex. After a string of heartbreaks, she decided to just focus on her job and her ministry at church. She was shocked that after a year of doing this, she wound up gaining 80 pounds and had to go on antidepressants. During a conversation, I revealed to her that I have a problem with having positive expectations of rich men and needed to work on this area. Katie responded, "Well, I have negative expectations of all men and they always disappoint me." I told her what the Lord showed me after a bad date with a very rich and handsome man: God revealed that we are "precious daughter of the Most High King. He is King of Kings and Lord of Lords. God can do all things, fix all things and solve all problems. Our daddy loves us." Something clicked in Katie and she began to realize that this is true. We should live in positive expectation that our daddy is able to provide us with someone wonderful. We must trust him and wait for him to do things in his perfect timing.

The Woman Who Needed a Man with Money More than Christ

Melanie is a beautiful exotic looking woman who came to Christ after having a baby out of wedlock. She was rejected by her Arab family and she joined a Houston mega-church who took her in and gave her the love and forgiveness that she needed. She got very involved in the life of the church and even joined several ministries. She eventually met a handsome engineer who swept her off of her feet. After about three weeks, he decided that he did not want to see her anymore, but she was hooked on the lifestyle that he provided. She began to call him five, ten and sometimes twenty times a day. She would camp out in front of his apartment building daily and cry. She would sneak into the building to his home to leave desperate letters, begging for him to return. He filed a restraining order against her and she backed off for a while. Eventually, he felt bad about it and apologized to her. He was fascinated by her son and wanted to be a Father figure for the boy. For the next several years, Melanie and the engineer maintained a relationship based on the guy's friendship with the son. Melanie now had the perfect excuse to call the engineer three to five times a day and drop by his home. She was inexperienced with men and had never been wooed by a man. This strange one-sided relationship seemed normal to her. She considered this man her boyfriend even though he had no real interest in her. She never spent the holidays with him and he never gave her anything or did anything for her.

Melanie and I met 3 months after she finally had the courage to break up with the man who showed no interest in her. It was amazing to see a woman in her forties who knew so little about men. She reminded me of myself when I was 16 or 17 years old. She was frustrated about dating and she was trying to understand her new boyfriend. The new boyfriend really liked her, but he was concerned about her constant calls and her habit of showing up at his job with gifts. Luckily for her, the new guy understood her lack of relationship skills and showed patience towards her. She changed her obsessive ways once a team of Christians revealed to her that she was engaging in the serious sin of idol worship. She was making the man in her life God and trying to get from these men what only God could give her. I told her that she needed to learn to trust God and then he would give her the ability to trust a man and relate to men correctly. She immediately realized her need to repent for this obsession and she began to relate to her boyfriend in a more normal way. She is still seeing her boyfriend and she is at peace for the first time in years. She is shocked that men are so sweet and wonderful when we stop trying to manipulate them and allow their feelings to unfold naturally. She called and said, "Wow, for the first time a guy actually shared himself with me and I did not even have to ask him fifty questions to get him to open up. He actually wanted to tell me about himself." She was shocked that she wasted so much time chasing men when there are plenty of guys out there that would be willing to chase her.

The Man Who Could Not Control Himself

The most disturbing dating disaster occurred between a Christian man and my spiritual but not religious coworker. My coworker went on a date with a man who claimed to be a serious Christian on a famous online dating site. They visited a famous Houston Mega-Church for their first date. This gentleman raped her on the way home from church. Luckily this same co-worker was older and extremely grounded. This experience did not shake her faith in God and she continued to date men on the same online dating site and met a wonderful husband. She took the bad experience as a critical life lesson. A Christian rapist sounds like an oxymoron. However, any of us are capable of doing almost anything if we fail to guard our hearts and minds against sin and lust. It starts out with a thought and it is better to fight lust at the thought level. If he meditated on that thought through pornography or masturbation, it was probably just a matter of time before he acted out his fantasies. Many of us live by the mistaken notion that the flesh must get what it wants. This is simply not true. When we submit the flesh to the Spirit, the flesh can lose its grip. There is never an excuse for a man to rape a woman. However, if a rape does occur, the woman must be careful to forgive the man because bitterness will simply eat up her soul and this will make the rape a double tragedy. Any man who rapes should ask for forgiveness from the woman and repent before God. If he got away with it, he really should turn himself in and stop living a lie. God is able to pick up the pieces from the most broken of situations, but we must first give those pieces to him.

My Shortest Date Ever

I personally visited a very popular Houston mega-Church and a member of the Pastor's staff followed me out the door and asked for a date. I was truly honored that a minister would ask me out. It was icing on the cake to find out that he was also an engineer. He picked me up and during the drive he pressured me to explain why a pretty woman like me did not have someone. I made the mistake of saying, "It could be because I do not believe in pre-marital sex." He answered, "What? You don't believe in premarital sex! Let me take you home then." The guy ended the date at that moment. He would not even buy me a Burger King hamburger and this was a youth pastor! The senior pastor of this same church eventually lost his wife after she found out that he was cheating about three years later. I warned the youth pastor that his behavior is unacceptable and shows a lack of Christian character. Luckily, I had a strong faith in Christ when this happened. There are millions of other women who could have lost their faith in Christ because of his behavior. I was hurt for 2 weeks after this happened. Then I decided to share this story with my co-workers. When I saw them laugh so hard that they cried, I realized that this was not my fault and an indication that something was wrong with me. They pointed out to me that this man was acting like a jerk and I am better off without him wasting my time. Sometimes when we share things with others, even things that we are embarrassed about, it can bring about healing and insight about the root of the problem. I was depressed for two weeks for no reason at all. I realized that this man simply needs lots of prayer.

My Most Disturbing Date Ever

After church service ended at a wonderful and spirit-filled church in Southeast Houston, a rather handsome man stopped me and told me how pretty he thought I was. He seemed like a really nice guy and I was impressed that he was a minister to the homeless. He called and arranged for us to meet at the movies on the weekend. I just knew that this would be a great date. Unfortunately, it turned out to be the second worst date ever. This guy started out wrong when he showed up on the first date wearing a football jersey and jogging pants while I was dressed in a cute top and jeans. When we approached the theatre, he attempted to skip everyone in line. I had to tell him that we must go to the back of the line. Even though we were watching a great Denzel Washington movie, he started snoring loudly after I told him to stop groping me several times. Next, as we exited the theatre, he opened the door so hard that he hit a teenager in the nose with the door. Instead of asking if the kid was OK, he yelled "man, what is wrong with you? You need to watch where you are going!" I felt that I truly deserved a free meal after enduring a movie with this man, but this meal almost costs me my sanity though. This minister talked about his homeless shelter and the fact that his last girlfriend was one of the homeless women he took in. When he found out that she was cheating on him with another homeless man, he kicked her out of the shelter. As I recovered from being upset over the outrageous story he told, he bragged, "Look, I make $40,000 a year and there are 15 women for every one man in Houston. You better get on this gravy train while the getting is good." This guy caused me to eat too many onion rings as I kept myself from screaming, "I would not get with you if you were the last man on earth." For a long time after dating this guy, I was actually afraid to date Christian men, especially pastors. Eventually, God showed me that I must marry a Christian man, but I would have to be patient and wait for the right one. Many of us like to leave a date like this and vow not to ever date again. Satan loves our vows. He wants for us to be so hurt and disappointed that we give up on each other. We must ignore that impulse and press on. Many of us have given up when a wonderful man could be just around the corner. God is full of surprises.

The Sex Addict with a Broken Spirit Who Wants to Change

Sometimes we think that we have discovered how God always operates, but God cannot be put into a box. God works in the most mysterious ways and we will never fully understand his plans and purposes. We like to have formulas and structure for everything while God loves to surprise us. We must remember that God is always in control and each person that he allows to enter our lives is there for a reason. This is why we must be prayerful about each person that we meet. Several months ago, a guy from my past kept trying to contact me and I was very difficult to reach. He called about nine times and I was extremely slow about returning his calls. Finally, I decided to cook some gumbo and felt that inviting him over for gumbo would be the perfect way to apologize for being so difficult to find and slow to respond to his calls. He came over in the middle of me cooking and I had Billy Graham on TV. He did not comment and sat and listened. We enjoyed a wonderful meal of gumbo, salad, and bread. We talked and laughed. Then at about 10:00 he said, "Do you realize how big your behind is?" I answered, "Yes, I am trying to get rid of some of it too." He answered, "Don't do that! I came over to turn you out (have sex with me for all dinosaurs who hate bad English), but you confused me by having Billy Graham on TV. It made me remember when my dad used to always play Billy Graham. My dad was a travelling pastor and he was my hero until he left my mom and me. When he left, I felt so rejected and angry. When he rejected my mom, I felt that he was also rejecting me. I turned to sex as a release of my pain. I went on a mission to have sex with as many women as possible."

I answered, "There is never enough sex to fill that void. Just like Billy Graham said, 'only Jesus Christ can fill that void that is in each of our hearts. 'God loves us so much and he wants for us to be happy. Sex is a physical expression of our spiritual relationship with him. It is sacred and he wants for us to enjoy it in marriage. It is the union of two souls and he does not want for us to bring soul ties of other people into this sacred bond." The guy answered, "You know, I am either having sex, about to have sex or just finished having sex. I like to have sex with married women because they have had fewer partners. I am over 40 now, and this is getting real old. It is too dangerous out there now. I am getting this strong desire to settle down and have something real. I don't know if it will be with you, but I am not happy with the way that I have been living." I went to him and held his hand saying, "Jesus Christ loves you and he died for you. He wants for you to come to him with your pain and confusion. These women will never satisfy this deep need in your soul." He was almost crying when he answered, "I know, but I am not quite ready to change just yet, but it is coming soon because I am getting tired." Whether he completely changed or not, I really do not know. However, I felt that God had arranged a divine appointment for him that particular night. I thought that it was to share a meal of gumbo and he thought that it would be an opportunity to have amazing sex, but God had his own plan and purposes for our meeting. Christians must realize that people's souls are at stake. If I would have been willing to have sex with him, I just would have been another example of a Christian hypocrite pointing him away from Jesus Christ and away from the church. Instead, I pointed him back to Christ and hopefully the next person that comes into his life can point him a little further in that direction. We must remember that the goal of dating and everything else that we do is to glorify God, not to satisfy ourselves.

The Only Solution: Jesus

Jesus Christ loves us exactly where we are. Jesus told the Jews who were about to stone the woman caught in adultery, **"He that is without sin among you, let him cast the first stone"** (John 8:7, KJV). When all the Jews left one by one, he told the adulterous woman **"Woman, where are those accusers? . . . Neither do I condemn thee: go and sin no more."** (John 8:10-11, KJV) Scripture tells us **"Brothers, if someone is caught in a sin, you who are spiritual should restore him gently. But watch yourself, or you may also be tempted. Carry each other's burdens, and in this way you will fulfill the law of Christ"** (Galatians 6:1-2, NIV). Paul was aware that in the world, there would be many temptations. Today, we have the added distractions of the television and the internet. There are so many things in the world to get us off course that attending church and having accountability in friendships is essential to keeping the faith. We live in a secular humanist society in which all points of view are acceptable except for the biblical view. Many became angry when President Obama stated that we are not a Christian nation. Unfortunately, he was stating a sad reality. Postmodern Christians have been taught that the views of the bible are just one of many possible views. Many of us have lost trust in the only reliable standard for relationships and living: the Holy Bible. The beauty of a standard is that it will let us know if we are travelling in the wrong direction. Without a standard, many of us are living shipwrecked lives and don't even know it. Luckily, we serve a God who specializes in making thing that are shipwrecked better than new. However, we must return to him and give him all the broken pieces. There is no problem so great or so big that Jesus cannot handle.

Some churches may need better accountability practices for its pastors and members. There needs to be an emphasis on Christian character and the importance of holiness that results from honoring God. Too many churches have made grace their central focus and it has resulted in a more casual form of Christianity for some. Churches that emphasize accountability along with grace are far more scandal resistant. These scandals can be used to open up conversations among Christian singles about sex and sexuality. Rather than sweep our mistakes under the rug, we need to look at our mistakes and learn from them. Our mistakes can be used to help others to learn and grow as well. Kids appreciate transparency and trust those who tell them the truth. The church may need to provide classes for adult singles on sexuality, dating and relationships. Singles and young adults need a relevant, biblical based message from the church that is not cloaked in legalism and patronizing half-truths. The church has made the mistake of embracing the man-made rules of the Pharisees who only care about appearances while underemphasizing the clear directives in scripture about how to interact in relationships. Many will not date, but they are perfectly willing to fornicate. Many will not associate with unbelievers, but they will form Christian clicks and avoid following the Great Commission to win others to Christ. Many will protest against gays without upholding the sanctity of their own marriages. The church is broken in the area of dating and relationships. Luckily, God specializes in putting broken things and people back together again.

We need to become a church after Jesus Christ's own heart. Rather than holding picket signs to get prostitutes and their clients arrested, Jesus ate with them and told them how they could be freed from their life of sin and receive eternal life. Paul warned that it is not our place to judge the world. Our job as Christians is to attract the world with the gospel of Jesus Christ. This message is very attractive if stated in love and respect. During the Essence Music Festival, I shared the beauty of God's plan for love and marriage with 3 different men in divinely appointed situations. I explained to them that sex is an act of worship that represents our intimacy with God. It is beautiful and God wants for it to be done in the context of marriage because it involves the bonding of two souls. God does not want for us to enter our marriages with soul ties to other people. He loves us too much for that. Each man was very thankful and told me that they know I told them the truth and they are getting tired of dating and having sex with so many different women. As they thanked me and we exchanged information, I thought about the fact that the men in the church could start telling this message to other men to bring more brothers to the body of Christ. This is so much better than trying to get other men arrested or protesting for morality. If the church would spend more time explaining the message Christ and his wisdom about relationships to the world, members of the church would have a lot less to complain about. Is the world going to benefit from more arrests or will the world benefit from hearing the good news of the gospel and God's beautiful plan for sex and relationships?

CHAPTER 6

A Deeper Understanding
of the Christian Dating Myths

The major problem facing most single Christians is that they have the additional baggage of holy sounding dating myths that keep them from taking the required steps to be successful with the opposite sex. The most common dating myths that Christian singles have to deal with are:

"Dating is a sin."

"It is wrong to desire a mate."

"God will send the perfect person to you if you just wait patiently."

"You can never be alone with the opposite sex before marriage because the sexual temptation is too great."

These myths virtually guarantee that many Christian singles will never get the practice that they need relating to the opposite sex in a positive way. Christians who believe in dating myths will often go months and even years without any real interaction with the opposite sex on a one-on-one level. This causes them to have even poorer relationship skills than most non-Christians. Their idealized marriages often turn into a nightmare if they are ever lucky enough to find someone. This is most likely the reason for the high divorce rate among Christians. Often when Christians do meet "the perfect one", their relational skills are so poorly developed that they find it difficult to keep this person. Others who feel that dating is a sin never make it down the aisle in the first place. Jodi is one such young lady. She attends an awesome church in Houston and took all the classes that emphasized keeping us pure and avoiding premarital sex. She was a 32 year old virgin when I met her. She was so afraid that she would never meet someone and so frustrated that many of the young men who took the vow of purity seem to be afraid to ask her or anyone else out on a date. She said, "Sometimes I question God's sovereignty because I thought that he would have arranged me to be married by now. Less Godly guys ask me out all the time, but I cannot go out on a date with them. I feel that God wants for me to date a Godly man and these guys do not ask anybody out." I tried to explain that it is OK to date and this may be the only way to ever connect with someone. She responded, "a prophesy speaker from Africa told me to wait for my mate to come to me and I don't think that God wants me to date." While this may have sounded spiritual, she had actually exchanged trust and dependence on God for trust and dependence on an opinion based on man-made rules.

The biggest issue is that most Christians do not understand the purpose of dating. They assume that dating is all about sex and using people. While premarital sex and using others is a sin, dating is not. In reality, dating should be an opportunity to interact with the opposite sex in a loving way. The best way to learn patience is to practice being patient with the people that you encounter on the dating scene. The best way to learn how to be kind and merciful is to practice being that way with someone. The best way to learn how to be unselfish and forgiving is to practice these skills. To wait until you are married to learn and understand these virtues is not the greatest idea. The more practice with loving others that we get before marriage, the more fulfilling and enriching our marriage will be. Marriage is easier when both parties come to the table with good relationship skills. When people have been living in a world of make-believe and waiting on Prince Charming or Princess Leah, the realities of marriage being hard work can be overwhelming. If our entire life has been about "me, myself and I", it is going to be difficult to start thinking in terms of "we" and "our" all of a sudden. Those who eventually want to get married should remember that they are already married to the Lord. If we cannot submit to him, we will not be able to submit to a human husband either.

We have made dating seem like something bad because we have bought into the cultural lies that a good date always ends in sex. Others have bought into the common church lie that each date is an interview for marriage. Both of these false beliefs are guaranteed to kill any enjoyment and spontaneity on the date. Dating is about having fun and enjoying life while sharing your ideas and wisdom with another person. Some of us fail to enjoy dating because we approach it as lawyers who are there to cross-examine. Now there is a time and place to interview a person, but it is not on the first date. If we want a second date, we need to make the first one fun and memorable. There is plenty of time to find out a person's financial records and dating history. Instead of being lawyers, we should be servants who want to make the lives of the people we date better and introduce them to Jesus Christ.

After running into dozens of people who swear that Christians are the most crazy and promiscuous ones on the dating scene, I have come to believe that the myths about not dating and "waiting on God to send someone" actually leave many Christian singles lonely, horny and with less self-control when they finally do get alone with the opposite sex. This "no dating rule" keeps many Christians from developing the required social skills for dealing with the opposite sex. The idea that Christians must always date in groups to avoid sexual temptation probably causes more problems than it cures. It is hard for two people to really connect when there is a group dynamic going on. It also fails to give the individuals practice in the area of self-control. When these men and women accidently find themselves alone with someone, they are more prone to lose control. It is like a dieter who has been told that she is addicted to sugar and chocolate and must take major steps to keep these things out of the house and away from them. When that party or picnic at a friend's house finally does occur and there is plenty of chocolate cake and other goodies available, this same person will probably eat twice as much chocolate and other forbidden food as those who have a more healthy relationship with food and have chocolate around the house all the time. Focusing on the power of sex or food to control our lives somehow makes sex or food more prone to control our lives. By the same token, knowing that Christ can strengthen us to overcome all temptation can make temptations seem less daunting. It helps for us to remember that God sees everything that we do. He is like a Father that is with us at all times. Like our human Fathers, even though he will forgive everything we do, he will not let us get away with anything.

One of the biggest issues with Christian singles these days is that they are growing up in a Christian pop culture that separates singles from married. Married couples get to read excellent books like Kendrick's **Love Dare** and John Bisagno's **Love is Something You Do**. These books emphasize sacrificial love and unconditional forgiveness which are good traits for all Christians to develop. Christian singles today are bombarded by books like "I Kissed Dating Goodbye", "Single and Satisfied" and "The Power and Purpose of Singleness". These books emphasize self-esteem and having pride in one's singleness which are traits that many singles already have. These books view singleness as a desired state rather than a place in which we are being prepared for marriage. These books give Christians the idea that singleness is a more holy state. Blogger, Elysse Barrett wrote an interesting blog entitled, "Five Reasons My Generation is Not Getting Married and What Can Be Done about It". She even mentioned how this state of prolonged singlehood gives many in her generation an excuse to avoid growing up and dealing with real life. Ms. Barrett wrote the following:

Unfortunately, pop-Christianity implies, and sometimes out-right states, that being in the state of singleness allows for knowing and serving God better. I certainly grant that there are opportunities to serve as a single person that one simply cannot do once married, however there is not one shred of Biblical evidence that one should embrace singleness as a holier state than marriage. The issue here is not being single; it is a need to re-think our singleness in light of correct reasoning. Unfortunately, because it is often viewed as a more holy state, I have seen young people—guys and girls alike—turn away from pursuing marriage, for intensely selfish reasons, and use the "holiness of singleness" as an excuse. It breaks my heart to know that they will regret that decision in years to come. And for those who view singleness as the time of preparation (which indeed it is), far too often one is expected to remain single until they have "arrived," whatever that means. For some, they are expected to be debt-free, for others, they must be debt-free AND have a certain amount of money in the bank. For others, it means having all their beliefs and convictions solidified. While these are great goals and we should strive towards them while single, I see no strong Biblical basis for excluding relationships and marriage until one has 'arrived'" [(1)].

This prolonged state of singleness is a fertile playing ground for the devil. A single may go five, ten even fifteen years without dating in this subculture and completely mess up the first time a person of the opposite sex touches them. In ***Forbidden Fruit***, Mark Regnerus shows that the sex lives of young Christian singles is identical, if not more X-rated than their non-Christian peers. Our youngest adults hear the extra-biblical message about not getting married too soon loud and clear. However, they are not heeding the biblical part about waiting until marriage to have sex. Paul knew that waiting years to have sex is too difficult for most people to handle. At a time in which people married in their teens and early 20's, Paul warned married couples, **"Do not deprive each other [sexually] except by mutual consent and for a time, so that you may devote yourself to prayer. Then come together again so that Satan will not tempt you because of your lack of self-control"** (1 Corinthians 7:5, NIV). The situation of people holding off on marriage until the late 20's, 30's and 40's was not even an issue back then. Now, if Paul were alive today, his warning to modern 20-somethings and 30-somethings would have to be "get married so that Satan can stop tempting you and taking advantage of your lack of self-control."

Prolonged singleness is also fertile playing ground for depression and other emotional problems to develop. Singles that are waiting until they arrive at some mythical state of perfection before marriage are just setting themselves up for disappointment. Most of us never arrive and are never fully ready to walk down the aisle. Marriage is about two imperfect people coming together to go through life's ups and downs together. It is about two people growing in the Lord as a team. It is about two separate people becoming one flesh and this is not always easy. When we have read too many romantic books we may have a fantasy view of marriage that makes us unable to accept the reality of it when it arrives. Many women and men who kissed dating goodbye are now emerging as bitter and confused single adults who fear that they may have wasted their best years dating in groups and avoiding male-female relationships. Some of these singles have decided to just give up on Christianity altogether. Others have decided to give up on dating altogether. They decide that God must want for them to be single and that there is no need to look. Many churches may need to take a second look at its "Kissing Dating Goodbye" stance. The church needs to also ask if the teachings to be "single and satisfied" are making it more difficult for men and women to connect. If people are avoiding the opposite sex, how are they going to be able to relate if and when they do get married?

Most important, we must ask ourselves if the modern "Wait on the Lord" teachings are just another way of making women say to themselves "I Don't need a Man". Christian women are getting a double whammy of bad dating advice that leaves them less desirable to the opposite sex. There is the secular world telling them to be a "strong, independent woman who does not need a man" and there is the Christian Community telling them that "all you really need is the Lord." There is a nugget of truth to both messages; however, women who wrap their mind around these teachings are going to have a lot of trouble attracting men. If a woman honestly feels this way, then she can continue to live by this motto and enjoy singlehood. However, if a woman really wants to find a man, it would be better for her to be honest about how she feels. Going around with an "I don't need a man" attitude is usually going to result in a self-fulfilling prophecy coming true.

Famous psychologist, John Gray explored this issue better than any other writer. He noted that there is one type of woman that is very likely to never get married: the woman who thinks that she does not need a man. According to Dr. Gray,

Many women remain single even when they want to be married. They wonder, "Why am I still single? Why can't I find a man who will commit?" This frustration has nothing to do with looks, personality, level of success, or the availability of men. It does involve their style or approach. These women mistakenly approach their relationships with men the way that they want men to approach them. They are repelled by the thought of a needy man, so they are very careful to not need a man. When asked if they need a man, they are proud to acknowledge that they don't. These are some of their responses: 'No I don't need a man. I can take care of myself. I just want to be with a man because I choose to, not because I need him.'; 'No, what do I need a man for? I can completely support myself. I just want a companion.' Although these responses sound reasonable and positive, they reflect an attitude that clearly does not attract men, or at least does not attract men who will become motivated to make a commitment . . . They have spent years becoming self-sufficient believing that this would make them more attractive . . . When they first hear that men need to feel needed and men are most attracted to a woman who needs what he has to offer, they become confused [2].

Modern women must understand that men need to feel needed. A man is naturally wired to be attracted to someone who needs him. When women are trained to be stand-offish and feel no need for men, men are not encouraged to pursue them. Christian women who desire to be married need to understand that it is OK to desire a mate. Jesus only requires first place in our heart, not the only place in our heart. In fact, our relationship with Jesus Christ gives us a special insight into why men need to feel needed in the first place. We know that Jesus Christ died on the cross for our sins. He loves us unconditionally and desires relationship with us. When we live as if he is not important to us, this displeases him. Imagine dying for someone and giving up everything for them only to find out that the person you died for does not even care. This was his warning to the Church of Laodicea and the Church at Ephesus in book of

Revelations. He threatened Ephesus and Laodicea with being removed and spit out for their "I don't really need you attitude" towards him. We usually find our lives falling apart when we forget to make Jesus the center of our world. He does not force himself into our lives, but he is pleased when our hearts seek him out. A Christian cannot be in right relationship with Jesus Christ unless he or she understands that Jesus is a requirement like air and water. As head of the body Christ, he holds the body together. Similar to how blood is required for human tissue to live, the blood of Christ is required for the Christian to function. Any tissue that loses access to blood will die. Any Christian who loses touch with Jesus will die spiritually. In the same way, a woman cannot be in proper relationship with a man unless she needs him. To get an idea of how a man feels when we say that we do not need him, we can look at how Christ probably feels when we as Christians say, "I can make it by myself, and I don't need Jesus or God as crutch." No man wants a woman who is so independent that she would be perfectly fine without him.

This is such a serious issue that we need an army of brave and Godly men and women to bring up these issues at their churches. We will not have a large number of Christian singles to choose from unless the dating and marriage myths are confronted. Married people need to be honest with singles instead of pretending that they were perfect and never went on a date. How can people get to know each other if they don't date? How can people learn relationship skills unless they relate to others? There needs to be more discussions and helpful advice to help singles navigate a very sexually charged world filled with bad advice.

Successfully Confronting the Christian Dating Myths

Dr. Henry Cloud wrote a compelling book called "How to Get a Date Worth Keeping" that confronted these dating and relationship myths. Many of the singles who followed his advice found the husband or wife that they were seeking and benefited from the relational skills developed from active dating. Lilly, an attractive woman who had not had a date in two years, was a victim of the "God will send the perfect person to me" myth. Lily told Dr. Cloud, "I always thought that I would be married and have children by now . . . but God hasn't chosen that for me . . . Well, I believe that God brings the man into your life you are to marry, and he hasn't bought that man to me yet . . . Or he hasn't given me the feelings I would need for the men that he has brought into my life." Lilly did not understand that finding a mate required action on her part and sitting at home waiting for God to deliver "the One" was going to most likely end up in disappointment. Dr. Cloud explained to Lilly and the millions of others like her the following: *Many people have been taught to view dating the same way that Lillie did: 'God will bring the person to you. Just wait.' And they think that this approach is spiritual. But in reality, it negates the dual track of the Bible that teaches God will guide the way, but we have to actively walk in that way and fight the battles"* [3]. Once Lily took Dr. Cloud's advice and began active dating, Lily was married within two years to a wonderful Christian man. Similar to Lily, many of the women that Dr. Cloud had coached had not had a date in years. They were approaching 40 without any prospects and wondering why this is the case. They did not realize that we must plant the seed before God can water it and cause it to grow. If we have not planted the seed, then there is nothing for God to water. If there is nothing for God to water, we should not expect for anything to grow. Ecclesiastes tells us to plant multiple seeds because we have no idea which will be the one to grow. This means instead of waiting around for someone to magically appear, we should start planting seeds by joining clubs that attract other singles, going online and letting friends and family know that we are interested in meeting someone. Sometimes we may even have to change the places that we hang out. For example, instead of going to the Starbucks in the suburb that attracts housewives and their children, we can go to the trendy Starbucks in the city that attracts lots of singles. According to Ecclesiastes 11:6, (KJV), "In the morning sow your seed, and in the evening withhold not [your] hand; for [you do not know which] shall prosper, either this or that, or whether they both alike shall be good."

Life Coach, Jenna Turton noted that in her earlier years, she was a victim of the book, "I Kissed Dating Goodbye." She wrote the blog about the problem with kissing dating goodbye. She wrote, *"I grew up in the era of "I Kissed Dating Goodbye" . . . . I attended conferences where I was encouraged to not only save myself for marriage, but also avoid the dating scene altogether . . . . I kept men at arm length. I studied them critically . . . . I managed to save myself a lot of needless heartache, but I also managed to stay very single! I lost a lot of priceless experience . . ."* [4]. Eventually Ms. Turton realized that these "thou shall not date" rules were going to most likely keep her single forever. After reading Dr. Cloud's book, she began dating and enjoying herself. She gained valuable experience as well as confidence that she can meet and marry the right mate. I am looking forward to seeing the blog on her wedding one day.

Many churches or groups within churches have adopted the "I Kissed Dating Goodbye" philosophy and have never dealt with the impact of this thinking on singles in the church. I will never forget attending a single's bible study in which the main message of the class was to be "single and satisfied" and "kiss dating goodbye." It basically taught the message that we must simply wait on the Lord for our mate and there is nothing that we can do. The elder insisted that this be the main message because she did not want to turn church into a "club." I poured my heart out to the Elder in charge of the class because I was concerned about the younger students. They seemed very sad and confused as they were told to forget about a desire for marriage. This elder's statements were identical to Lilly's: she essentially said that we should not date or seek a mate in any way and just wait on God to bring the perfect guy into our lives. While this sounded good, it was also unrealistic and left the younger singles vulnerable to just give up in frustration. Most of the youngsters eventually left the singles class and the singles class did have to be disbanded just as I predicted. This elder, like so many other

Christians, simply has no understanding of the needs of young singles in this culture. She had been bombarded by books and seminars promoting the "be single and don't hope for marriage" message. She, like so many other Christians, is totally unaware of the following statistics:

- According to USA Today. 70% of Evangelical and Mainline Protestants leave the church by the time that they are 23 years old, but 35% of those who left did eventually return by age 30. [5]

- Barna studies show that less than 10% of Christians have a biblical worldview. [6]

- Statistics show that 65% of young adults rarely attend church service, 67% of young adults do not read the bible and only around 50% of them believe that Jesus is the way to heaven. [7]

Christians like the elder fail to realize is that most young adults do not fully trust the bible or the teachings of the church. Young adults have taken psychology and sociology courses that have made the bible seem more "primitive" and the philosophy of secular humanism more relevant. It is hard enough for us to follow the rules that are actually written in the bible. To add more legalistic rules like "no dating allowed" and "no thinking about marriage allowed" on top of what the bible commands us to do is just going to make most of us run away from the church even faster. Indeed, our faith has already been tested by seeing dozens of church scandals, seeing the lies of the money loving preachers on television making false promises, and listening for hours to humanistic teachings at school. In addition, as modern young adults, we are bombarded with secular messages by friends on facebook and twitter, as well as dozens of television programs and songs on the radio with worldly themes. Instead of more pizza parties, legalistic teachings and shallow teachings, we need strong biblical teachings that challenge the messages from pop-culture and make the bible seem relevant to our lives. In the PEW research study on millennials, the combination of Humanistic beliefs mixed with Christian beliefs was so great that Raines estimates that only 15% of the young adults surveyed who claimed to be Christians were actual Christians [8]. Lots of work needs to be done for younger Christians. A big start would be to come up with a relevant biblically based message about dating and sexuality for them.

Modern youngsters do not feel any stigma about being single because the majority of their friends and family are single as well. If anything, we are trying to wait as long as possible before getting married because we fear divorce. We have seen parents and friends of the family go through one or more divorces and we want to avoid it if it is possible. Can any of us name a person in their early 20's that feels bad about being single? A single class that tries to address the stigma of being single is just not relevant to this age group-especially since the average age at marriage is 25 for women and 27 for men [9]. Rather than discussing the stigma of being single, young Christians need Godly instructions on how to deal with sexual temptation, how to date in such a way that honors God and how to share their faith with others without fear in an age of tolerance for everything except biblical Christianity.

My cousin confided that her single Christian friends are lonely and desperate and a few are even suicidal. Unfortunately, my cousin, similar to many people in the church, tells these women that "some women were just not meant to get married." This advice is similar to telling a childless woman who wants a baby that "some women were just not meant to have children." It is like telling a poor homeless person, "Some people were just not meant to have a home." These harsh statements make people more depressed and desperate rather than bring them comfort. My cousin would be very upset if someone told her "maybe your husband is going to leave you this year." She would instantly see the arrogance and presumption of this statement, but she and other married people rarely see these same qualities in their advice to singles. Instead of arrogant and patronizing pats on the head, singles need to be encouraged by the truth. The truth is that we do not know what will happen tomorrow, but knowing the one who knows will bring us peace and comfort regardless of what that will be. It is unrealistic to expect for most women to lose their desire for having a mate or for most men to be comfortable without having sex for the rest of their lives. Few are given the grace to live such a "holy" lifestyle; yet, this is often the only advice given to singles in modern churches. It is no wonder that Christian singles often bring scandal to the body of Christ rather than bring people closer to God.

Dr. David Jeremiah, Dr. John Bisagno, Pastor Gregg Matte and Pastor Terrence Johnson have some excellent sermons and books on marriage and singlehood. Many other churches are producing excellent relationship material for singles as well. I personally enjoyed the T.D. Jakes series of teachings for singles. However, many churches leave Christian singles horny and clueless. This is rather tragic since singles often come into contact with more non-Christians and we are often not prepared to be Godly witnesses. The men need real practical ideas about how to treat women and practice self-control. Men need to hold each other accountable when it comes to sex and their treatment of women. Instead of laughing at disrespectful jokes and comments, there should be an army of Christian men with the message, "respect women or I will put you in check." Christian men should be the best dates and mates, not the worst. Many people in the church erroneously tell men not to approach women when there is no such rule in the bible. When these men finally do approach a woman, they have not had the same practice in social skills as other men and tend to say the wrong thing. Christian women need better instructions about being Godly singles as well. While Christian men often seem socially inept and unable to control themselves, Christian women often seem horny and depressed or prudish and judgmental. Christians should model their behavior after Christ.

God's Call to Freedom Instead of Legalism

My favorite piece of legalistic advice was from a popular psychologist who talks to Christians all over the country about dating. He came up with the rule that we must introduce each date to our spiritual mentors for their approval. He claimed that failure to do this would result in serious issues and cause singles to constantly sleep with the wrong person. In reality, following his advice results in serious issues. There is a war that goes on in each one of us between the flesh and the spirit. We determine who wins by who we feed. If we feed the flesh with worldly advice, watching the wrong TV shows, listening to explicit music and daydreaming about sex, the flesh will most likely win. However, if we spend a significant amount of time in prayer, praise and worship and reading the bible, the spirit will most likely win. What makes this psychologist think that the Spirit of God is too weak to keep us chaste? What makes him think that a certain mentor or mentors hear from God in such a way that they can pick our mate for us? What makes him think that singles are unable to hear from God for themselves? The real secret of making the right decisions is for us to grow in love with God to the point that we would be grieved to ever displease him. Christ did not die on the cross to give us more rules; rather, he died on the cross to give us more freedom in him.

God is our Father who sees everything that we do. Paul explained, "**For as many as are led by the Spirit of God, they are the sons of God . . . [We] have received the Spirit of adoption, whereby we cry, Abba, Father. The spirit itself [bears] witness with our spirit that we are children of God**" (Romans 8:14-16, KJV). God is such a loving Father that he was willing to send his only Begotten son, Jesus Christ to die on the cross to save us from our sins. If Jesus could die for us, then the least that we could do is die to our fleshly cravings. We must make up our own minds to follow the Spirit instead of the flesh; no one can do this for us. Paul explains, "**For what the law could not do, in that it was weak through the flesh, God sending his own Son in the likeness of sinful flesh, and for sin, condemned sin the in the flesh: that the righteousness of the law might be fulfilled in us, who walk not after the flesh, but after the spirit. For they that are in the flesh do mind the things of the flesh: but they that are after the Spirit the things of the Spirit. For to be carnally minded (fleshly) is death; but to be spiritually minded is life and peace**" (Romans 8:4-6, KJV). Many of us feel powerless against our flesh because we do not realize that we have the power of God to help us. We do not understand that submitting to the Spirit may be difficult, but it is easier than following the flesh and losing our peace. Nothing is more precious than being at peace with our Heavenly Father.

Accountability is an excellent idea; however, it should not be our only reason for avoiding sin. A pastor who is in the awkward situation of having a beautiful lady knock on his door for counseling should not feel completely helpless with this temptation. He should not have to have a deacon following him around all day in order for him to avoid sin and temptation. We need to develop our own personal relationship with Jesus Christ and develop our own sense of personal integrity through prayer and bible study. We must do what Paul did-die daily to our own flesh and our own agenda. There is an epidemic of weak-willed Christians who are quicker to sin than the unsaved and they will use the excuse, "oops, my accountability partner was out of town, so I had an accident." Or they will say, "The spirit is willing but the flesh is weak." Many of us simply do what we want to do when we want to do it and we use the weakness of the flesh as an excuse. Unfortunately, there is an unsaved world watching us do this and we fool no one but ourselves. Many refuse to believe in Christianity because they have observed too many weak-willed Christians with this attitude.

We must come to the realization that God is holy; in fact, he is so holy that he could not even be in the presence of sinful man. God desires a relationship with us, so we can only come into the presence of God our Father through Jesus Christ. Our sin does not stop God from loving us, but sin does keep us separate from him. We must come to the point that we desire being with him more than satisfying our fleshly craving. We must come to the point that we care more about building the kingdom of God than we care about feeling good. The problem today is that too many Christians have lost their focus. Instead of trying to share the love of Christ with the world, too many of us have allowed the world to make us forget about the love of Christ. Most important, we must come to the point that we do not want to grieve the heart of our Heavenly Father. When we sin, we hurt God's heart the same as a parent is hurt when their child gets in trouble at school or steals something and goes to jail. God is a good daddy and he deserves our respect and praise. We should live lives that honor and please him.

While we must live lives that honor God, we must also ignore holy sounding advice about dating that is found nowhere in the bible. These excessive man-made rules place us under legalistic bondage and keep us from enjoying the freedom and success in dating and life. One lady at a singles bible study came up with the rule that "all Godly women must talk on the phone for four months before seeing a guy in person". She admitted and made it quite obvious that she had not dated in several years. She would constantly make comments about not needing a man and the importance of not dating until Prince Charming has been found. When we are in the presence of such a person it is important to listen, but observe the fruit of their lives and simply ignore their ideas. If someone giving advice has not had a date in years, it is probably because they live by their own advice. Another Christian came up with the rule that you must be friends with a guy for at least a year before ever going on a date with him. This is found nowhere in the bible and I can only imagine how few people this person could get to follow this man-made rule. These legalistic rules limit our choices and keep us from enjoying dating God's way.

Today, too many Christian women feel that it is against God's will for them even talk to a man or flirt. They really think that God will send a husband to them at the proper time. Joy is one such woman. She is a very lovely lady who divorced 10 years ago. She has only had five dates during that ten year period. She continues to wait for the Lord to send her someone, but it does not look very favorable for her. In reality, the probability that God will deliver a husband at our door is as likely as the stork delivering a baby at the door. It is similar to waiting for an employer to walk up to our door and ask if we need a job. No one ever got a job sitting at home watching TV and saying, "I name and claim a job now. Man from Exxon call now, call now I decree, call now!" In the same way, no one ever got a mate by staying at home watching TV saying, "The next delivery truck will bring the delivery of my man, I decree it and it shall be-sum num num num." It is ironic that the same people who tell us "to wait on the Lord" to send a man down from heaven are the same people who would call us lazy if we did this in any other area of our lives. We live in a culture that calls people who won't go out and look for a job lazy. We call people who complain that they have no friends unfriendly and unwilling to go out and meet people. However, many try to label Christians who sit at home saying that the Lord will send a mate someday as "spiritual." The only time that this could be considered spiritual is if this is exactly what the Holy Spirit prompted us to do. If not, we are just engaging in delusional thinking and missing dozens of opportunities to meet people.

It is not about formulas; rather, it is about having the Spirit of God lead us. The truth is that after we have prayed about our dating situation, we need to follow any promptings that the Holy Spirit gives us. Sometimes, the Holy Spirit will direct us to follow what may seem like legalistic rules. Sometimes the Holy Spirit will prompt us to be friends with a guy for a year first. Sometimes he will not. Sometimes the Holy Spirit will prompt us to get the approval of our parents and mentors before dating a particular person. Sometimes he will not. He works differently for each person because each person is unique and has a different set of needs. However, we should not assume that some technique is the answer to our dating woos. What works for one person may not work for another person. God created each of us differently and we must be humble enough to seek his wisdom about what approach works best for us. We have to be in the habit of praying for God's direction and wisdom as we navigate the dating scene. We should listen to these promptings by the Spirit, but we should not assume that any extra-biblical practice is some magical way to get what we want or a formula that works every time. If these man-made ideas do work, it is only because God gave the grace for them to work. The power is not in the technique, it is in the grace of God. When we rely on techniques instead of God's wisdom and direction for our lives, we often move further from the type of relationships that we want. These man-made rules can put us in a cocoon that no one sees or knows about when there is great freedom in Christ. Christ does not put a heavy yoke on us that we cannot handle. I cannot handle Sister Super Christian's 100 dating standards that she has made up, but Jesus' standards are no burden. Jesus Christ himself will give us the grace to handle his rules and precepts.

It may come as a surprise, but God even allows us to hang out with nonbelievers. We must remember that Jesus allowed a sinful woman to sit at his feet. He did this out of love to show her that he was willing to forgive her of all her sins and give her the free gift of eternal life regardless of her past. Some of my best dating experiences have been when I shared the gospel with unsaved men on a date. One of the guys even came to Christ on a date with me. We should follow in Jesus' footsteps as we navigate the dating scene. If we view dating as a way of meeting interesting people and sharing the love of Christ with them, then we can date just about anyone. How can we win nonbelievers to Christ if we refuse to talk to them or associate with them? Jesus left us with the great commission; yet, many of us have become comfortable in our Christian clicks in fear of any association with the outside world that needs us. There is a rule with this though—if the world impacts you more than you impact the world, then you should leave that particular ministry alone. In other words, if the person is more likely to bring us down, than we are to lift them us, then we need to avoid getting too close to that person. Sometimes we have to avoid certain settings and situations as well. For example, alcoholics and sex addicts should not witness in bars until a complete healing has occurred. Also, former drug addicts should not witness around crack houses unless he has been away from drugs for a very long time and it is no longer a major temptation.

Dating God's way is fun and exciting, not boring and legalistic. Most of the marriages in the bible were arranged by the family. Today we are lucky enough to be able to pick our own mate. If we fail to take an active role in this process, we are going to let our choices walk on by. Smart women know that they must go where the men are—sporting events, sports bars, parties, outdoor concerts and festivals, health clubs, civic organizations, conventions, church events, singles events and even on-line. There is simply no verse in the bible that states that women must stay home and never desire anything but holiness. God wants for us to enjoy life, not just endure it. We become our most attractive selves when we approach life with this state of mind. The desire for a mate to share one's life with is a natural desire that God puts in our heart, but it should never eclipse our desire for God himself.

CHAPTER 7

The Danger of Making Men Our Idols

Spouse hunting should never become an idol in our lives. God must always be the first priority for each of us. God will usually allow us to find a Godly mate as we pursue God's will for our lives. If we are really doing everything that God has called us to do, we are probably coming in contact with lots of other single people. If God has called us to something solitary that does not allow us to meet anyone but the UPS driver, we can still go to events that interest us on the weekend. The important thing is to make what God called us to do our first priority. For men, there is no verse that states that a man cannot pursue a woman that he is interested in. The bible simply does not instruct people to stop living and sit under a rock to wait for Jesus. Rather, the bible says, **"Seek ye first the Kingdom of God and his righteousness, and all of these things shall be added unto you"** (Matthew 6: 33, KJV). In other words, as we put God first, he will take care of the rest for us. We can still pursue an income, pursue relationships with both men and women, pursue good health and pursue community involvement. However, these other pursuits must come second to our pursuit of God and his righteousness.

Mary

Mary was a woman who made finding a man her full-time obsession. All of her conversations were about men and finding the right man. Even when she would talk about God, she seemed to only relate to him in terms of his ability to help her get a man. She drove her friends insane with this obsession. She would ask her friends to take pictures of her constantly so that she could post them on facebook, Match.com and Plenty of Fish. She would wear these awful Daisy Duke short shorts and hang around hotels and restaurants hoping that men would notice her. When the guys from the internet would show interest, she would find out where they lived and camp out in front of their home every night. She was very scary to the men that she dated. She would call ten times in a row or beg for the guys to take her out instead of waiting to be pursued. Her real issue was that she did not trust God, so she was incapable of trusting men. I told her that she did not even need to start dating until she trusted God because all she was doing was wasting time and driving men away from her with her intense desperation and fear. She did not realize that God is the ultimate matchmaker and we have to trust him throughout the dating process. Mary had to learn to relax and quit searching so hard. She had to realize that we cannot force guys to like us; in reality, we can only be the best that we can be and leave the results to God. Once she laid down her guard and trusted that God would bring her the love that she desired, men started responding to her in a different way and she became a successful dater.

Marge

God is jealous when other pursuits win first place in our hearts. Marge is a beautiful Hispanic woman who had to learn this the hard way. She could not figure out why so many tragic things happened to her and why she had such bad luck with men. She would talk to her friends for hours about her male problems and anyone who hung around her for over an hour knew that she was obsessed with men. She was constantly e-mailing or texting her guy of the moment. When she would walk with friends, she had her phone in her hand to check if a guy was trying to reach her. She signed up with Match.com and Plenty of Fish. She would figure out where a particular guy lived and check out his house. She was constantly sending intrusive e-mails to men to get more and more information about them. She would show up to a guy's job unexpected if he said that he had to work late. She claimed that she did this because a guy had cheated on her when she was in her 20's and it was difficult for her to trust men. She claimed that she trusted God in every area of her life except for romance because she never had any luck in this area. She felt very justified to have this mistrust of men and God because of her past hurts. Unfortunately, she never experienced being pursued by a guy. She claimed that she did not want to be pursued by a guy because it would cause for her to lose control. Her attitude was that she would do whatever she wanted to do and no God or man could tell her anything. Her pattern with men was strange to say the least. She would express her feelings of love and devotion to these men, then without warning she would call them stating that she wanted nothing to do with them and delete them from her facebook page and block their phone number. Next thing you know, she would show up at their home expressing regret and vowing to love them forever. Her behavior was consistently very child-like and erratic. She would behave the same way with God. One moment, she would claim love and devotion to God as long as it looked like he was going to give her what she wanted. The next moment she would hurl the greatest blasphemies ever known towards God for failing to give her what she felt entitled to get. It was very painful to listen to her hurl these insults at God.

The Lord gave me the grace to be Marge's friend and gave me supernatural patience with her. She was constantly asking for prayer for her relationships or "pseudo-relationships." I would always direct her to pray for herself and develop a personal relationship with Jesus Christ. Even though she claimed to be saved, she seemed to have no understanding of what I was talking about. One night, Marge got very angry and upset that God was putting her through so much grief with men and said, "I have been so good to God and he treats me so bad. I am so tired of seeing these women with their children happily married when they were sluts with their husbands while I tried to keep myself pure. Now I am in my 40's and it is too late for me. I wish that God would just kill me if he is going to treat me like this." This greatly alarmed me and I sought help for Marge through the church.

Several weeks later, the Lord revealed the real issue that Marge was having with both God and men. Since several people at the church were praying for her, she was able accept God's wisdom about her issues when I revealed it to her. I called her and she met me at a restaurant. I told her the following: "We have been doing a bible study at church and it has been on the book of Judges. In this book, the Israelites were constantly coming under God's judgment and being placed into captivity. Guess why God was so angry with them? "She said, "I don't know." I responded, "He was angry because they engaged in idol worship. Idol worship occurs when we place someone or something above God. God created us to be in relationship with him and when we chase other Gods, it causes him to become jealous. Whether the idols are wood and stone images or actual people, God looks at idol worship the same way that a husband looks at a wife who has been sleeping with another man. Throughout the Old Testament, he called the Israelites adulterers, whores and prostitutes for worshiping other Gods. He would allow their enemies to capture them whenever they committed spiritual adultery by worshiping these false gods. By the same token, if you ever watch Lifetime or see court cases of men who found their wives cheating, you would find that they become incredibly enraged. Some would burn their wives or tear their bodies apart. Usually when a man finds his wife cheating, he has a lot of trouble forgiving her. Women will forgive cheating in a heartbeat, but men seem to remain angry for a very long time." Marge responded, "And I have been in captivity for 12 years. That is why things have not worked for me and I have felt so sorry for myself. I have been under judgment. I did not know that idol worship was such a big deal to God. If I would have known, I would not have done it."

Marge once again tried to explain her erratic behavior with the guy she is currently dating. She said, "I feel so insecure because my man has female friends that have a home, a nice car and great careers. I have nothing. How am I supposed to compete with a woman who has everything?" I explained to her that she is absolutely right. She has nothing of value to offer her man the same way she has nothing of value to offer God. I said, "God owns everything. We come before him completely naked and bankrupt. There is nothing that we can give him that is not already his in the first place. There are only three things that God really wants from us: he wants us to trust him, respect him and be faithful towards him. Marge, you do not trust God because you are constantly trying to remain in control and do his job for him. When God would prompt you to do something, you feel that it is your right to tell him no because you control your own life. Instead of submitting to God, you treat him as your cosmic servant. You do not respect God because you are trying to boss him around and blaspheme him whenever it seemed that he is not agreeing with your personal agenda. You have been so ungrateful towards God until it is painful for anyone who loves God to watch you disrespect him the way that you do. God deserves our praise and thanksgiving whether we realize it or not. You were spiritually unfaithful because you idolized men and their status instead of idolizing God. A real man wants the same things from you that God wants from you. A real man is not interested in how much money you have because he knows that he is the real provider. A real man simply wants his woman to trust him, respect him and be faithful towards him. When you show up to this man's job uninvited, you prove that you do not trust him. When you refuse to give him the space that he needs or honor his requests, you show your lack of respect for him. When you constantly delete him on facebook and show a lack of commitment you prove your unfaithfulness towards him. This lack of stability and tendency to change your mind with the wind is proof that you are not quite ready for marriage. Marriage starts from a foundation of commitment. God is not going to send you his best man if you are not the best woman for that man."

Marge was disappointed that she wasted so many years of her life chasing idols and wound up with absolutely nothing. This is the nature of idols: they prove to be useless in the end and the sad thing is that we never really loved them in the first place. I explained to Marge, "You don't really love these men that you idolize and this is probably why God hates idol worship so much. It pulls us away from him, the only real source of love. It also causes us to fail to pursue our true purpose in the world: to be conformed to the image of Jesus Christ and bring others to Christ. We have so many gifts and talents that could be used for God's glory. Unfortunately, if we busy ourselves chasing idols, we bury these gifts and talents and everyone suffers as a result of our selfishness and God gets no glory from our lives." The time that Marge spent chasing these men could have been spent helping poor kids learn to read in a tutoring program, working with abused women or some other venture to make the world a better place. Instead, she wasted her days away making herself miserable, the men in her life miserable and making God angry. Marge was searching just like Mary was searching. These women did not realize that they already have everything they really need in Jesus Christ. Jesus Christ is our only true source of love and happiness.

One of Marge's primary problems was that she failed to understand the meaning of love. Our culture tends to define love as a fond feeling towards others. In reality, love is an action. The King James Version of the bible uses the word charity instead of love. The King James Version describes love or charity as long-suffering, kind, faithful and truthful. Charity is said to not be envious, arrogant or selfish because it does not seek its own good, but rather seeks the good of the other person (I Corinthians 13:4-6, KJV). Charity implies action not just feeling. Marge, like so many other women, lived by her feelings and this would result in the most unloving behavior without her realizing it. She would do whatever she felt like doing without thinking about how her decisions impacted other people. I explained to Marge, "Before you delete someone from facebook or show up to someone's job uninvited, you should ask yourself, 'Would I want for someone to do this to me? Is this action in the best interest of this person or am I just trying to make myself feel better? Am I acting selfishly or am I doing this out of a true love or concern for this person?' Love begins with commitment. We cannot say that we love someone if we plan on dismissing them from our lives for every little thing that they do." Marge began to learn that love is acting in a way that gives the other person what he or she needs versus satisfying her selfish feelings and wants. She vowed to stop acting selfishly and start showing love towards the men in her life. This is a smart first step to take because according to scripture, love never fails (I Corinthians 13:8, KJV)

The Truth: Messed Up Theology= Messed Up Life

Marge is also an example of the importance of knowing theology. In our modern culture, we often hear people say that theology does not make a difference because God is simply love. God is love, but he is so much more than that. He is also holy and all-powerful. He is the creator of both heaven and earth. We were right when we sang as kids, "he holds the whole world in his hands." He is the King of Kings and Lord of Lords. There is no one or nothing above him. When Marge would blaspheme God for not giving her what she wanted, she did not realize her true position before God. She thought that her purpose was to use God to get what she wants rather than to use things and relationships to glorify God. She put herself above God because she simply did know who he is and what he does. She did not realize that we exist for God's purposes and not the other way around. C.S. Lewis once wrote, "*In God you come up against something which is in every respect immeasurably superior to yourself. Unless you know God as that-and therefore, know yourself as nothing in comparison-you do not know God at all. As long as you are proud, you cannot know God . . . How is it that people who are quite eaten up by pride can say that they believe in God and appear to themselves very religious? I am afraid it means that they are worshiping an imaginary God . . . And any of us may at any moment be in this death—trap*" [1]. When our concept of God is small, we have a tendency to become too casual with him. We follow in Satan's footsteps by believing that we are smarter and wiser than him. We start to think that we deserve the glory instead of God. Satan was kicked out of heaven for this very crime (Isaiah 14). We simply can't see the seriousness of the sin of worshiping ourselves or other people as God when we do not take the true God seriously. Tim LaHaye and Ed Hindson noted, "*Even in religious circles, there is a growing tendency to view God as someone who exists to meet our needs. Psychologist Larry Crabb writes, 'We Christians cannot talk about loving God until we come to grips with our raging passion for ourselves. We cannot and will not love anyone but ourselves until we meet God in a way that stirs us to race after him with single-minded intensity, until our deepest desire is to get to know him better.' He summarizes his appeal by adding:*

'I must surrender my fascination with myself to a more worthy preoccupation with the character and purposes of God. I am not the point. He is' [2].

The bible gives warning after warning about glorifying man and idols instead of glorifying God. In the Old Testament, good kings were the ones who led the people away from Idol worship and bad kings moved the people towards idol worship. Before there were Kings of Israel, God would send judges to lead the Israelites. Time and time again, the Israelites would whore after false Gods and then God would allow their enemies to overtake them. Then the Israelites would repent and God would prepare judges to lead them out of captivity. According to scripture, **"And the children of Israel did evil in the sight of the Lord and served Balaam: and they forsook the Lord God of their fathers, which brought them out of the land of Egypt and followed other gods. [These were the] gods of the people that were round about them and [they] bowed themselves unto [these false gods] and provoked the Lord to anger"** (Judges 1:11-13. KJV). In the New Testament, when the people saw Paul and Barnabas do miracles, they tried to worship these men as Gods. Paul told the people, **"Sirs, why do these things? We are men of like passions with you and preach that [you] should turn from these vanities unto the living God, which made heaven and earth, and the sea and all things therein: who in times past suffered all nations to walk in their own ways"** (Acts 15: 15-16, KJV). Paul and Barnabus knew the grave sin of making themselves a God and failing to give God the glory. Unfortunately, King Herod was not so wise. According to Acts 12:21-23, KJV, **"And upon a set day Herod, arrayed in royal apparel, sat upon his throne, and made an oration unto them. And the people gave a shout saying, 'it is the voice of god, and not of a man.' And immediately, the angel of the Lord smote him, because he gave not God the glory: and he was eaten up with worms and gave up the ghost."** In the first chapter of Paul's letter to the Romans, Paul explains God's just anger towards mankind for making idols for themselves instead of serving their creator. He wrote, **"For the wrath of God is revealed from heaven against all ungodliness and unrighteousness of men, who hold the truth in unrighteousness. When they knew God, they glorified him not as God, neither were they thankful; but became vain in their imaginations and their foolish hearts were darkened. Professing to be wise, they became fools and changed the glory of incorruptible God into an image made like to corruptible man and to birds, and four footed beasts and creeping things . . . [They} change the truth of God into a lie, and worshipped and served the creature more than the Creator, who is blessed forever. Amen"** (Romans 1:18-25, KJV).

God is so awesome and amazing that he can do all things and fix any situation if we trust him. Marge and other women who are "independent" must remember that they must ultimately be dependent on this wonderful God as singles. We must remember that the single woman is married to the Lord. This does not mean that God expects for us to only seek him. It means that we enter our relationships with the full knowledge that God is our provider, protector and the nourishment of our souls. Most of us still have feelings for the opposite sex, but these feelings are secondary to our feelings for God. A lady once got angry when I said, "the single woman is married to the Lord." I explained that this did not mean that she can never date or desire a mate. This means that she enters her relationships with full knowledge that before marriage, the only man that she is fully submitted to is God as she navigates the singles scene. In my own life, this improved my relationships instead of causing me to become lonely and dateless. It allowed me to take the pressure off of my dates. I was not as anxious to hurry up and find a man to provide for me and protect me. I was self-assured that God would somehow take care of these things in whatever way he seemed fit. This allowed me to view each man that I dated as a human being to be treated with respect, not as my last chance to find someone to provide for me and protect me. Knowing that God is the ultimate provider and protector takes the desperation away. We lose that sense of insecurity when we realize that our security is ultimately in Christ. Confidence and self-assurance are attractive qualities and tend to ensure more dates, not less dates. We are not all called to be monks. However, we are all called to follow Proverbs 3:5-6 KJV, which states, **"Trust in the Lord with all thine heart and lean not to thine own understanding. In all thy ways acknowledge him and he shall direct thy paths. Be not wise in thine own eyes: fear the Lord and depart from evil."**

The apostle Paul made it clear that being single is preferable to being married if one wants to dedicate his life fully to serving the Lord, but he does not forbid marriage. A single person simply has more time to do the things that build God's kingdom and help others. However, the apostle Paul also made it clear that it is better to marry than to burn with lust. In a letter to the Corinthians, Paul explains, **"It is good for a man not to touch a woman. Nevertheless, to avoid fornication, let every man have his own wife, and let every woman have her own husband . . . I speak this by permission, and not of commandment. For I [wish that] all men were [single] as myself. But every man has his proper gift from God . . . I say therefore to unmarried and widows, It is good for them to [remain single] as I. But if they cannot contain [their sexual desire], let them marry: for it is better to marry than to burn"** (1 Corinthians 7: 1-2, KJV). In reality, both the single woman and married woman are married to the Lord because they are a part of the church which is the bride of Christ. The married woman just has to make sure that she allows Christ to meet her primary needs while making her own husband the number one person in her life to meet her secondary needs. The married woman has to take the extra step of making Jesus number one and her husband a close number two as he is her physical representation of Christ. This can sometimes become a difficult juggling act, but it is what married women are required to do.

CHAPTER 8

Finding Success Dating God's Way

We do not have to make men the center of our lives and deal with disappointment after disappointment. By the same token, we do not have to settle for legalistic rules made by people who were never able to follow them in their own dating lives. We can date God's way as outlined in the Holy Bible. There is a freedom in dating God's way. There are only four strict rules when dating God's way:

- Let no man become an idol that takes the place of God. (Exodus 20: 2-6, Matthew 22:37-39)

- Treat others the way that you want to be treated. (Philippians 2:2-4, 1 Corinthians 9:19-22, Colossians 3: 12-22, Matthew 22: 37-39)

- Do not get serious about a mate unless the mate is serious about God. (2 Corinthians 6:14-16)

- No premarital sex (Rev 22:15, Colossians 3:5-9, I Thessalonians 4:3-8)

We must remember that each date gives us the opportunity to glorify God. We get to practice giving and receiving love and we gain valuable experience in relating to the opposite sex. When we receive God's love by spending personal quiet time with him, we are able to share God's love with others. When our love tank is on empty it means that we need to spend more time with the God himself who is the only true source of love. Our relationships do not work out because they often involve two empty people coming together to see if the other could fill them up. We greet each other asking, "What can you give me to make my life better or complete?" We should greet each other saying, "How can I bring more richness and joy to your life and bring you closer to God?" God must remain our primary focus as we date. All roads point to him, not us. God is love and sin is anything done that does not show love for God and love for others. The best way to avoid sin and strife is to spend as much time as possible praying to God and praising his Holy name. When a date disrespects us or treats us poorly, we do not have to return evil for evil. If the Lord prompts us to say something, we must pray about it and ask, "Will these words bring God glory or does this just make me feel better about being hurt?"

As we remember to make our primary objective to glorify God by bringing others closer to him, we can trust God for the results. We were not meant to marry every person that we date. Many women and men meet a person and start treating that person as "the one" before they even know the person's last name. We often beg God to make our relationships work when God never intended for the relationship to occur in the first place. God is not our cosmic servant who is there to do our will. He is our King and the Lord of our lives. He does whatever he feels like doing with or without our permission. We are unhappiest on the dating scene when we approach God feeling entitled to get the end result that we want. When God does not deliver the results of our program, we get mad and frustrated with him. In reality, we should be mad and frustrated with ourselves for allowing a particular guy to mean so much to us that we would harm our relationship with God. If we find ourselves obsessed with a guy, that guy has become our idol instead of God. God does not promise to give us our idols, he only promises to destroy them or remove them from our lives. We must remember that if we seek God, he will give us many of the things that we desire. We must always remember that God is sovereign and he is not obligated to give us what we want. However, if we seek things and forget God, we will most likely lose both the thing that meant so much to us as well as fellowship with God. God does not tolerate idols for very long.

The freedom that comes from dating God's way cannot be enjoyed until we kill the dating myths and embrace the bible's teachings about interacting with others. We must treat our dates the same way that we would want to be treated. We should always ask, "Am I doing this for his good, or am I doing this to make myself feel better?" While there is no rule in the bible that people should not date as many Christians try to make up, there is a rule that we must follow God's law to love and respect each person that we allow into our lives. Paul told the Galatians, **"You my brothers, were called to be free. But do not use your freedom to indulge the sinful nature; rather serve one another in love. The entire law can be summed up in a single command: Love your neighbor as yourself"** (Galatians 5:13-14, NIV). Love does not act in its own interest, but does what is in the best interest of the other person. For example, when a guy disrespected me a few months ago, the Lord prompted me to lovingly tell the guy that I forgive him and to advise him to treat women better because he never knows who his blessing would come through. Instead of cursing him out which is what I felt like doing, I asked God, "What do you want for me to say so that you can be glorified in this difficult situation?" The guy responded by apologizing and asking for my forgiveness. I treated him with the same kindness that Jesus gives me when I mess up.

We should turn to the bible and pray to get wisdom about how to treat each other. There are many famous courtships in the bible: Ahasuerus and Esther, Boaz and Ruth, Isaac and Rebecca, Jacob and Rachel and Samson and the Philistine woman. Dating is our opportunity to meet new people and serve others. Our prayer before each date should be the following:

Lord, whether this person is coming into my life for a moment, a season or a lifetime, please bless our interaction and give me the wisdom to encourage and edify this person. May my interaction with this person be a light that brings them closer to you, oh Lord. Please remind me that I go on this date to bring you glory, not to glorify myself. In Jesus name I pray. Amen.

Dating is the time to find out if a man would make a good husband. We get the opportunity to observe how a person acts in a variety of situations. We can use these observations to determine if this is the type of person that we can spend the rest of our lives with. The time to screen a man is before marriage, not after marriage. After marriage it is too late. It is so sad to see married women going through their husband's clothes and showing up on their jobs when they could have found out about him and his ways during the dating process. If a guy is under the assumption that he can do whatever he wants to do, what makes us think that he will respect our bodies and avoid soul ties with other women? We must remember that a Christian wife agrees to respect and obey her husband, so we need a mate who is willing to respect and obey God. We must use dating as an opportunity to see if a man is willing to grow spiritually with us in the future. If a man refuses to go to church with us and does not know how to pray, that is a red flag and the best advice is to run. How can we ever hope to submit to a man who refuses to submit to God? We need someone with wisdom and all wisdom comes from God. If a guy is not under God's authority, exactly whose authority is he under?

We must always remember that God's rules about sexuality are there to protect us from getting hurt. They also protect others from getting hurt as well. We do not want to cause harm to anyone's future mate. We simply don't know if we will walk down the aisle with a person until we have actually done it. We cannot be presumptuous about our future when only God knows what will happen tomorrow. We must remember that sex creates soul ties and we only want soul ties with our future husband and not someone else's husband. Sex is beautiful and God invented it to represent our intimacy with him. If we maintain our intimacy with God, then we have the real thing and don't need a cheap imitation that does not glorify him. There is no rule that people cannot hold hands or be alone as many other Christians try to make up. However, a good rule of thumb is to make sure that you do no more in private than you would do in front of your earthly Father. We must always remember that God our Heavenly Father knows everything that we do. He can even read our hearts.

As we read the bible, it is clear that God is not all that concerned with whether or not we get married. God's main concern is that we are being conformed to the image of His Son, Jesus Christ, and that our lives glorify Him. It is our modern day obsession with finding a "soul mate" that keeps us in a spooky state of mind during the dating process. Each person has many soul mates. I could have married many different men and each of the marriages would have been just fine. There is God's best mate for me. It is the mate that allows me to be the best that I can be. The best mate for me is the man that is willing to support my ministry and help me to grow spiritually. This is why we should pray before choosing a mate. It is important to avoid anyone who wants to keep us from going to church or who will not allow us to exercise our spiritual gifts. This is why one of the few rules that God has in regards to marriage is to be "equally yoked."

The bible contains all the wisdom we need to live fulfilling lives as single Christians. We can listen to Sister Super Christian or Pastor Deacon Dr. Duh give us a hundred rules for singles even though they are married and followed none of these rules during their courtship or we can follow the advice contained in God's word. We can listen to our friends tell us the worldly way to get a man, but if it does not line up with God's word, God will not bless it. We have been bought by God for a price-we must commit to living holy lives in front of our Holy Father who sees everything, even those things done in the dark.

Three Things Every Christian Single Should Do

There are three things that every single woman or man should do whether a mate is desired or not:

1. Pray

2. Prepare

3. Profess

Everyone should pray before seeking a mate or seeking celibacy for the rest of his life. According to Philippians, we should "**be anxious for nothing, but in everything by prayer and supplication with thanksgiving make your request be known to God. And the peace of God which is beyond all understanding will keep your hearts and mind through Jesus Christ** (Philippians 4:6-7, NIV). God always answers prayers with the answer yes, no or wait. The promise of God is that he will give us peace regardless of which answer he chooses. Prayer gives us a win-win situation. If the answer is no, God's grace will sustain us by giving us the strength to handle temptation and live in peace. If the answer is yes or wait, he will give us

The Christian Woman's Ultimate Love, Sex and Relationships Manual

the wisdom to know how to prepare for our upcoming mate. A person wanting to get married should also seek the advice and prayers of older wiser people. James 5:16 states "**confess your faults to one another and pray for one another . . . The fervent prayer of a righteous man availeth much**" (KJV).

After one has prayed about a mate, one should prepare for their mate. In the story of Ruth, the prayers and instructions of Naomi were essential in Ruth obtaining a suitable mate. Naomi told Ruth, "**My daughter, I must seek a home for you that will please you. Now is not Boaz, with whose servants you were, a relative of ours? . . . So bathe and anoint yourself; then put on your best attire and go down to the threshing floor . . . uncover a place at his feet and lie down. He will tell you what to do**" (Ruth 3: 1-4, NASB). Ruth prepared for her mate by putting on her best clothes and following the customs of the people that she had grown to love. Ruth probably did not understand why Naomi told her to do certain things to attract Boaz, but her obedience to an older wiser person's instructions paid off. She did become Boaz's wife. The story of Ruth is also an example of how putting first things first works. Ruth left her own land to be with Naomi because it was the right thing to do. Sure, she could have put herself first and let Naomi fend for herself, but she chose to do the right thing and God honored that choice. She got to experience Psalm 37:3-4, KJV: "**Trust in the Lord and do good . . . Delight yourself in the Lord, and he will give you the desires of your heart.**"

Esther prepared for her future husband, the King who reigned from India to Ethiopia, in two ways: she spent one year receiving beauty treatments and she spent years following the teachings of her noble uncle Mordecai. The beauty treatments were important because the King could have any woman he wanted, so any woman going before him would have to be pleasing to the eye and be the type of woman that he could show off to all of the people that he ruled. The bible says "*of this period of beautifying treatments, six months were spent with the oil of myrrh and six months with perfumes and cosmetics.*" (Esther 2:13, NASB) Esther was also lucky enough to be raised by her Godly uncle Mordecai. She was raised by him to be a kind and virtuous woman. This kindness allowed her to "**obtain favor in the sight of all them that looked upon her**"(Esther 2: 15, KJV). The combination of Esther's beauty and virtuous spirit won the heart of the king. Esther displayed humility and love which make one more attractive than all the make-up in the world. Esther was what the king was looking for in a woman. He had just been burned by a beautiful, but proud and unloving wife and he did not want anyone with any signs of these qualities. Queen Vashti did not lose her royal estate to Esther because she was not pretty enough; rather, she lost her royal estate because she was disrespectful towards her husband. Esther's humility truly touched the heart of the King and according to scripture, "**the King loved Esther above all the women, and she obtained grace and favor in his sight more than all the virgins; so he set the royal crown upon her head instead of Vashti**" (Esther 2:17 KJV). A combination of beauty and character caused an orphan girl to be elevated to the status of queen.

In my own dating experience, I can testify that a combination of enduring beauty treatments and developing a Godly character is a winning combination with most men. Getting a makeover can make a big difference in your ability to attract members of the opposite sex. In my own case, a short visit to the fashion fair make-up consultant at Dillard's Department Store resulted in going from 1-2 guys approaching me every 3 months to three to five guys approaching me per day. This significantly increased my chances of getting married because there were simply more men to choose from. During this time, I also spent hours each day reading the bible and reading the Mars-Venus series of books by John Gray. These books contained the wisdom of our grandmothers that has been lost in today's "do what you want-anything goes" society. As a result of approaching dating God's way, nearly every man that I came into contact with stated that he would love to marry a woman like me.

It was not my looks-I weighed over 200 pounds when I received most of my marriage proposals. Instead, it was a sweet quiet spirit that came from spending hours with God. When I was younger, I had nothing but bad luck with men even though my measurements were 36-26-38 with the legs of Tina Turner. The proposals occurred when I was more of a bear can than a coke bottle. Everyone sees gorgeous men with plain or fat girls all the time. God does this to show us that he can favor whoever he chooses. God controls what happens and he can make crooked things seem straight or straight things seem crooked. God can do anything.

You don't have to be a perfect 10 if God is giving you favor for obeying him and humbling yourself before him. At the same time, men are human and they do like for their women to be attractive and shapely. My ex-husband eventually confided in me that a part of the reason that he wanted a divorce was that I had gotten up to 265 pounds and he met me at 210 pounds. When he saw me years later after the weight was lost he said, "I would have never left you if you looked like you do now. You are absolutely gorgeous!" I noticed that as I lost weight, most men would treat me better and better. At 265 pounds, I met 1 man a year. At 245 pounds, I met 1 man a month. At 235 pounds, I met one man a week. At 200 pounds, I meet one or more men a day. It may not be right, but men are visual creatures and women should do the best they can with what they have if they want favor with the opposite sex. This means eating right and having the best body possible. At the same time, women should not obsess about their weight. The first step to losing weight is to accept the body that God has blessed you with. The 2nd step is to commit to eating as healthy as possible and exercising. The rest will fall into place. Many guys do not like bigger women; however, there are some guys that love them. There is someone out there for everyone.

The last step for one seeking a mate is to profess an interest in the opposite sex. Women do not profess their interest directly by saying "I really like you and let's get together!" This generally turns men off because men are programmed to be the pursuer. Rather, women profess their interest by being receptive to a man's advances. Each time that I have pursued a man, I was rejected. Similar to many modern women, in my early years, I fell for the lies of the Women's Liberation Movement. The only thing that this movement liberates women from is their chances of ever finding and keeping a husband. The idea that women should walk in front of men instead of beside them is unnatural and completely against the teachings of the bible. Before learning God's way, I tried to play the man's role and made myself and the men in my life feel very uncomfortable. Once I denounced the false teachings of this movement and allowed the man to take the lead in my relationships, dating became fun and exciting for my dates and I. Over the years, many men have told me that they have never had so much fun with a woman. This was not the fun of a sexual experience-it was the magic experienced when a woman plays the role of a woman and allows a man to truly feel like a man. Women's liberation dictates that men and women should go dutch-that means the woman pays for her meal and the man pays for his. This is a big mistake that most people make because this takes away the man's role as provider. Men simply feel better about themselves when they are playing their God-ordained role as provider. Women's liberation also dictates that a woman can open her own door; however, when a woman graciously accepts a man opening the door for her, it allows a man to feel good about himself as he exercises his role as protector. Women also feel better when they are being provided for and protected. These traditional dating practices allow the man to feel more like a man and the woman to feel more like a woman. They allow each person to bring out the best in the other.

Men must profess directly. So many men miss out on the woman of their dreams because they are too shy to approach her and tell their intentions. One of my male students would always ask my advice about girls and I told him that women like men who are confident enough to just be themselves and state what they like. I told them to listen to the Charlie Wilson song and take notes (Hello, How are you doing? My name is _____, last name _____. I would like to _____. Here is my number . . . .) Men must understand that women like a man that is confident enough to approach her. If a woman says no, then that just isn't the right woman. Men should be like a telemarketer: they should be undisturbed by a series of "no's" because all they really need is one "yes."

God is the greatest source of wisdom about dating and marriage because he invented both. The bible is the world's best relationship manual. We are foolish to believe that our way is better than his way. God's way leads to favor and honor while our way leads to heartbreak and disappointment. Proverbs 28: 26 states that "**he that trusts in his own heart is a fool**" (KJV). This is the direct opposite of pop culture's advice to follow your own heart and live by feelings. God's way of dating is different than our way, but God's way works.

Why be Equally Yoked?

Paul says, "**Be not unequally yoked together with unbelievers; for what fellowship hath righteousness with unrighteousness? What communion [has] light with darkness?**" (II Corinthians 6:14, KJV). Paul's warning to be equally yoked should be taken seriously even when it seems hard. Many men who are not Christian may seem like a dream person to date and marry, but they are not in the same family as Christians. According to Christian doctrine, we are either children of God or children of Satan. We are all in Satan's family until we accept Jesus Christ as our personal Lord and savior and are born again. The warning that Jesus gave the Jews who wanted to kill him is the same warning that he gives to nonbelievers today: "**If you were Abraham's children, you would do the works of Abraham. But now you seek to kill me, a man that has told you the truth . . . . You do the deeds of your Father . . . If God were your Father [you] would love me: for I proceed forth and came from God . . . You are of your father the devil, and the lusts of your father [you] will do. He was a murderer from the beginning, and abode not in truth, because there is no truth in him. When he [speaks] a lie, he [speaks] his own: for he is a liar and the father of it. And because I tell you the truth, [you] believe me not**" (John 8: 39-45, KJV). When we marry a non-Christian we are combining two opposite Spirits.

Satan is so clever that he could easily allow a non-Christian to be smooth and sweet during the dating process and turn into a tyrant once married. This is exactly what happened to me during my first marriage. My ex-husband was the most romantic and wonderful man imaginable while we were dating. As he became more successful during our marriage, he became a completely different person. He later admitted that he was not saved during our marriage and only pretended to be to win me over. Luckily, now he is saved. This exact same thing happened to wonderful lady in the church who was married for over 30 years. Suddenly, her husband became extremely abusive and even threatened her life. He got deep into witchcraft and voodoo. This wonderful lady was lucky to escape the situation with her life. The reality is that all Christians have a flesh, but they also have the Spirit of God in them. A Christian husband can never be a happy wife abuser. He may do wrong, but the Holy Spirit is going to mess with his conscious. With a Christian, there is a definite limit to the amount of evil because of the conviction of the Holy Spirit. When a Christian marries an unbeliever, light and darkness are being mixed together. Light cannot mix with darkness. Either the light is going to win or the darkness will win. There is no guarantee of a bright future in this type of relationship. In some instances, the Christian wins the non-believer over. In other instances, the Christian almost loses his or her faith or sanity. If two are unequally yoked, they are not walking in the same direction and a crash is bound to occur.

It pains me to see women like Deborah Cooper write articles like, "How Black Churches Keep African American Women Single and Lonely." She declared that the worst men are found in churches. According to Ms. Cooper, *"Going to church for a single black woman is a waste of time . . . Some women will argue that there are lots of nice single men in church . . . Without a doubt, the vast majority (98%) fit into one of four categories: A loser working a 12-Step Program; openly or in the closet gay men; opportunistic players on the prowl; elderly reformed players"* [1]. I can honestly say that I have met all of the types of men that Ms. Cooper described in her article. However, her advice that we need to stop going to church is simply wrong. It was Jesus Christ who healed my broken heart after these so-called Christian men treated me poorly. There is nothing that can keep me away from the church house to worship him. With Jesus, I know that all things are possible, including finding a Godly Christian man. She talks about how good men would not be caught dead in a church. In reality, there are lots of good men in the church, but most of them are already married. Ms. Cooper is correct that single Christians need to go to different places and meet different people if they ever want to get married. However, the church is our foundation. We should not go there looking for a man, but we should go looking for a deeper relationship with Jesus Christ. I think that if more single ladies would invite the men that they meet other places to church, the church would be full of good single men. Christians need to start thinking outside of the box. Christian singles tend to only associate with other Christians when there is a big world out there that needs to see the love of Jesus Christ. Once we bring men from the clubs to the church, the men would find that they like it. I have done this and no guy has ever complained about going on a date to church. When I invite them again, they usually say, "yes." As Christian singles, we need to stop trying to conform to the world and start boldly witnessing about Christ and inviting others to church. The world needs to hear about Jesus Christ and the world is more open to us than we think.

We must guard our hearts and avoid letting Satan use our experiences as an excuse to grow further away from Jesus Christ or as an excuse for marrying a non-Christian. We need to allow these bad experiences to bring us closer to Jesus Christ, the healer of our souls. He does not want for us to become bitter; rather, he wants for us to become better. We must remember God uses our bad experiences to help us grow closer to him and to help us to understand others. Romans 8:28, KJV, says, **"And we know that all things work together for good to them that love God, and to them are called according to his purpose.** "What is our purpose? We are here mainly to **"be conformed to the image of God's son, Jesus Christ"** (Romans 8:29, KJV). We must remember that God loves us and Jesus is there for us when we are hurt. There is no burden or bad date that is too much for Jesus Christ to handle. Paul reminds us that no one can **"separate us from the love of Christ [and] in all things we are more than conquerors through him that loved us. For I am persuaded, that neither death, nor life, nor angels, nor principalities, nor powers, nor things present, nor things to come. Nor height, nor depth, nor any other creature, shall be able to separate us from the love of God, which is in Christ Jesus our Lord"** (Romans 8: 35-39, KJV). God's love is enough to handle any hurt or situation. Rape is not too much for him. Abuse is not too much for him. Promiscuity is not too much for him because he can handle anything. The frailty of the men who disappoint us reminds us to put our trust in God instead of man. Only Jesus Christ can satisfy our thirst for a perfect man and a perfect love. Man can let us down, but Jesus Christ can always be trusted to be there for us and give us whatever love and comfort that we need. This was the point that Jesus made to the woman at the well who had five husbands and a current live-in boyfriend. Jesus is the only living water that can cause us to never thirst again.

Is it OK to Date Non-Christians?

The bible tells us to avoid marrying an unbeliever but it does not say that we cannot date one. What if we redefined dating as an opportunity for two people to enjoy each other's company, learn more about each other and practice giving and receiving acts of love and kindness? If we embrace dating as an enjoyable opportunity to show the love of Christ, then it is really OK to date just about anyone. Also, we cannot really tell who is a Christian or who is not a Christian when we first meet someone. C.S. Lewis makes a very good point: "*The world does not consist of 100% Christians and 100% non-Christians. There are people who are slowly ceasing to be Christian but will still all themselves by that name . . . There are other people who are slowly becoming Christian though they do not yet call themselves so*" [2]. Our job is to motivate as many people as possible to move towards the Christian side. When we date, we do not know where a person will be 5, 6 or 12 months from now. We can only hope that they will be closer to Christ and fully Christian, but there is no guarantee. When we refuse to date unbelievers, we may be rejecting someone who is going to be a great Christian 3 months later because we invited them to church several times. Our ability to determine someone's status as a Christian is quite limited until many months of knowing someone. Even then we are limited in our knowledge. Dating unbelievers is perfectly fine as long as we do not mistake dating for marriage. Dating does not need to involve sex or plans for marriage. Premarital sex and marrying an unbeliever is the sin, not dating. Unbelievers often make the best dates and we can learn a lot from them about how to relax and enjoy life. God wants for us to enjoy life and he does give us the freedom to do so. Each date teaches us a little more about ourselves, a little more about men and a lot about life in general.

It was a non-Christian who gave me the best example of someone acting lovingly even when they did not feel like it. Fred is a handsome Ethiopian guy with the sweetest spirit. He was an atheist when we parted years ago. Once we reconnected, our first date was at a Karaoke club and we had a wonderful time. To my surprise, he revealed that he was thankful to God for blessing him financially. He said that he was attending Joel Osteen's church and becoming more open to Christianity. Even though Fred was not a Christian, he would display more Christian character on a date than anyone that I had ever seen. He was always kind, gentle, courteous and generous each time we would go out. He always portrayed a quiet, peaceful confidence that made him quite attractive to women. One day he invited me to dinner at a Mexican restaurant. I had told my friend Mary that he and I were going out and she wanted to join us. I did not think that she would actually come on my date, but she actually showed up about 10 minutes after Fred and I ordered the food. I was mortified and afraid that Fred would curse me out. To my amazement, Fred showed no signs of anger or shock that someone interrupted our date. He asked Mary if she wanted anything to eat because he would treat her to it. He was kind, gracious and gentle as he answered Mary's rather invasive questions. Watching Fred handle this awkward situation with such grace and care really touched my heart. I began to think, "This is really a wonderful guy. If I were him, I would be livid." A few months later, Fred confided in me that he was not very happy when Mary intruded on our date. He told me, "I decided to just pretend to be happy and this resulted in everyone having a good time." As he spoke, I thought about the Christian men who I had dated would never display such patience and kindness while irritated. Fred's secret was to just pretend. He understood that somehow when we act lovingly, loving feelings and positive relationships often follow. As a result of Fred's plan to "just pretend", Fred had a good time and my friend and I left the restaurant thoroughly impressed with Fred. Mary called after the date and said, "Boy, I wish that there were more Christian men like Fred." I said, "I completely agree."

My favorite date occurred during the Essence Music Festival. I was walking in the Hilton hotel lobby and this guy stopped me to ask if I wanted to watch a boxing match on his computer with him and friends. I told him that the last time I saw a fight was when Tyson fought against Holyfield and bit his ear off. We laughed and then his cousin arrived. His cousin found me very attractive and started flirting. He said that he does not like fights and invited me out for ice cream. I told him, "Don't try any funny stuff!" and he agreed. We had the most wonderful time. We stopped and played video games. He was number 40 on the score board and I was number 41. Even though we were dead last in scores for the game car racer, we were first when it came to laughing and enjoying ourselves though. As we left the hotel, we saw the bicycle carriage ride person. My ice cream partner insisted that we go on a ride through the French Quarters and find an ice cream shop on the way. We had the most incredible time. I cannot remember having so much fun on a date. My date told me that he has not had that much fun in years. He said that his original intentions of going out with me were not good, but he enjoyed my company so much that he forgot his original bad intentions. I told him that it had been a long time for me to have that much fun as well. Both of us learned a lot from each other. He taught me the importance of being open to all that life has to offer and to enjoy new experiences. I had never played that video game before in my life and it was so much fun. I had never gone on a carriage ride through the French Quarters, but it turned out to be totally exhilarating. I taught him that he could have fun with a woman even if the evening does not end in sex. I got the opportunity to share the lesson that I learned from Fred: when you act lovingly towards others, it makes you feel loving towards them as well. I was just so thankful to the Lord for allowing me to have such a wonderful time, especially after a major heartbreak. We both knew that we would not be walking down the aisle together, but that did not mean that we could not enjoy each other's company. God wants for us to enjoy our relationship with him and our relationships with each other. He only gives rules to make that enjoyment possible.

We don't have to be uptight and upset all the time when the joy of the Lord is our strength. The joy that God offers us comes from knowing him and being in right relationship with him. Once we fully trust God and his wisdom, we can learn to enjoy our relationships with others. A true Christian does not have to sin to be happy. In fact, sin takes us out of fellowship with God and God's peace is better than any momentary pleasure. God is our daddy once we have surrendered to him. He loves us so much that he allowed his only Begotten Son to die so that we could be in proper relationship with him. Our daddy, God, owns everything on earth and he made this wonderful world for us to enjoy. He wants for us to drop those legalistic rules and enter his rest as we do things his way. In his kingdom, we find heaven on earth. With him, there is "**righteousness, peace and joy in the Holy Ghost**" (Romans 14:17, KJV). He is so wonderful that once we have met him, we cannot help but to delight in him.

CHAPTER 9

Picking the Right Person

Steve Harvey's Statement on the Role of a Man has a Biblical Basis

Steve Harvey's statement that the role of the man is to profess, provide and protect a woman has a lot of truth to it. According to Harvey, "If your man loves you, he is willing to tell anybody and everybody, 'Look man, this is my woman.' . . . In other words, you will have a title . . . If he introduces you as his friend or your name, that is all you are . . . . Once we've claimed you, and you have returned the honor, we're going to start bringing home the bacon . . . . A man who truly loves you will never make you ask for money for necessities-he would try to make sure that you need and mostly want for nothing . . . . Once he says he cares about you, you are a prized possession to him and he will do anything to protect that prized possession" [1] A single woman can evaluate if a guy is good for her by his willingness to do Steve Harvey's 3 P's: profess, provide and protect. Every man that has ever proposed to me would do these three things before proposing: 1.They would profess their love for me to their friends and family; 2. they wanted to make sure that I was financially OK; and 3. they wanted to protect me by showing a concern for my safety and mental well-being. Guys just looking for fun usually did one of these things, but never all of them. Steve Harvey gives women a very useful tool for evaluating the men that we date. The quicker we identify time-wasters, the quicker we can meet the man of our dreams.

The first question we should ask before picking a mate is, "Is this person proud to be seen with me or is this person trying to hide me?" I have observed that men who eventually proposed would always make sure that friends and family knew me as his woman. They enjoyed taking me to fun places and showing me off. Guys who were just looking for fun would try to make the first date at their house as if they were ashamed of me. Men who could care less about me would introduce me as their friend instead of their girlfriend. In my 20's I fell for this foolishness and each time I came up disappointed. Once I started dating God's way, I realized that it would simply be a waste of time to date a guy who wanted the first few dates to be at his house or who was not willing to introduce me to his friends and family after a certain period of time. According to scripture, a guy who is to be a Godly husband will think of his wife as an extension of himself. The bible says that similar to the way that every member of the church are members of Christ's body, in marriage, a woman becomes a part of the man's body. Ephesians 5:30-31 (KJV) states **"For we are members of [Christ's] body, of his flesh, and of his bones. For this cause a man will leave his father and mother, and shall be joined unto his wife, and they two shall be one flesh."** So if a man is not willing to introduce you to his friends and family, he is not going to give you the type of marriage in which he will willingly put you ahead of all others. In fact, such a guy either has other women or does not really want to be seen with you, which means that he is probably not that interested in marrying you either.

The second question we should ask is "Are we capable of being good friends or is this just a physical or emotional attraction? It is important for us to marry our friend, not just someone who looks good or has money. Many dating experts claim that the depth of friendship is one of the greatest predictors of whether a marriage will last. Friends do not have to have the same interest in sports or the same hobbies, but they do need to have the same general values. For example, a strong organized Christian is going to drive himself insane if he marries a free-spirit who does whatever she pleases. A parent who is a strong disciplinarian is going to fight constantly with a spouse who believes in spoiling children. People with opposite value systems rarely sustain relationships. The husband and wife are to become one flesh. Oil and water cannot mix. This is why a believer should not marry a nonbeliever. The two are not moving in the same direction and there is always a good chance that the couple will simply drift apart. There must be a sense of unity in purpose within the relationship. How can two people walk in unity with one another if they do not share the same spirit?

The third question that we should ask is "Would this man be a good provider?" According to the bible, "He who loves his wife loves himself. After all, no one ever hated his own flesh, but he feeds and cares for it-just as Christ does the Church" (Ephesians 5: 28-29,NIV). A part of the "care" in this verse involves money. A lot of us like to pretend that this is not important, but money is cited as a major reason for many divorces. Men who eventually proposed would also try to make sure that I was well provided for. Even when they were broke, they would make sure that I never had to pay for a date. If it meant borrowing money from a friend, they made sure that I was taken care of. If I mentioned that something was broken, they would immediately volunteer to fix it. Men who could care less would ask to go dutch or demand that I paid by the third date.

When we continue dating men who do not care, we set ourselves up for disappointment. A man rarely values something that comes too easily or cheaply. If he did not pay a high price for it, he is going to assume that it is of little worth. In the same way, when a man feels that he does not have to do anything special to earn our loyalty and love, he does not usually consider us that important. When a man is not acting as provider, he does not usually grow in affection towards the woman that he is dating. I have observed that any time I paid for a date within the first month or so, the relationship would always end suddenly. Women do need to reciprocate, but it needs to be later on in the relationship and it should not always involve money. Dating is most smooth when the man successfully provides for the woman and the woman shows gratitude and appreciation for whatever the man is doing. This is probably because in the scripture, God (allegorically the male) is our provider and not the other way around. The woman acting as provider makes the man feel uncomfortable and makes the woman feel resentful and cheated. Chris Rock never spoke a truer statement when he said that the best way to get a woman to lose interest in a man is to get her to start paying for everything. Our parents and ancestors had certain dating rituals for a reason. These rituals were used to make a man feel more like a man and the woman feel more like a woman. This bought out the best in both parties. When a woman plays a man's role she is cheating herself and her man. When a man plays the woman's role, he inevitably feels like less than a man and less enthusiastic about being around a woman who makes him feel that way.

Money should not be a primary consideration in marriage because God is the ultimate provider for both husband and wife. When we go after a man strictly for his money, we are putting our faith in the wrong thing. God can strip a person of his riches in a split second. That guy who is a millionaire today can get sued tomorrow and lose it all. We must marry a man who we both like and admire. We need a man who is led by Christ so that we can trust him to lead us. We can go gold-digging or we can find pure gold in Christ. Jesus Christ is our ultimate provider and we must never forget this fact. In my own life, after my divorce money was extremely tight. I was $200 short each month and often had to live on credit cards to make ends meet. I was looking forward to the day when I could remarry a rich man so that I did not have to worry about supporting myself. I even became friends with a gold-digger and wanted to learn her techniques. After several months of dating nothing but millionaires, I was extremely frustrated because these millionaires wanted sex before sharing their money and I did not believe in pre-marital sex. One day my earthly Father helped me to discover the real truth about my Heavenly Father. I told my dad that I was looking for a good life insurance policy because this guy said that it is a good way to borrow money and have protection. My dad responded, "That is such a dumb idea! Don't you realize that I am your life insurance policy? I will give you whatever you need." This statement really touched me and I realized that this is also God's message to me: God is my life insurance policy and he provides full protection. After a while, I gave up my quest for a rich man and decided that God is my protector and provider and he will make a way for me somehow. I do not even have to worry about how the bills will be paid: this is God's job.

The book of Isaiah states that the single woman is married to the Lord and he will take care of his bride. As soon as I made this declaration, God began to bring man after man into my life who actually wanted to provide for me. Looking back, I now realize that God would not allow these rich men to take care of me because I would have been tempted to give these men the credit instead of God. God knew that if I worshipped a man for providing for me, it would lead to spiritual death and I was very prone to committing such a sin if left to my own devices. God did not allow me to have what I wanted because he loved me and knew that I could not handle it. God gave me something more than money or a rich man could ever buy, he gave me his peace and a deeper relationship with him through Jesus Christ. It was through this experience that I received the revelation that God is my daddy and I can trust in him to provide whatever is needed. I began to understand Jesus' instructions to his followers, "**Do not be worried about your life, as to what you will eat or what you will drink; nor for your body, as to what you will put on. Is not life more than food and the body more than clothing? Look at the birds of the air . . . [They] do not sow, nor reap, nor gather into barns, and yet your heavenly father feeds them. Are you not worth more than they? And why are you worrying about clothing? Observe how the lilies of the field grow; they do not toil, nor do they spin; yet I say to you that not even Solomon in all his glory clothed himself like one of these. But if God clothed the grass of the field . . . will he not much more clothed you? . . . Do not worry then, saying, 'What will we eat?' or 'What will we drink?' or 'What will we wear for clothing?' For the Gentiles eagerly seek all these things: for your Heavenly father knows that you need these things**" (Matthew 6: 25-32, NASB).

Sometimes circumstances dictate that the woman must be the main provider; however, this should be avoided as much as possible. When a man loses his job and the woman is forced to be the breadwinner, it will create lots of stress for both parties in the marriage. Each person must anticipate that their partner will be a little more irritable and frustrated than usual. In order to preserve the marriage union, such a couple will need to pray together more, read the bible together more and seek spiritual guidance and counsel. Otherwise, when a man is unable to provide for his woman, it can cause her to lose respect for him and become overwhelmed by the increase in responsibility. In the same way, he will often suffer a loss of respect for himself and he could become quite sensitive about everything. This is fertile ground for the marriage to begin to unravel.

Respect is the primary need for most men. Love is the primary need for most women. When these primary needs are met, the marriage runs smoothly. When they are not met, things begin to unravel quickly. One reason that so many marriages fail is that men often try to give women what men need while women give men what women need. Relationships work best when we try to meet the actual needs of the other person. It is like me loving Gucci watches and my husband loving computer equipment. If I buy him a Gucci watch for Christmas, he is not going to be nearly as happy as he would have been if I bought him a computer or some type of gadget. We must give our partners what they need, not what we need. Since God created us, he knows what each of us needs. These primary needs are outlined in Ephesians 5:33: it says, "**Let every one of you love his wife even as himself; and the wife see to it that she reverence her husband.**" Similar to how Jesus summarized the Ten Commandments as love

God and love your neighbor as yourself, Paul summarized the proper attitude of husband and wife as the following: the husband is to love and cherish his wife and the wife to respect her husband. A husband should ask himself, "Am I willing to put her needs ahead of my own?" He should also ask "Do I like her enough to sacrifice for her?" By the same token, before a woman agrees to marry a man, she must ask, "Do I respect this man enough to submit to him?" The bible says, **"Wives submit to your husband as to the Lord . . . Now as the church submits to Christ, so also shall the wife submit to her husband in everything"** (Ephesians 5:22-24, NIV). As woman, we must make sure that we trust a man's judgment before saying "I do." When we marry men that we do not truly respect, we treat them like children. The man will stop wanting to even be around us. No man wants to be a woman's charity project or child. Men want to be our hero, not constantly reminded that they are a complete zero. According to the bible, it is **"better to live on a corner of the roof than share a house with a quarrelsome wife"** (Proverbs 21:9 NIV). Men have a basic need to be respected and when we women fail to provide this basic need, the marriage begins to unravel.

Anyone can observe that when a man really loves a woman, he wants to protect her. I noticed that marriage minded men like to make sure that I walk on the inside of the sidewalk so that if anything happens, they will be in a better position to protect me. Men who are thinking in terms of marriage do not like to see me driving by myself at night or even take the bus. Men who could care less would often walk in front of me or leave me behind without any regard for my safety. I will never forget when a guy friend wanted me to meet him at a deli at 10:30pm. Luckily, I was already out and I agreed. We arrived at the deli at the same time. When he got out the car, we hugged and then he proceeded to walk into the place leaving me behind in a poorly lit parking lot. This was not a very protective thing to do at 10:30pm at night. At that moment, I realized just how little this guy cares about my safety and well-being. It also dawned on me that no guy would ask a girl to meet him at 10:30pm unless she was an afterthought-a woman to take the place of the woman that he had previously asked to go out. This particular friend had been burned in a bitter divorce and tended to think of women as gold-diggers. I realized that this bitterness may have caused him to have problems providing for or protecting the women in his life. He could make a good husband in the future once a certain degree of healing has occurred. Or it could be that he just did not care much for me-either way, wisdom dictated for me to let him "walk on by."

Real men always protect their women. The bible says that a man should "Love [his] wife like Christ loved the church and gave himself up for her to make her holy and present her as blameless" (Ephesians 5:25-27, NIV). That means that a man should be willing to die for his woman. If an intruder enters the home, he should not be trying to use his wife as a body shield. His priority should be to protect his wife first. For single women, this means that a guy who calls at 10:00pm and asks for you to come over to his home most likely cares nothing about your safety or about you. A guy who walks in front of you and leaves you behind clearly cares about his safety more than yours. "Booty call men" usually never ask the woman for marriage in the first place and they prove to be a serious time waster.

Biblically, men are told to provide, protect and profess in marriage. However, these habits should be practiced during the courting process as well. We can use a man's willingness to do these things and a woman's willingness to accept these things from a man as a good gage for whether the couple should even consider getting married. One of the reasons why so many marriages fail is that people jump into marriage without any idea about how to pick the right mate or how to live with another human being "till death do us part." Men and women should be preparing themselves for marriage much sooner than 2-3 months before the marriage begins. Churches like to give 3-6 week marriage preparation courses to engaged couples. This is simply too late. People need to know about what to expect in marriage and what to look for in a mate much sooner than that. It is too late to find out that you have probably picked the wrong marriage partner a few weeks before the wedding. It is too late to find out that you have a year's worth of growing up to do two months before you walk down the aisle. Many couples would have never picked each other in the first place if they would have had better instructions earlier. In my own case, I realized the mistakes I made only after my divorce. All singles need good instruction about what qualities to look for in a mate and how to live with others unselfishly and with a forgiving spirit.

Good teaching about the beauty and spiritual nature of marriage is important even throughout the teen years. A young girl who looks forward to meeting a man who loves her like Christ loves the Church is not going to be as tempted to let Pooky down the street climb through her bedroom window for a quick thrill. She will want a man who would not put her in harm's way with her parents. She would be willing to wait for someone who is really special. My cousin's older friends who want to commit suicide because no one has ever asked them to marry them would begin to realize that being a single woman married to the Lord is better than settling for less than an Ephesians 5 marriage. They would also have better insight on which guys to choose. Most women who have never received a marriage proposal have probably been wasting lots of time with men who are not marriage material or marriage-minded. They have probably been waiting by the phone for a booty call man to text them. They have probably been dating guys who walk in front of them or ask them out at the last minute all the time, not realizing that this indicates a lack of care and concern for women.

Understanding how to biblically choose a mate can keep us from making the wrong choice in marriage partner. One woman had the man of her dreams, but he said that he wanted for her to stop singing in church and even going to church. She automatically knew that a man who is not led by God cannot lead her. I recently had to let go of a wonderful man who I could not fully respect. He worked off-shore for several years, so he could be a good provider. He was kind and willing to introduce me to friends and family. He even wanted a baby soon and this really impressed me. However, he was younger than me and had piercings and tattoos all over his body. He even told me that he would get more tattoos. I was perplexed because he had 80% of what I wanted in a man. However, when I had to ask myself some key questions, I had to admit that the answer would be "no". I wondered "Could this guy be a good spiritual leader for the household?" The answer was a clear "no." I wondered, "Would I be willing to respect this guy's judgment?" The answer again was no. I wondered, "Could I proudly introduce him to my ultra-conservative friends and family?" Again, the answer was "no". Most important, "Would I slip into mothering this guy or would I willingly submit to him?" The answer to that was "he would nickname me mommy dearest" if we tied the knot. Knowing that it would never work, I had to let a truly wonderful guy go. However, I know that I made the right decision even though it still hurts.

God wants for us to enjoy ourselves during the dating process. Dating gives us the opportunity to show love by serving others. Our goal should be to enrich the lives of those we date. Everyone comes into our lives for a reason: some come for a moment, some for a season and some for a lifetime. We need to be ourselves and enter God's rest as we date. Our part is to do the best we can with what we have to offer. Only God can determine the results. We plant the seed. God does the watering and allows it to grow. If he chooses not to water the seed that we planted, maybe he has a good reason for it. When I was in my 20's, I would have jumped at the opportunity to marry a man with tattoos all over his body and numerous body piercings. That would have been the coolest thing in the world to me. When I would date guys like that, things would never work out back then and it would always end abruptly. I thought that I was being rejected and felt bad about myself, but now I realize that God was keeping me from messing my life up with the wrong type of guy for me. God allowed for this type of guy to fall for me in my late 30's because he knows that I am now mature enough to realize that a relationship with a "bad boy" would never work. God gives us only those things that we can handle. We must remember that we have a loving Father who wants what is best for us. When things don't work out, it is because God has something better for us and our loving Father knows what is best. He knows better than we do and that is why the wisest thing for us to do is to just trust him.

CHAPTER 10

Three Secrets to Being the Best Catch When Men Go Fishing

Secret 1: Glorify God Instead of Self

We are not called to results, but we are called to obedience. Success in dating does not mean that we get that man of our dreams and live happily ever after with the next man that we meet. Success in dating really means using each date as an opportunity to glorify God. We have successful lives when our lives glorify God and we walk with God in peace and joy. There are too many married people who are absolutely miserable for anyone to persuade me that marriage is the ultimate goal of life. We must always remember that our goal is to know Jesus and be known by him. We are his bride and he loves each of us. Marriage is only a physical manifestation of the spiritual reality that is our relationship with Christ. Whether married or single, we are married to Christ. Christianity is not so much about rules and bargaining with God as it about a relationship with Jesus Christ. Jesus wants what is best for us, but unfortunately, we do not always know what is best for ourselves. We often assume that money and marriage will somehow make us happy and pursue these as goals. This usually leads us to disappointment. God warns that any single-minded pursuit except pursuit of him is going to leave us empty-handed. God is not so much concerned with whether we are rich and happy as he is concerned with whether we are being conformed to the image of his son Jesus Christ and growing closer to him. As we seek God and obey his word, we find something better than happiness from good circumstances: we find a righteousness that we did not earn, a peace that is not dependent on circumstances, and a joy that is unexplainable. In other words we get the opportunity to experience a little piece of heaven on earth. When we have the right goal, we will usually get the right results. My favorite scripture explains that if we would seek God, the things that we need will be thrown in (Matthew 6:33-6:34). I have named this principle "The Law of Focus". It works in all areas of life, but especially in spiritual areas. As Christian singles, once we focus on the goal of glorifying God and growing closer to Jesus Christ, dating and all other areas will fall in place and maximum success will be achieved. We are successful daters as long as we are focused on building God's kingdom and being more Christ-like in each of our interactions. These goals are so powerful and profound that marriage proposals and great relationships are almost inevitable by-products.

God attempted to teach me the powerful lesson of having the right focus when I was in graduate school. Towards the end of my stay in Detroit, I met four of the most amazing Christian women. These ladies were pretty in their own way, but not gorgeous. Yet, they were all male magnets. Men were just drawn to these women for unknown reasons. Ironically, even though they did not know each other, they all gave me the same advice: trust God and do what God says and he will take care of your every need and concern. One of these women was 56 years old and looked 38 years old. She was the mother of a very famous boxer from Detroit. She met me while I was her other son's bimbo. She saw that I had no clue about men and needed spiritual guidance, so she tried to mentor me for a while. One day I was at her home talking to her son and heard the sweetest music from the other room. It was her spending hours in her room praising and worshipping God. This spirit-filled woman had something that I did not have at the time and I knew that one of the secrets to getting it would be to have a lifestyle of worship. She told me that at fifty-six, she had men of all ages trying to date her and she had a wonderful boyfriend. She said that as we delight in God, he will give us everything that we need. She said that she never worried about getting or having a man because God has always had her back. She was a living example that as we seek God, he can allow his blessings to chase us without us needing to lift a finger to make it happen.

As a Math teacher, I have a special understanding of the importance of having the right goals to get the right results. A lot of middle school kids have two main goals when they enter class: get a good grade and have fun in the class. These are good goals, but these are not the best goals. It is ironic that the students who care about their grades the most usually wind up scoring lowest on my tests. They often become nervous and spend too much time thinking about a final result instead of correctly going through the process of learning the concepts for the test. Some of these students will copy other people's homework or try to change answers for a paper to get a higher grade. I have to explain to these individuals that the secret to getting a good grade is to listen when I am instructing the class, ask questions as soon as you don't understand and practice by completing all homework each night. Many kids have heard me say over and over again: "If you do what you are supposed to do, the results will take care of themselves." As a teacher, my goal is to prepare the kids for the next level in Math and help them grow in character and integrity. The goals that I have for my students will last a lifetime. I don't really care about the outcome as long as my students are doing their best and doing it honestly. Kids who do what I tell them to do in the way that I tell them to do it are my greatest success stories. These kids usually enjoy my class the most as they find it very entertaining. The fact that the grades of my successful students are typically extremely high is just icing on the cake. Many of these students visit me years later to tell me about how they are earning good grades in high school and college because of some of the things that I shared with them. That is what makes me feel that my efforts are worth it. It is similar to how God's heart sings when we become more and more Christ-like by obediently following his word.

The Law of Focus was the secret to my grades in college. After my first semester of college, I had a nervous breakdown and cried for hours. I had too many things to do and not enough time to do it. My classes were too hard and it was impossible to keep up. Eventually, I cried out to the Lord to help me. He immediately started ministering to me that everything would be alright. I meditated on Matthew 6:33, KJV which states "Seek ye first the kingdom of God and his righteousness, and all of these things will be added unto you." This scripture gave me the confidence to continue on. I decided to change my major from biology to microbiology which was slightly easier. I dropped out of the honors college and started balancing my schedule between hard and easy classes instead of taking all hard classes. My grade point average went from 2.9 to 4.0. I maintained straight A's and B's for the remainder of college and graduated with the highest average in the Biology Department. The same thing happened in graduate school. Once again, I had to meditate on Matthew 6:33 to get the noise out of my head. This allowed me to leave graduate school with a 3.8 grade point average.

When I was 16, I saw this law work in the area of weight loss. Prior to 16, I had dieted at least a hundred times with little or no success. Then I decided to focus on praying to God to guide my eating and exercise. I walked daily for 30 minutes to an hour. God gave me the wisdom to have the attitude that I must eat to live not live to eat. He showed me that the donut stand was not going out of business and I did not have to act as if it were my last opportunity to get a donut. Instead of focusing on how many pounds were lost, I focused on eating healthy and getting as much exercise as possible. To my amazement, the weight just fell off at rate of 0.5 to 1 pound a day. By focusing on my health and ways to improve my health instead of focusing on the numbers on the scale, I was successful at weight loss for the first time. Most important, I focused on God and his ability to strengthen me to eat correctly and exercise.

In the area of relationships, once we focus on being a vehicle of God's love and bringing others closer to Christ, we begin to see miracles happen. Even those relationships that don't work begin to have a special meaning. Christ takes the broken pieces of our life and relationships to make a beautiful mosaic. When Jesus fed the 5,000 men, he told them to gather all the scraps so that nothing is lost. Jesus uses every scrap from our lives for his own glory. Success in relationships did not begin for me until I started using this principle. God showed me that the law of focus gives us a win-win situation in every relationship. When our central focus is God, he will either give us the grace to succeed in our relationships or give us the grace to be content and learn from our rejections. Either way God is glorified. We either benefit from having the desires of our hearts fulfilled or we benefit from learning an important lesson to help us later on. It is ironic that God often gets the most glory from our most broken situations.

The Blessing of Brokenness

God uses our brokenness for his glory more than our perfect lives. My mother lived an almost perfect life and rarely did anything wrong. I am very proud of her, but her perfection was not useful for me growing up. I needed someone who was rough around the edges to show me the mistakes to avoid and the pitfalls of doing things my way instead of God's way. As a person who has made thousands of mistakes, I know what it is like to be down and get back up again. My most profound ministry experiences came after some of my greatest defeats. People's lives are changed when they see someone who was in their exact same circumstances who made it out and point to God as their source of strength. This is why people in leadership should be transparent. Sometimes we proudly try to hide our mistakes thinking that people will like and respect us more. In reality, people see through our phony façade of perfection and being a know-it-all. Many times, people are most blessed when we admit that we have fallen; yet, God was strong enough, wise enough and good enough to lift us up. My ministry did not become clear to me until I started sharing my mistakes and lessons learned with others. People were so blessed to hear someone else who faced their exact situation. The people that I ministered to poured out their thanks and love when I did not even expect it. We must remember that without a test, there is no testimony. Two different men taught me two of life's greatest lessons by breaking my heart to pieces. God revealed himself to me in the most powerful way and he gave me a platform to bless others. We should always write down the lessons learned from each person that comes into our life. This would give us a platform to share with our kids and grandkids or friends in years to come. We can point others to a God who specializes in putting broken people and broken situations back together again.

John—The Man Who Taught Me to Trust in God

I remembered the first time that we met as if it were yesterday. John was the most handsome man that I had ever seen in my life. He looked like a movie star. He was dressed in a pair of slacks and a tie with muscles bulging out of the shirt. He had perfect skin and bedroom eyes that could make a woman's heart melt. As I was walking through the Galleria in Houston, he stopped me and I was flattered that such a gorgeous man wanted to speak to me. He was so charming that it did not take much convincing for me to give him my number. I figured that he had lots of women so I was careful not to get my hopes up. To my surprise, he would text me a sweet message every day and call me every evening. He would even text me songs that he sang in the music studio. He was a hairdresser by day and an aspiring musician by night.

To my surprise, he was a really nice guy and I enjoyed talking with him daily. He would tell me about his future plans to launch a musical career and start several businesses. I felt like Cinderella when she just met her Prince. One day, I decided to invite him to church. I called him several times and he did not call back. I knew that something was wrong. Once we finally spoke, I got the most shocking news. He told me that his mother had just died in California and he needed to leave Houston to attend the funeral. The only reason that he was in Houston in the first place was that his Mother was going to MD Anderson for cancer treatment. My heart sank when I heard the news. I was sorry that he lost his mother, but I was also devastated that I was probably going to lose him. I knew that once he arrived in California, he would have little or no reason to return to Houston. Our relationship was too new for him to come back to Houston just to be with me. We talked a few more times and my worst fear was realized: he planned to stay in California to be with his family and launch his career. I spent the next five months trying to silently fight the depression that I felt. I did not want to date anyone but this guy; at the same time, it appeared that we would probably never be together. I tried to use work to bury my pain. I even felt that I was being selfish for focusing on my pain of losing him instead of his pain of losing his mother. Finally, in April, I realized that I must move on and start dating again. It was so strange that the very day that I had decided to move on, John called and decided to start pursuing me again. He told me that he really missed me and would love for us to get married. I missed his daily calls and I missed talking to him about our dreams to go into ministry together. In March, April and May, John pursued me and made plans to visit Houston again. Hearing from him became the highlight of my day. He sent pictures and we talked constantly about being together soon. John would always tell me, "people will let you down, but God will never let you down." I did not realize that our relationship would serve as an illustration of this lesson.

It was two weeks before school would end. As a teacher, I was in a frenzy trying to get grades done and get everything packed and secured for summer. John called me on the phone while I was on my way to meet two friends at the Country Club. He said that he would be in Houston the next day and I was elated. I told him that I was going to a meeting and would call him later. The meeting lasted longer than I expected. When it was over, my friend Mary asked to take pictures around the Country Club. As we were taking pictures, we got to speak to a politician who was having a fundraising event at the club. It was such a fun and exciting night that I did not call my boyfriend until 9:00pm. By that point, it was too late in his mind. He left the following text message on my phone: "Guess it was a long meeting. It seems like you have a lot going on. Maybe it is best that I be a part of your life when you are ready to settle down." I frantically tried to call him, but he would not speak to me. I was so hurt that I walked around in a stupor for the next three days. I was so depressed that I could not even bring myself to go to church that following Sunday. I simply could not muster up the energy to put a fake smile on my face and pretend like everything was alright. I felt that my pain was too great for church folks with pasted on smiles to handle. My heart had been ripped out of my chest because so many of my hopes and dreams centered on this man. I could not believe that the man that I loved and cared for the most would end things over such a minor misunderstanding. I used to always say, if everything is lost and I have Jesus, then I have everything that I need. I felt the same way about this man. I could be homeless with him and be happy. Now I had to deal with the fact that the man who meant everything to me had now rejected me for the strangest of reasons.

The Sunday after his rejection was difficult. Even though I could not deal with the people at church, I knew that I needed to reach out to someone instead of retreating into a shell and letting depression overtake me. I drove 40 miles to Sunnyside, Texas to see a friend of the family named Ms. Wessie. She poured out so much love towards me that she made me forget about my pain. Her brother stopped by and he prayed for both of us. The prayer was needed refreshment for my soul. Sometimes we are hurting so bad that we do not even know how to pray for ourselves. I left Ms. Wessie to get something to eat. As I drove down the road, I began meditating on the fact that the Lord is by my side as I go through this pain. Something kept telling me to keep my eyes fixed on Jesus and he would keep me in perfect peace. The Lord started bringing my boyfriend's favorite quote to my mind: "people will let you down, but God will never let you down." Each moment, I felt better and better and I knew that everything would be alright. I began to realize that Jesus is the great healer and comforter because he understands our emotions. There is no heart so broken that he cannot mend back together again.

Feeling much better and sensing God's peace, I drove to Chipotle in City Center to get something to eat. I must have parked further away than expected because the walk seemed to get longer and longer. Suddenly, I looked up and saw a young girl making strange noises with her head in between her legs. At first, I thought that she was a crazy drug addict. Then I thought about my own pain and realized that she was a young lady who needed to be comforted. I sat by the young lady and put my hand on her back and she began to sob profusely. After a few minutes, I asked her what was wrong. She answered, "My boyfriend and I had this huge fight. He was so cruel. We exchanged words and I am just so hurt." I told her that I just went through the same thing and the Lord comforted me by saying, "Keep your eyes on Jesus. Don't look to the left or to the right. Just keep your eyes focused on Jesus. Men will let us down, but Jesus will always be there for us." The young lady stopped crying and hugged me immediately. She told me her story and I listened attentively. I prayed for her and she hugged and thanked me. I left that bench with the most exhilarating feeling that anyone could imagine. I got my food from Chipotle and meditated on the awesome power of God to heal the brokenhearted. I went to evening church service with a renewed sense of peace, thanking God for giving me the opportunity to be used for his purposes. God comforted me and allowed me to share his wisdom to comfort another person. I got to experience Paul's message to the Corinthians: **"Blessed be God . . . the God of all comfort. [He comforts] us in all our tribulation, that** we may be able to comfort them which are in any trouble, by the comfort wherewith we ourselves are comforted by God. For as the sufferings of Christ abound in us, so our consolation also [abounds] by Christ" (2 Corinthians 1:3-5, KJV). It was so wonderful to see God use my pain to his glory.

The life of Joseph is a perfect example of God using tragedy and hardship to bring about good. In the story of Joseph, Joseph made the mistake of bragging to his jealous brothers about one day ruling over them. In a fit of jealous rage, they tricked Joseph and placed him in a pit to die. He was later sold to the Egyptians as a slave. Joseph did not let the unfair treatment that he experienced make him bitter towards God. God gave him favor everywhere that he went and blessed everything that he did. He was falsely accused and thrown in jail, but he even maintained favor in jail. Eventually, he became ruler of all of Egypt. As ruler of Egypt he managed to save his entire family from famine. Joseph's dream of ruling over his brothers did eventually come true, but in the most unusual way. Perhaps the days as a slave were used to humble him and teach him how to serve so that he could one day be a great leader. All great leaders are also great servants. Jesus himself told his twelve disciples, "**If anyone wants to be the first, he must be the very last and servant of all**" (Mark 9:35, NIV). Regardless of why God allowed Joseph to be sold into slavery, Joseph understood that it was a part of God's perfect plan that would allow him to save many from a famine. Joseph said, **"So it was not you that sent me [here] but God; and he [has] made me a father to Pharaoh, and lord of all his house, and a ruler throughout all the land of Egypt . . . But as for [you, you] thought evil against me; but God meant it [for] good, to bring to pass, as it is this day, to save [many] people"** (Genesis 45: 8, 50:20KJV). To the natural mind, much of Joseph's life appeared to be a failure. However, God used each negative experience as an opportunity to grow and mature Joseph so that he would have both the knowledge and character to handle being the Pharaoh's right hand man.

Sometimes devastating experiences result in a testimony that can bless millions of people. If we are too shy to reach millions, we can at least share our testimonies to bless friends and family. We have to always remember that it is not about us, but about Him. He is the almighty and powerful God who can mend our broken pieces back together again. Joyce Myer's was sexually abused by her Father and emotionally abused by her first husband. She was a smoker, had a bad attitude, and a host of other issues, but she loved the Lord. She shares her testimony to millions of people. She teaches us how to overcome adversity. She shows us how she dealt with the many mistakes she made as a young Christian and her wrong heart attitudes towards her husband and God. She has built an entire ministry off of sharing her secrets for changing her life. Beth Moore is often considered one of the best bible teachers. Women would stand outside waiting to get into her conferences. Similar to Joyce Myers, she pulls from her experiences and mistakes to offer thought provoking lessons for her audience. These women are just two examples of how God can turn our tests into testimonies. He has done this same thing over and over in my life. My desire to go into ministry did not occur until after my boyfriend disappointed me and the next guy I dated taught me life's greatest lesson. Our human mind expects the opposite: we feel that the qualifications for ministry are a perfect attendance record at church, having a perfect family, dressing perfectly and working hard for God. In reality, God typically uses the most unlikely people for his greatest purposes. He used servants for the miracle turning water into wine. He used a prostitute named Rehab to help the Jews gain key territory. He used a poor orphan girl to save the Jews from a planned genocide. God has the amazing ability to use our mistakes as our greatest teachers.

Secret 2: Know Who You Are

Sometimes a Bad Experience Can Show Us our True Identity

It was Sunday and my friend Mary was determined to meet a man so she insisted that we go to Uptown Park. I did not want to go at all, but I gave in to Mary's persistence. I told her that it was ghetto fabulous there and it would just be a bunch of millionaires and women trying to get them. She insisted that we go to the Wine Bar there. As we walked to the Wine Bar, we both noticed a rather handsome man staring at me. When I finally passed him, he said, "Hello" in the deepest most regal voice that I ever heard. I was hoping that he did not notice my knees shaking as I passed him. I told Mary "He is gorgeous!" Mary responded, "And he was checking you out too!" I said, "I know and he is the most amazingly gorgeous guy that I have seen in years." Since the Wine Bar was about to close, we decided to head to the 24 hour Starbucks on South Post Oak. It was interesting, but Mary quickly got bored and insisted that we hang out at Uptown Park. I suggested that we go home and get some much needed sleep, but she was far more persistent than I could ever be. When we arrived back to Uptown Park, I noticed that there was a nice looking guy sitting on the stool near Champs Sports Bar. I said to myself, "This is perfect! I can just sit here and talk to this guy while Mary does whatever she is planning to do." So the guy and I had a nice conversation while Mary stood hoping to be noticed. The guy had to leave and the handsome stranger that I saw at the Wine Bar came to sit next to me. I was so happy and excited. We talked for at least two hours straight. It was pure magic. I felt like Cinderella who had finally met her Prince. He said that he was from New York and attended Lakewood Church. He showed me a picture of himself with Joel Osteen and another picture of him with Brian McKnight. I commented, "Brian McKnight is not even handsome compared to you." The handsome stranger responded, "Bryan McKnight told me that I was the first guy to ever make him look bad." We both laughed and talked for another hour about every topic imaginable. He was half Italian and half Indian. His family was of a royal nature just as I suspected. Mary just stood and text messaged various friends while we spoke. I finally felt guilty for making Mary wait and told the regal Prince Charming that we needed to go. He walked me to my car and tried to kiss me, but I insisted that I don't kiss on the first date. It was so hard to resist though. He called me every single day for a week and I thought that I was falling in love. I was infatuated with him the same way that I used to be infatuated with boys in high school and college. I wish that this story ended in marriage and a family for me, but it ended in me learning the greatest lesson that I would ever learn about God and men.

When we planned our first date, he insisted that we have wine and dinner at his house. Normally this would have been a huge red flag for me. I tried several times to persuade him to change it to a public place, but he insisted. In the past, if a guy insisted that I go to his house on the first date, I had always refused the invitation and dumped the guy. This time, I was far too impressed with him and felt the need to compromise. I thought that he was too handsome and rich to be persistent with. I knew that many women were after him because the night we met, four women tried to give him their number. He also told me about various models and actresses that tried to pursue him. Unfortunately, my intrigue with his status and his appearance became more important than my own personal standards. This fatal decision to compromise my standards was also a decision to allow this guy to break my heart. Against the rules of common sense and the Holy Spirit's promptings, I went to his house. I was very uneasy about going to man's house so early. It had been a long time since I had done such a dangerous thing. I was acting the same as I acted during my "young and dumb" years in college.

His home was quite impressive and it was clear that he was very wealthy. He had beautiful 3,500 square feet 2-story home with a top of the line Mercedes Benz in the yard. His home was very neat and modern. He immediately offered me some white wine when I entered the home and I refused at first. He kept insisting, so I finally gave in. We watched an interesting Indian movie as we ate a delicious meal of tilapia, rice and veggies. He told me that he sensed negativity around me. I responded, "I did just break up with my boyfriend so there probably are some hurt feelings remaining but I will get over it." He said, "Some people come into our lives for different reasons. Are you having trouble forgiving someone?" I said, "I did just clear up some issues with 2 people at the church, but everything is OK now I think." He then tried to make me feel bad about my age and darker skin. I answered, "Those may be obstacles, but God is able to overcome any obstacle." Next, he tried to convince me to have premarital sex with him and I told him that I should leave. He backed off for a moment and changed the subject. He then started trying to make me feel bad about not believing in pre-marital sex. He said, "Your no pre-marital sex rule is just a way to keep men out." My heart began to sink as he said this. I was so hurt that my Prince Charming had turned into a frog. I told him that I needed to leave. He began pressuring me to have sex with him again and said, "If you don't want to have sex with me then why are you here right now?" At that moment, I woke up from my delusion. I left stating, "Sex without commitment and love is meaningless." He told me to leave and stop wasting his time.

The handsome stranger showed me that some people come into our lives to point out issues from the past that need to be dealt with. As I got in the car, I was as disappointed in myself as much as I was disappointed in him. He asked a very good question when he said, "Why are you here?" I realized that I had lowered my standards for this man because he was so rich and handsome. I would have never agreed to go to his house if he were a regular guy so my first sin was being a respecter of persons. James warned us, "**don't show favoritism . . . If you show special attention to the man wearing fine clothes . . . but say to the poor man, "You stand there" . . . have you not discriminated among yourselves and become judges with evil thoughts?"** (James 2:1-4, NIV). I felt the need to treat this extremely handsome wealthier guy differently because getting him to like me became more important to me than upholding my standards and pleasing God. Deep down inside, I was shocked that a man of his stature would be interested in me. It became clear that I had issues with rich men. I formed a habit of losing my fun-loving assertive personality to become a boring, passive, docile people-pleaser whenever I was in a rich guy's presence. I also realized that I was both angry and fearful of these men because of what happened with my ex-husband. My ex-husband was sweet and infatuated with me when we were struggling but he became very short-tempered and demanding with me once he started making six figures. I always wondered where we would be if he could have stayed the same person throughout the marriage. My fearfulness and mistrust of rich men is why I never could connect with them. At the same time, this fear of mistreatment did not stop me from having a deep desire to be swept off my feet by one and live happily ever after. This desire was not a result of love because true love cannot reside in a heart filled with fear and mistrust.

The pain of these realizations caused me to cry out to God in the car on my way home. God ministered to my spirit in the most powerful way once I turned to him. He said, "Stop trying to find a Prince when you have the God who created the universe as your King." He said, "You are a precious daughter of the Most High King. I am the King of Kings and Lord of Lords. I can do all things, solve all problems and fix any situation. There is nothing beyond my control." I pulled over by the side of the road to write these profound words down. Peace began to well up in my soul as God made it clear who he is and established that I am his daughter whom he loves dearly. I began to realize that I am from royal blood just like the handsome stranger. This guy may have been from a royal family on earth, but my daddy is his daddy's boss. My daddy establishes and tears down earthly kingdoms whenever he desires to do so. I became determined to never feel that a guy is better than me again.

Once we know who we are in Christ, our "who" can help to change our "do." If we know that we have the most awesome God, the creator of heaven and earth as our daddy, how can we possibly want to do something to displease him? How could we ever feel inferior or unworthy if we are from a royal bloodline? Once we know that we are children of the Most High God, we can no longer live small insignificant lives comfortably. We become aware that daddy loves us and has lots of work for us to do. We develop a need to please our Father instead of pleasing ourselves and others. We begin to realize that every mistake and every bad experience is an opportunity for God to show how powerful he is to change any situation. We should always pray to ask God what lessons we can take from a relationship. We can always use that wisdom in future relationships. I went home to look up the bible verses that are similar to what the Holy Spirit ministered to me and God did not leave me disappointed. I found the following scriptures to further minister to my spirit:

Insight: We are precious daughters (children) of the Most High King.

Jesus was "in the world, and though the world was made through him, the world did not recognize him . . . Yet to all who received him, to those who believed in his name, he gave the right to become children of God-children borne not of natural descent, nor of human decision or a husband's will, but born of God." (John 1:10-13, NIV)

"Those who are led by the Spirit of God are sons of God . . . . You received the Spirit of sonship. And by him we cry "Abba", father. The Spirit himself testifies that we are God's children. Now if we are children, then we are heirs-heirs of God and co-heirs of Christ, if indeed we share in his sufferings in order that we may also share in his glory." (Romans 8:12-17, NIV)

Insight: God is King of Kings and Lord of Lords.

"For the Lord is a great God and a great King above all gods." (Psalm 95:3, KJV)

"On [Jesus'] thigh a name [was] written, KING OF KINGS, LORD OF LORDS." (Revelation 19:16, KJV)

"The King's heart is in the hands of the Lord, as the rivers of water. He turns it [wherever] he will." (Psalm 21:1, KJV)

"For the Lord Most High is . . . a great King over all the earth . . . sing ye praises with understanding. God [reigns] over the heathen: God [sits] upon the throne of his holiness. The princes of the people are gathered together . . . for the shield of the earth belongs to God: he is greatly exalted. "(Psalm 47:2, 7-9, KJV)

"Do not put your trust in Princes, in mortal men, who cannot save. When their spirit departs, they return to the ground; on that very day their plans come to nothing. Blessed is he whose help is God of Jacob, whose hope is the Lord his God. The Maker of heaven and earth, the sea and everything in them-the Lord reigns forever. (Psalm 146:3-10, NIV)

"Thus [says] the Lord the King of Israel . . . : I am the first and I am the last; and beside me there is no God." (Isaiah 44:6, KJV)

Insight: God can do all things, solve all problems and fix any situation.

"And we know that in all things God works for the good of those who love him, who have been called according to his purpose." (Romans 8:28, NIV)

"It does not therefore depend on man's desire or effort, but on God's mercy. For the Scripture says to Pharaoh: 'I raised you up for this very purpose—that I might display my power in you and my name might be proclaimed in all the earth.' Therefore God has mercy on [who] he wants to have mercy, and he hardens whom he wants to harden." (Romans 9:16-18, NIV)

"Man's [steps] are of the Lord; how can a man then know his own way?" (Proverb 20:24, KJV)

The handsome stranger taught me the wisdom of developing a "Life's Lessons Journal". Instead of looking at negative situations as obstacles to our success, we should look at them as opportunities for personal growth. We may be able to use the wisdom that we gain from this journal to help us avoid repeating negative patterns over and over again. Most important, we can use our insights to help others in the future.

The following is an example of such a journal. This was my journal entry about the lessons learned from the handsome stranger:

JOURNAL ENTRY-Life Lessons from the Encounter with the Handsome Stranger:

1. **Problem:** I became more concerned with losing a man than pleasing God. I started thinking of ways to compromise God's rules so that this man would be pleased with me. In the end, neither God nor this man was pleased.

   Solution: Be a God pleaser instead of a people pleaser. Don't let the first priority be to please a man, but make the first priority be to please God.

2. **Problem:** I became more final goal oriented than process oriented.

   Solution: Remember the lessons from successful students. Students that pay attention in class, ask good questions, and do their homework tend to be successful. If we do the best we can, the outcome will usually take care of itself. Use each date as an opportunity to love others and bring others closer to God and the results should be quite positive most of the time.

3. **Problem:** I failed to find out God's plan for the relationship. I just set out to get a cute, rich guy without first asking God for his direction and wisdom.

   Solution: Pray before making key decisions. We are instructed to pray without ceasing. The very least that we should do is ask "What would Jesus do in this situation?" Doing things without prayer is like going on a journey without directions. It is similar to what happened to me on a date at Starbucks. A friend invited me to Starbucks in Katy several months ago. I got into my car and arrived at the Starbucks in Cinco Ranch. He was not there, so I called to see what happened. He said, "I am at the one on Kingsland." So I hopped in my car to go to the one on Kingsland. He was not there either. So I called and he said, "I am at the one on Kingsland Blvd. next to the Kroger shopping center. By the time I showed up, he had to leave for an appointment. We got to hug and he bought me a drink to go. Things would have been so much less stressful if I just got my directions straight first. That is the power of prayer. It focuses our mind and shows us the right direction to focus our attention.

4. **Problem:** I failed to uphold my own standards.

   Solution: Remember that our standards give us a basis for living. They keep us from getting off course. Whenever we compromise our standards, we are removing our primary protection from problems and pain. Our standards keep us from harm because they are rules for living that have stood the test of time. Standards become even more important when dealing with people of different class backgrounds. They keep us grounded and keep us from being used and abused. I should have used the same rule that I had with average men with the rich handsome stranger. If I would have upheld my usual dating standards, this situation would have never occurred in the first place. Steve Harvey always talks about this being the key to his current wife landing him. He was playing the fields and she sweetly told him that she wanted something different for herself and her children. She held on to her vision and Steve Harvey decided that he would give it to her. If she would have settled for "star" treatment, Steve probably would have counted her as one of many women to juggle along.

Psalm 95:3 says **"For the Lord is a great God and great King above all other gods"** (KJV). If God is for us then there is nothing that man can do to destroy us. God can take the scraps that seem like they are fit to be thrown away and make something amazingly beautiful with them. He is just that powerful. After my encounter with the handsome stranger, I became aware of the fact that I am a broken vessel that God can use to help and inspire other women. I had always known that God was calling me to ministry, but I had no clue about what that would actually look like. The experiences with John and the handsome stranger made me realize that I must share these insights with other women even if it makes me look bad. God gave me the supernatural revelation that it is not about me: rather, it is about him using me to bring others closer to him. This gave me the freedom to share these stories without any fear or concern about the consequences.

The first time I shared the story was with my cousin in New York. I told her that I learned the most powerful lesson when I went out with this handsome guy. Next I really touched her when I asked, "Do you know how a lot of women expect for men to dog them out and the men usually do?" She said, "yes and that would probably be me." I told her that there are a lot of great men out there and they are willing to treat us like a queen. I meet these men all the time. I have gone out on some wonderful dates over the years. I usually expect most men to treat me well and they usually do so. However, I expect rich men to treat me poorly and they seem to oblige. Sometimes, we can create a self-fulfilling prophecy by having wrong expectations and mixed feelings. God has revealed to me that he is the King of all Kings. He can do all things and fix all problems. He can bring us any man that he chooses because we are his beloved daughters." My cousin was moved as she realized that my problem with rich men is her problem with all men. She told me that she loves my inspirational stories and I really blessed her with that one." This made me feel so good. I went to the hair salon and shared the story again. I told the ladies at the beauty shop that "God can bring any man into our life that he chooses. When this handsome guy rejected me, I realized at that moment exactly who I am and the fact that all of God's daughters come from royal blood. The King who created everything just happens to be our daddy." The women at the beauty shop were spell-bound. They began sharing their stories and my hair dresser told me that I would one day become a great spiritual teacher. Next, I started sharing my story with young adults on facebook and they were so grateful to get some insight about men and life. From this bad experience a ministry was born. Somehow God took the scraps from really bad dating experiences and made them into a light to shine before others.

God's power is amazing and watching him make dating lemons into lemonade has been nothing short of miraculous. This experience left me in awe about God's ability to take broken people, broken relationships and broken situations and mix them together to bring us closer to him and to each other. We must realize that we are here to love and serve God rather than seek our own personal happiness. Somehow, when we focus on God's agenda, he usually focuses on our agenda. Dating becomes a fun and exciting adventure once our goal is no longer to meet the right man and get married, but to enjoy life and share the love of God with others. We must stop looking at dating as an activity to just pass time or to look cool. We must also stop looking at dating as an activity to avoid. Each date is an opportunity for us to learn and grow and help others to learn and grow. Stop asking the question "What do I have to do to get him to do what I want?" Start asking the question, "What do I have to do to bring glory to Jesus Christ by pointing others towards him? Or, "Lord, how can I use this situation to bring glory to your name?"

Secret 3: Know What Others Typically Want and Know What You Need

There is so much misinformation out there on the dating scene that there could be three or four books written on common dating myths. Two myths that we hear from men over and over again are that women want a man that they can control or that women like bad boys. In reality, we want a man that will not allow us to control him. Most of us want a real man with good character. We want a leader who leads, not a man who asks for permission to lead. We want for him to be flexible in things like picking clothes or picking a movie to watch. However, we like a man who has a core set of values that are just non-negotiable. We tend to like a man who is confident and knows where he wants to go in life. We rarely respect or appreciate men that we can control. At the same time, we usually do not want a bad boy who is disrespectful and rude. Every woman respects and appreciates a confident man who puts the needs of the woman first, but sticks to his core principles and commands respect. We do not seek a bad boy, we actually seek a man who could be bad and chose not to be with us. We know when a man is being nice out of fearfulness or insecurity. This is a turn-off. We want a man that makes us feel special. We need to feel loved and cherished.

When my male students ask me about the mystery of women, I always give them the same advice: just be yourself and the right girl will be that one girl that likes and appreciates the real you. This is the lesson learned in the movie "Zookeeper". The main character realizes that he should not have to change everything about himself just to get a particular woman. If he needs that much changing, then it is probably the wrong woman. Every man was not intended for every woman. It is good for people to have different hobbies or be interested in different types of music. However, people should be on one accord when it comes to things like career, finance, children, and religion. If a man is a welder and the woman only relates to PhD's and MD's, the couple is going to clash. If she wants 2 children and he does not want any children, serious resentment is just around the corner for that couple. If a woman is a Baptist and a man is an atheist who wants to forbid her from going to church, World War III will soon break out in that house.

Most studies indicate that women want a man who is financially stable and intelligent. When it comes to looks, the only possible deal breaker is when the guy is much shorter. However, if he has millions, as in the case of many of Hollywood's leading men, this can be overcome as well. According to C.D. Mohatta,

What do women prefer—Looks or money? If you ask some men around you about what they desire in women, good looks may come out as a common answer. What about women? Does a good-looking man attract women or they are more attracted by a man having more money and a man with ambitions? Please ask some women and you will be surprised to know that even very good looking women are not necessarily looking for a partner with great looks, if he has no money. Women desire men with money, power and ambition more than looks [1].

Women like men with money and power, but few are willing to accept a guy if this is all that he has got. Men with money need to spend time developing something that money cannot buy: character. We women are biologically programmed to seek a man who would be able to take care of us and our children both financially and emotionally. If that emotional component is missing, the financial component often cannot make up for it. This is why some of the most miserable women are rich housewives with emotionally unavailable husbands. There are some things that all the riches in the world cannot make up for. Women need a guy who is honest, fun to be around, considerate and unselfish.

A confident man who knows how to treat a lady is a female magnet every time. Men like Denzel Washington and Blair Underwood make women scream because of their confidence and charisma. Men don't have to be rich, but they do have to have the ambition to make it. Women have a basic need for security. We do not want to deal with a man that will have us going from homeless shelter to homeless shelter. At the same time, we do not want a man who keeps us in the psychiatrist chair either. We need a hard-working man who can support the family and act as a great leader. In other words, we just want a real man.

Men's Deal Breaker Can Give Us a Clue about What Men Want

A man likes a woman that looks good on his arm. Beauty and youth are definite advantages for women. However, many men are beginning to look deeper. They are discovering that looks are not everything. The funniest facebook status ever seen was done by Michael Baisden. In the blog, he asked men to list their deal breakers-those things that make a man run away from a woman. When men listed the things that they want in a woman, it was clear that they have a strong desire a traditional woman who has the additional qualities of being strong and sexually responsive. While women's liberation changed women, many men are similar to their grandfathers. Most of the deal breakers listed deal with the failure of women to live up to the traditional roles. Some of the most common deal breakers listed on the blog involved women failing to cook, clean and be submissive. Men also complained of women being loud, obnoxious and failing to listen. What is funny is that it seemed as if there were more women commenting on the men's comments than men actually commenting. About a fourth of the deal breakers involved men being frustrated that women were answering the question for the men [2].

It is clear that the mythical "strong independent black woman" is not admired by most men. Men made it clear that they need to feel needed and respected. Women who wear the "I-don't-need-a-man" label across their foreheads do not realize how unattractive this makes them to men. Two blogs give us a clue about how we really look to men when we are "Ms. Independent":

- *Women who talk about being "independent" need to also talk about how the label has gone way too far, to the point where it is now inconsistent and in many ways cartoonish, mannish and just plain unattractive. In fact, I often cringe when I hear women talk about being "independent" because it usually means that they are not. In the quest for so-called "independence," some women have given up substantial portions of their womanhood-the very things that many men look for in a woman. Most of what remains in "independent women" is aggressiveness and negativity . . . . Women can say what they want about their liberation, but we have not evolved to the point where an aggressive woman is desirable and we never will. The overwhelming response by some women to men's repulsion to aggressiveness and negativity is that a "strong woman" is hard to handle. It may make you feel good to declare that men can¹t handle a strong woman, but you have to ask yourself what it is that is really repelling them* [3].

- *Statistics are showing that more than half of black women in America are not married. More black women are graduating college, and becoming successful in their jobs. Because of this, some women develop this I don't need a man attitude. Now, don't get me wrong, there is nothing wrong with being successful. I wish everyone could graduate college and get a good job. But there is something wrong with people thinking that a certain amount of money and a piece of paper makes them so good that they don't need any companionship. That's just silly. I don't blame a man for not wanting to be around a woman who constantly reminds him of his shortcomings and what he has NOT done. Then, when "the good" black men gravitate toward women of other races, they are considered sell-outs* [4].

While traditional values are high a lot of men's list, practical values are just as important. It appears that men really do want a helpmate. They want someone to add to their life, not make their lives miserable. They need someone who they could trust because they don't like the drama of a scandalous woman. It turns out that character really does count. On the famous dating website, e-harmony staff gave a list of five deal breakers that women really need to think about.

The Christian Woman's Ultimate Love, Sex and Relationships Manual

- The first deal breaker is failing to have your own life. If our first priority is a personal relationship with Jesus Christ, this is not a problem. However, when we start idolizing men, we usually wind up disappointed. When a woman chases after a guy because he is the only thing in her world, it usually scares the guy off.

- The second is bad habits like getting drunk, smoking or being messy. If we follow the advice in proverbs and adopt a biblical worldview, this does not concern us.

- The third is dishonesty. I personally know of two guys that test every woman they meet to see if a women keeps her word. This is a big one. Men must have a woman that they can trust.

- The fourth deal breaker is a lack of confidence. This is very important because men don't want to spend every moment propping a woman up. Both men and women like to have a confident person by their side-it just feels better.

- The last is the most important: cheating. Years of observation has shown me that men rarely forgive infidelity. Women who try to make their boyfriend jealous by using another man are playing with fire. These men usually get more angry than jealous and there are rarely second chances with this one [5].

Women were promised greater freedom with the Women's Liberation Movement, but we just wound up with greater responsibilities. In addition to the traditional responsibilities, now men expect for us to also bring home a certain amount of money and be ready, willing and waiting for sex when the man wants it. This means that after working 10 hours, we are expected to also cook, clean and pamper her man. She is also expected to be the primary person to take care of the kids. It is simply overwhelming for a lot of women. This was a serious issue in my own marriage. I wanted to be a submissive traditional wife, but I also worked 10 hours a day and I found it impossible to be superwoman. Women in this situation should not burn themselves out like I did. We must talk frankly to our men about what we can and cannot handle in a relationship. The unrealistic expectation that women can do it all is probably a cause for many fights and divorces in our modern marriages. Once married, we must communicate with each other about what we can realistically handle and find ways to divide the chores in a way that is fair to all parties.

It is important for each of us to identify our own individual deal breakers. During the dating process, we should be aware of our expectations and constantly evaluate a person based on their ability to meet these expectations. Once married, our goal should be to support and accept our mate rather than make him into an improvement project. The best thing that we can do is make our own list of things that we must have in a mate and make a good choice before marriage. My friend Lynn told me how a clear idea about what we want and need will protect us from marrying the wrong person. She was ready to settle down with a guy who she dated for a very long time. Then she met the man of her dreams at a wedding in another state. She was torn about what to do, so she developed a list of essential things that she needs in a mate. It turned out that the original guy had less than 40% of the traits that were important to her while the man that she met at the wedding had 100% of the traits that she really wanted. Her list saved her from marrying the wrong guy and she has been happily married for the past seven years to the man of her dreams. She told me to develop my own list and avoid settling for less than the best person for me. As a Christian, I decided that I must have an Ephesians 5 marriage. My list is the following:

1. He must love God and seek God's wisdom before making decisions.

2. He must be willing to strive towards an Ephesians 5 marriage: He loves and adores me enough to put my needs ahead of his own; he commands respect from me to the extent that it is easy to submit to him.

3. He is a good provider and he wants to protect me.

4. He is open to having kids, but not desperate for some.

5. He lives by integrity and takes marriage seriously.

6. He likes to dance and have fun.

7. He is honest, reliable and dependable.

8. He likes to travel.

9. He is willing to stand by me as I go into ministry.

10. He is not intimidated by me in any way. He knows that he is the man and he is ultimately in charge. Yet, he chooses to honor and respect my opinions and wishes within reason.

11. We are moving in the same general direction.

12. Most important, God is the center of his life. He realizes that I am no substitute for God, but I am a great companion on our journey to get to know each other and God better.

The Christian Woman's Ultimate Love, Sex and Relationships Manual

CHAPTER 11

Marriage and Family: The Building Block of Society

Marriage is considered to be a contract between one man and one woman who agree to go through life's difficulties together and raise a family. With our current 50% divorce rate, many obviously do not consider this contract to be binding. Some have tried to solve this problem by forming covenant marriages. Real marriage is a covenant between a man, woman and God. This covenant must occur in the human heart and no piece of paper can make it work. There are many great debates about why marriages are failing these days. Some say that it is due to women entering the workforce. Others feel that people just don't know how to pick the right mate. There are hundreds of books telling people the secret of finding Mr. or Mrs. Right. Unfortunately, few of these books address the root of the problem: man's refusal to follow God's divine order and obey his commandment to love one another unconditionally and forgive one another.

God is a God of order. The original order of the family was God as head of the entire family; man as head of the woman; and parents as the head of the children. According to Paul, "**the head of every man is Christ, the head of the woman is the man: and the head of Christ is God**" (1 Corinthians 11:3, KJV). Paul admonishes the children to honor their parents: he wrote "**Children obey your parents in the Lord, for this is right. Honor thy father and mother; which is the first commandment with a promise; that it may be well with thee, and thou may live long on the earth**" (Ephesians 6:1-3, KJV). The new secular humanist order is children running the household, with momma telling daddy what to do or not do. When something is out of order it simply does not work. The modern humanistic family has been a dismal failure. God equipped men, women and children to take on certain roles. When they take on the opposite roles that they were equipped to take, everything falls apart. In fact, children who control their parents and women who control their husbands are some of the unhappiest people that I know. These unnatural roles don't even bring happiness to the person who takes the leading position, let alone the humiliation of men for allowing women or children to lead them. Some women honestly believe that women should take the lead and be independent. They foolishly follow in Queen Vashti's footsteps. They feel that the idea of the man taking the lead is sexist. Similar to queen Vashti, these women pay a high price for their lack of understanding regarding male-female relationships. Similarly, kids who run their household usually have to learn the lessons that their parents should have taught them in jail or on the streets. These kids often lead the most tragic lives. This is why the bible warns that parents must "**discipline [their] son, for in that there is hope; do not be a willing party to his death**" (Proverbs 19:18, NIV). The bible not only warns of physical death being a possibility for an undisciplined child, it also warns of spiritual death: Proverb 23:13-14, KJV states "**Withhold not correction from a child: for if thou beat him with a rod he shall not die. Thou shalt beat him with the rod and shalt deliver his soul from hell.**"

God, knowing that men desire to be respected and women desire to be cherished gave us the perfect illustration of the perfect marriage in Ephesians 5: 22-33 KJV:

Wives submit yourselves unto your own husbands as unto the Lord. For the husband is head of the wife as Christ is the head of the church: and he is the savior of the church body. Therefore, as the Church is subject to Christ, so let the wives be subject to their husbands in everything. Husbands love your wives as Christ loved the Church, and gave himself for it. That he may sanctify and cleanse it with the washing of water by the word. That he might present it to himself as a glorious church not having spot or wrinkle . . . but that it shall be holy without blemish. So men ought to love their wives as their own bodies. He that [loves] his wife [loves] himself. For no man ever hated his own flesh, but [nourishes and cherishes] it even as the Lord the church . . . Let every one of you so love his wife even as himself and the wife see that she reverence her husband.

This is the perfect win-win situation for men and women. The wife gets her dream of a man who loves her so much that he is willing to die for her and put her needs ahead of his own. The husband gets a wife who follows his lead and shows respect towards him. God knows what is most important to both men and women. When we follow his advice to enter marriage putting the partner's needs ahead of our own, the marriage becomes solid as a rock. How hard could it be for a woman to follow a man who is willing to die for her? How hard could it be for a man to be kind and generous to a woman that treats him like a king and honors him among his friends? When two people begin a marriage relationship thinking about how they could please their mate instead of what they can take from their mate, divorce is most likely never mentioned. Selfless love is the glue that can hold any marriage together. Selfishness only tears our relationships apart. The idea that pride is good causes many people to enter marriage with a "What's in it for me?" attitude. This may be at the heart of the high divorce rate in our churches. Instead of people focusing on serving one another in marriage, they come to marriage expecting to be served and face great disappointment.

God ordained men to be the spiritual head of their households. It is sad that many of today's men have been swept by a sea of humanism-thinking that they can forge their way by self-will and self-effort without first consulting God. Many men have abandoned going to church and leading the family in prayer and spiritual practices. One must stop and ask, "How can a man lead his family if he is not first led by God?" Women see this void in leadership and feel that they must take over the man's job. Other women have Godly men willing to lead, but these women have been swept by the rhetoric of the Women's Liberation Movement. We need to return to the only true source of knowledge about marriage and relationships: God himself. He created marriage to represent his relationship with his people. His word contains all the wisdom that we need to make our marriages work. We need to use our bibles as the relationship manual that they were meant to be.

Our relationship with Jesus is the spiritual manifestation of our relationship with our spouse. Jesus made it very clear that we are to be unselfish and avoid letting anyone or anything become an idol that takes His place. Jesus warned that pride and self-centeredness would lead us to destruction. Jesus said, "**Anyone who loves his father or mother more than me is not worthy of me; anyone who loves his son or daughter more than me is not worthy of me; and anyone who does not take his cross and follow me is not worthy of me. Whoever finds his life will lose it, and whoever loses his life for my sake will find it**" (Matthew 10: 37-39, NIV). This statement is true about our physical marriages as well. We are to put our spouse ahead of father, mother, children and even ourselves. The bible states, "**[From] the rib that the Lord God had taken from the man, [he] made woman, and brought her unto the man. And Adam said, 'This is bone of my bones and flesh of my flesh: she shall be called Woman because she was taken out of the man.' Therefore shall a man leave his father and his mother, and shall cleave unto his wife: and they shall be one flesh**" (Genesis 2: 22-24, KJV). A lot of our marriages are unraveling because we do not realize that the spouse is the most significant person in our lives. We mistakenly assume that the kids are more important or parents are more important. Some of us even think that our friends or job are more important. In reality, just as our marriage to Christ requires that we give our life away to Him, our marriage to our husband requires giving our life away to our spouse. The bible clearly says that our body is not our own in a marriage.

The idea of giving our life away to another person is scary at first. However, once we actually do it, we find that life gets even more exciting and our relationships get better and better. It is our pride that keeps us from turning to the only true solution for our relationship woes: God himself. We are like two year olds who want to handle everything ourselves. We forget that marriage is far too difficult without God in the union. He made the union and he is the only one who knows how to keep it functioning. It reminds me of the song, "What a friend we have in Jesus". As the song says, "what needless pains we bear when we fail to carry everything to him in prayer." Today, people are consulting their daily horoscopes, the local psychic or counselor instead of God. Isaiah warned about such practices when he said, "**When men tell you to consult mediums and spiritists, who whisper and mutter, should not a people inquire of their own God? Why consult the dead on behalf of the living?"** (Isaiah 8:19, NIV). God is the source of all knowledge and wisdom. Still, we go to friends and family hoping that they could make us feel better instead of consulting an all-powerful God that could take the problem away or change us so that the relationship would change. We must return to the only valid source of wisdom about marriage: God through his holy word the bible. As Jimmy Evans always says, "your marriage has a 100% chance of success if done God's way."

The Ten Commandments for a Healthy and Happy Marriage

1. **Pray and read the bible daily either together or during personal quiet time.** We should consult with God through daily prayer and bible reading for wisdom about how to navigate through the ups and downs of marriage. This is something that we often put on the backburner, but it is the most essential tool for a healthy and happy relationship and life. Satan does not want for us to spend time with the Lord because God is the ultimate source of love. When we spend time with him, we become filled with the love needed to handle our spouse's faults and issues. When we neglect this practice, we often become cranky and self-righteous. Things that are not even important begin to bother us and make us desire to leave the relationship. One couple at church admitted that things go so much better when they spend time praying together and reading the bible. When this activity is neglected, every little thing that would occur during the day bothered them and resulted in lots of unnecessary fights. The old saying is true: "couples who pray together stay together." Prayer is how we communicate with God himself. God is the only perfect source of love and wisdom that we have at our disposal. We are programmed to seek advice from friends and family or a popular psychologist; however, the advice from these sources is imperfect because all people are imperfect. There is only one perfect source of knowledge and information: Jesus Christ. From Genesis to Revelation, the bible points us to Christ as the ultimate satisfier of our souls who can fulfill our every need. The bible is the greatest relationship manual ever invented.

2. **Keep God at the center of your relationship and the relationship will become nearly impossible to break.** Paula Whidden wrote that couples who stated that "God is the center of our marriage" were 26% more likely than other Christians to claim to be "Very Happy in marriage, with only 1% of husbands and wives stating a proneness to divorce" [1]. We must remember that a true marriage is between three people-the husband, the wife and God. God is the glue that holds the whole thing together. According to Ecclesiastes, "**Two are better than one . . . For if they fall, the one will**

lift up his brother . . . . and a three-fold cord is not easily broken" (Ecclesiastes 4: 9-12, KJV).

3. **Seek God as the ultimate source of happiness and joy rather than our spouse.** We cannot make another person responsible for our happiness. It could be estimated that 90% of us in unhappy marriages could trace the root of the problem to the fact that we tried to make our spouse play the role of God or we tried to play the role of God for our spouse. Pastor Greg Matte noted that *"In any marriage or close friendship, there is a potential temptation to make someone else a priority over the Lord. God never intended for anyone else to play His role in our lives. A spouse will never be able to withstand the pressure of playing God. Neither will a dear friend. We were never meant to be God. But so often we look to other people to fulfill the role that only he can fill . . . Human beings were created to worship God, not each other. Only Christ can satisfy. People can only play their proper role in our lives when we are not depending on them for too much"* [2].

4. **Date throughout the marriage to avoid becoming roommates instead of lovers.** Couples who make a real effort to spend quality time together and nurture their friendship are the happiest. It is easy to get into a rut of going to work, coming home and then barely speaking to each other. When this happens, we lose focus on how much our spouse means to us. We become more likely to want a divorce because our spouse ceases to add value to our lives. The only way to avoid this is to make an effort to do the things that drew us together in the first place. A fresh and exciting marriage is a usually a strong marriage.

5. **Be a selfless giver instead of a selfish taker.** We must remember that the secret to making any relationship work is to seek to satisfy the other person instead of seeing what we can get from them. What we must remember is that men and women want different things. Women want a strong man that makes her feel loved, secure and protected. A man wants a woman who respects him, admires his wisdom and shows loyalty and faithfulness towards him.

6. **Be honest about problems and issues rather than pretend that everything is going well.** Some people like to deal with conflict by not dealing with it. This is a big mistake. When we bury our feelings and pretend that everything is alright, we are acting dishonestly with ourselves and the other person. Instead, we should call a meeting and loving state what is wrong. This avoids bitterness and resentment from setting in. When we pretend that everything is OK when it is not, we just turn our hearts colder and colder and it is only a matter of time that our true heart condition will be revealed.

7. **Plan for conflict rather than react to it.** Conflict is a part of life. Anytime we live under the same roof with a person, we are guaranteed to have disagreements. It is a good idea to develop a plan of action when this occurs. Screaming and yelling is not the best solution. One technique to use when explaining issues is to say I feel _____ when you _____. Could you please_____? This avoids placing judgment on the person's character or assuming that we know a person's motives. Most conflict escalates when we judge someone by his actions or pretend to know what is in someone's heart when we really have no way of knowing this. Only God can accurately read hearts. We as mere humans should address what we can see which is the behavior. If a wife feels like she has no help around the house, there is never a need to call her husband stupid or lazy or anything else. It is far more effective to say, "It makes me feel overwhelmed when I have to come home and cook, clean, do the dishes and look after the kids. I need some help so that I can be a better wife. Could you please start tending to the kids while I am cooking and could you dry the dishes when I wash them?

8. **Be disciplined and follow the proper chain of command.** This means that husbands must be submitted to God; wives should be submitted to husbands; and children should be submitted to their parents. It is important for each member of the family to know his or her role and do it. We get along with others best when we live lives of excellence. Success is often a matter of doing what we are supposed to do when we are supposed to do it.

9. **Do not make the family our idol.** Anything that we place before God is an idol that brings us pain rather than joy. When we make our spouse our idol, they usually crumble under the pressure because no one can replace the one true God. Kids find the same pressure. They crumble under the pressure of parents who live vicariously through them and expect them to be perfect.

10. **Enjoy sex as the precious gift that God intended it to be.** Sex is God's gift to the married couple. It is an act of intimacy that brings the husband and wife closer together. It is the wife surrendering to her husband while the husband provides the wife with his seed. It is a physical manifestation of what happens at salvation. The believer surrenders his entire body to God while God plants his Spirit in him. Sex for the wife is the ultimate form of surrender. Sex for the husband is the ultimate form of giving. It is a beautiful act of love that we should cherish and enjoy. Anything that is pleasurable is allowable on the marriage bed. Husband and wife should be able to present their naked bodies to each other without feeling any shame. The marriage bed is the place that the fig leaf is removed and discarded. Two souls become one in an act of total freedom and pleasure.

The Christian Woman's Ultimate Love, Sex and Relationships Manual

Confessions of a Divorced Woman

Sometimes a minister's confession of faults can be life-changing for those listening. One Sunday, a visiting pastor at First United Methodist Church in Houston preached the most honest and thought-provoking sermon. She discussed how she often questions God about why he allows children to die early and why the best people have the worst luck. She wondered why a good God would allow these things to happen. This pastor also confessed that she was often guilty of just going through the motions in her ministry. Sure she would do what she was supposed to do-but it was in the spirit of "I got to do this because it is my obligation." It was not in the spirit of gratitude and wanting to please God, our loving Father. As she spoke, I realized that I was guilty of the same attitudes towards God. As I entered deeper thought, I realized that this also described my attitude towards someone else. For the longest time, I could not figure out who else I treated like that. Then it finally hit me: I treated my ex-husband with the same apathy and lukewarm spirit that I had towards God. This revelation transformed my relationship with God and men.

Prior to this sermon, if you would have asked me to explain why my marriage ended, the automatic response would have been, "my ex-husband cheated and he did not take marriage seriously." This sermon made me realize that my "ungrateful, just going through the motions attitude" was hurtful towards my ex-husband in the same way that it had been hurtful to God. When I got home from church that day, I spent hours crying and praying for forgiveness for my attitude. I thanked God for everything that he had done for me and called my ex-husband to apologize for having the wrong attitude during our marriage. I told my ex-husband, "Today, I realized how I contributed to the breakup of our marriage. I did things out of obligation instead of out of gratitude for all of the wonderful things that you had done for me. I allowed my job, my health club membership and a hundred other things to be first place in my heart. You were just at the very bottom of a very long to-do list and acted as if I were too tired for you." I then asked if this was why he was so mad at me and wanted a divorce. My ex-husband was almost crying when he replied, "that is exactly why I wanted a divorce-I just could not quite put it into the right words." Since that conversation, the Lord has continued to give me insights about marriage and relationships. It is too late for my ex-husband and me because he has remarried, but others can learn from my mistakes.

Once I apologized to my husband, the Lord allowed me to get favor with other men again. Before the apology, I was meeting a lot of unhealthy men and constantly complaining about the men in Houston. Similar to many modern Afro-American women, I assumed that the problem was that too many black men were dating women of other races or that I was too old or too fat. In reality, the problem was that I needed closure from my first marriage. I needed to acknowledge my mistakes in the first marriage so that I would not repeat these same mistakes again. I also needed to make sure that any bitterness or resentment towards my ex-husband was gone. Once all bitterness was healed by God, my heart was open to love again. After I repented to God and my ex-husband, every guy that I dated for more than two months had asked me to marry him. This led to several marriage proposals after the divorce. Men are magnetically attracted to love. Men find the love that only Jesus can give attractive when they see it in a woman. Jesus is love and love cannot reside in a heart that is filled with bitterness or resentment. According to the bible, **"For this is the message that we have heard from the beginning, that we should love one another . . . We know that we have passed from death to life because we love the brethren. He that [does not love] his brother [abides] in death. Whosoever [hates] his brother is a murderer: and [we] know that no murderer has eternal life abiding in him"** (1 John 3:11-15, KJV). It pains me to see so many women stuck with bitterness that prevents them from attracting the right man. They assume that all the good men are taken or all the good men are dating women of other races. Some think that they need plastic surgery or a new weight loss program. In reality, the issue is most likely spiritual. Often, their bitter hearts must be healed before they can have the ability to attract a good man. The poison of bitterness is eating their very soul and they do not even know what is wrong.

The major lesson that I learned from my first marriage was that one must avoid allowing a marriage to become lukewarm. It is amazing how God uses natural things to represent spiritual realities and vice versa. In the book of Revelation, Jesus tells his ungrateful-just going through the motions church the following: **"because [you are] lukewarm, and neither hot nor cold, I will [spit] thee out of my mouth"** (Rev 3:16, KJV). In the same way, the desire for divorce is strong in a lukewarm marriage. My ex-husband was deeply wounded by my ungrateful ways and lack of desire for him in the same way that Christ is troubled by our tendency to put our desire for other things over our desire for him. Even though the bible says that we "should leave Father and Mother to cleave to our husband", many of us put friends, family, children, television and the Oprah Magazine above our mate. In the same way, spending quiet time with the Lord, praying, reading the bible or worshiping God is often at the bottom of our to-do list when it should be first. This is why Jesus summed up the whole law of God in one statement: **"Love the Lord your God with all of your heart, mind and soul. This is the greatest and the first commandment. The second is like it. You shall love your neighbor as yourself"** (Matthew 22:37-39, NASB). According to the bible, the most important neighbor to love as yourself is your own spouse.

Loving our spouse is difficult when we are proud. As a divorced woman, I can testify that when two proud people live in a house together, there is serious trouble. Each proud person has an inflated idea about what he or she deserves from the other. Pride was the true source of my "ungrateful just going through the motions" attitude and it was also the source of my ex-husband's exaggerated response to it. During our marriage, my ex-husband went from making $40,000 a year to making six figures. Women began to notice him and he would arrive home and say, "You better get your act together and start treating me like a king, do you know how many women gave me their number today?" I would look at him and think, "Who does this fool think that he is? How dare he say that to me?" Then I would respond to the man who thought that he was a king, "They can have your sorry a_ _! Don't be coming in my house throwing other women in my face. Are you crazy?" Of course, these unkind remarks did not go over well with a man who considered himself to be a king. The equation for a bad marriage is the following:

Proud Wife + Proud Husband = Serious Marital Conflict

It is our pride that makes it so difficult to love or forgive. If our spouse snubs us or says something that we don't like, we think, "How dare he do that to me. I could do better than this." Proud people always think that they deserve more than what they are getting. Proud people in marriage forget to pray for each other or pray for the ability to overlook faults. Forgiveness is an act of humility. Our pride only gets in the way.

We are blessed that God is merciful and patiently waits for us to return to him unlike many natural husbands who often just want to put us away. In the Old Testament, the marriage relationship was used to symbolize God's relationship with Israel. Israel's tendency to seek other Gods was considered to be adultery in the eyes of God. The book of Hosea chronicles God's treatment of his adulterous wife, the nation of Israel. God told Hosea to marry a whore and forgive her in the same way that he forgives Israel. He wanted for Hosea to feel what it was like to be a God that provides for his people, protects his people and professes his love for them only to see his people turn towards other Gods. God said to Hosea, **"Go take to yourself an adulterous wife and children of unfaithfulness because the land is guilty of the vilest adultery in departing from the Lord. So he married Gomer . . ."** (Hosea 1:2-3, NIV). After a brief anger, Hosea was instructed to forgive Gomer's adulterous ways in a similar manner to how God would forgive Israel. Hosea was told to **"Go show your love to your wife again, though she is loved by another and is an adulteress. Love her as the Lord loves the Israelites even though they turn to other Gods and love the sacred raisin cakes. So he bought her . . . and told her 'You are to live with me many days; you must not be a prostitute or be intimate with any man, and I will live with you.' For the Israelites will live many days without king or prince . . . Afterward, the Israelites will return to seek their God . . . They will come trembling to the Lord and his blessings in the last days"** (Hosea 3:1-4, NIV). God's love for Israel allows him to forgive Israel even though they do not deserve it and in the same way we are called to forgive others even though they do not deserve it. God expects for us to extend the same love that he gives us to each other. He especially wants for us to extend the love and forgiveness to our spouse.

Love and Forgiveness: A Radical Way to End Divorce

The movie, **Fireproof**, was a wonderful movie based on the book *Love Dare*. In the movie, a couple was going through a divorce and both husband and wife did a lot to hurt each other. There was one scene in which the husband listed all the things that he had done for his wife even though she continued to be unresponsive, distrusting and ungrateful towards him. As the husband ranted to his Father about his ungrateful wife, both he and his Father realized that the husband had been treating God the same way. The dad pointed out that the husband could forgive his wife in the same way that Christ has forgiven him. When I saw this scene, it reminded me so much of the day that I realized that I had treated both God and my husband in a lukewarm unconcerned fashion and needed to ask both God and my husband for forgiveness. That movie reminded me that we have to learn how to forgive every single offence every time because that is what God does for each of us.

Peter is my favorite disciple because he seemed so much like me. In the area of forgiveness, I would love to have a policy of three strikes and you are out. Similarly, in the book of Matthew, Peter advocated to Jesus that there should be a seven strikes and you are out policy for forgiveness. Peter said**, "Lord how many times shall I forgive my brother when he sins against me? Up to seven times?"** (Matthew 18:21, NIV). Similar to me, Peter only planned to do this forgiveness stuff a limited number of times. However, Jesus refuted our "limited forgiveness theory" by saying, **"I say not [seven times] . . . but seven times seventy"** (Mathew 18:22, KJV). That means at least 490 times which can be translated as each and every time we are to forgive. It is interesting to note that Jesus never said to only forgive those minor offenses a set number of times. We are called to forgive everything even though the person may not deserve it. Jesus gave us our example of how to do this as he forgave even those who crucified him. Jesus cried out on the cross, "Forgive them Lord, for they know not what they do."(Luke 23:24) . . . If Jesus could forgive people as they were killing him, then surely we can forgive someone we live with for leaving the toilet seat up or forgetting to take the trash out.

Ruth Graham Bell once called marriage the union between two continuous forgivers. When we are single, if someone gets on our nerves, we can just avoid that person. However, in a marriage, the person who gets on your nerves sleeps next to you and has done a hundred things to make you mad. Sometimes, you may have to forgive your spouse every hour, but that is what God calls us to do. Marriage is a union only for those mature enough to put "hate the sin and love the sinner" into practice on a continuous basis. We are all sinners; therefore, we all have faults. When we live together, these faults cannot be hidden, but are magnified. God calls us to treat the faults of others with the same mercy that we give to ourselves. He also calls us to remember that he forgave us even though we do not deserve it, so we should do the same for others. C. S. Lewis noted, "*This means loving people who have nothing lovable about them. But then has oneself anything lovable about it? You love simply because it is yourself. God intends us to love all selves in the same way and for the same reason: but He has given us the sum ready worked out on our own case to show us how it works. We have then to go on and apply the rule to all other selves. Perhaps it makes it easier if we remember that this is how He loves us. Not for any nice, attractive qualities we think we have, but just because we are these things called selves"* [(3)].

God forgives because he is love and love covers a multitude of sins. He loved us so much that he was willing to allow his only begotten Son to die on the cross as atonement for our sin. John 3:16 says "**God so loved the world that he gave his only begotten son, that whosoever believes in him shall not perish, but have everlasting life.**" If Jesus could die for our sins, then the least we could do is die to self for him. He gives us his love so that we can share it with others. He does not pour out his love for us to hide it or just keep it for ourselves. He wants for us to grow perfect in our love for one another and share what he has freely given us. Paul explains that "**Love is patient. Love is kind. It does not envy, it does not boast, it is not proud. It is not rude, it is not self-seeking, it is not easily angered, and it keeps no record of wrongs. Love does not delight in evil but rejoices with truth. It always protects, always trusts, always hopes, and always perseveres. Love never fails**" (1 Corinthians 13:4-8, NIV).

The ability to forgive is not a mere human trait. This ability comes from God himself. I will never forget the time when I worked for a very racist boss who treated me less than human. I hated her with all my heart; yet, I could sense that this hatred was displeasing to God. I would come home and complain about her to all my friends and my boyfriend. Many people stopped wanting to be around me because I became so negative. Finally, I started reading the bible every day and praying on a regular basis. I felt a prompting to buy my boss a boss's day present despite her treatment of me. As I purchased a boss's day mug, I felt really silly buying something for someone that I did not even like. Once I presented it to her, she cried and said that no one had ever done anything so kind for her. Suddenly, to my surprise, all of the mutual hatred and animosity that we had for each other over a six month period just magically disappeared at that moment. God supernaturally healed our relationship once I obeyed him by doing well to an enemy. I did not realize that a single act of obedience to God could have such powerful results. We began to treat each other with respect and other people became magnetically drawn to me again. By this time, my boyfriend had left me, but other men started asking me out all the time. My friends started seeking me out as well. God honors us when we honor him by obeying his precepts. God clearly states that we must "**love one another, for love comes from God. Everyone who loves has been born of God and knows God. Whoever does not love does not know God, because God is love. This is how God showed his love among us: He sent his one and only Son into the world that we might live through him. This is love: not that we loved God but he loved us and sent his Son as an atoning sacrifice for our sins.**

Dear friends, since God so loved us, we also ought to love one another" (1 John 4:7-11, NIV).

I did not realize that my hatred of one person was contaminating all my other relationships until I saw the results of doing things God's way instead of my own. Husbands and wives can use this same principal in their marriages. When a spouse does something wrong and we feel angry, we can pray for them and do something nice. This loving act of obedience to God will then allow God to use his holy spirit to heal our wounded soul. Obeying God's command to forgive is hard. When someone wrongs us, we all have the human impulse to want to slap them or knock them out. However, God blesses those who obey his will. The principles of the bible do not make sense to the natural mind, but they do work by the power of the Spirit.

Many Christians mistakenly assume that offering forgiveness is optional. However, Jesus made it very clear that if we expect to be forgiven for our sins, we have to forgive others of their sins. In Matthew 6: 14-15 (KJV), Jesus said, **"For if you [forgive] men their trespasses, your heavenly father will also forgive you. But if [you] forgive not men their trespasses, neither will your Father forgive your trespasses."** As someone with thousands of trespasses to be forgiven, I have to take that verse very seriously. It does not say that you have to forgive everyone but your spouse. Your spouse is included in the people that God expects for you to forgive. Jesus told a parable to illustrate his point about forgiveness. According to the parable, there was a servant that owed the Master a huge debt. The Master was merciful and forgave the debt. Someone else owed the servant a much smaller debt and the servant would not forgive the much smaller debt owed to him. The other servants were upset about this and told the Master. The Master told the unforgiving servant, "**[You] wicked servant . . . I forgave [you] all that debt . . . Should you not have compassion on [your] fellow servant, even as I had pity on [you]? And the Master delivered him to the tormentors till he should pay all that was due . . .**" (Mathew 18:32-34, KJV). Forgiveness is simply a non-negotiable requirement for all Christians. We are forgiven to the extent that we forgive others. Ouch!

God hates divorce because marriage is the physical manifestation of our relationship with him. This relationship is characterized by unconditional love and a willingness to lay down one's life for another. We can use the relationship between Christ and the Church to see how man and woman should relate to each other. The best advice that I ever heard about marriage came from Dr. John Bisagno, author of *Love is Something You Do*. He was a guest speaker at the church that he formerly pastured called First Baptist Church of Houston. He preached a sermon called "Marriage Deception" in 2010 and he offered the best wisdom that I have heard about marriage and relationships. It was as if he summarized everything that God had taught me over the last five years after my divorce. He introduced me to an even deeper understanding of how Christ's relationship with the church parallels our relationship with our spouse. Dr. Bisagno had noticed that after six months to 2 years almost every couple who came in for counseling had the same complaint: they would say some variation of "it is just not the same, I do not love him/her like a used to love them." This was the same complaint that my ex-husband and I had towards each other. This wise minister began to realize that every marriage reaches a point in which the infatuation and "being in love" wears off and the couple feels cheated. He discovered that the best part of marriage could actually be after the infatuation wears off. Once the feeling of infatuation is gone, we can transition from being in love to actually loving another human being. He began searching for a remedy for the problem of marriages turning dull and loveless over time. He found the cure in the most unlikely place: the Book of Revelation. Since his discovery, he has counseled hundreds of couples who claimed that they had lost their passion and love for their mate. He claims to have a 100% cure rate when couples use the principles in the book of Revelation to heal their marriages [4].

According to Dr. John Bisagno, The Church of Ephesus had the same heart condition towards Jesus that many married people have towards their mate: they had lost their passion and zeal towards Christ just like many of us lose our passion and zeal towards our marriage partner. The same cure prescribed by Jesus to the Church of Ephesus can be used to heal this heart condition in marriage. Jesus told this church the following: "You have forsaken your first love. **Remember** the height from which you have fallen! **Repent** and **do the things you did at first**." (Revelation 2:4-5, NIV). The first thing to do is to **REMEMBER** how the relationship was at first. Talk about old times and the fun you used to have when the love was new and fresh. Remember how you used to treat your mate and go back to treating your mate with the same degree of respect. Thinking about the good times will always make the bad times seem less important. The next step is to **REPENT** or ask forgiveness of each other for falling short in the relationship. If this is difficult read what Jesus said happens to you when you refuse to forgive in Matthew 18. The marriage partner should be first on the list of priorities. Many women mistakenly put their family or children ahead of their spouse. Many men often put work ahead of the family. However, scripture shows us that "a man [shall] leave father and mother, and shall be joined unto his wife, and the two shall be one flesh." (Ephesians 5:31, KJV) We also have to repent before God because God is love and when we find ourselves lacking love for others, it is a clear indication that we have not been spending enough time with God or honoring him. The last thing is to **DO** the things that you did at first. Relationships grow stale when people stop dating and enjoying each other. It is so easy to get caught in a boring routine. A vacation or a date night is the perfect cure for a boring relationship. Dating rituals are designed to create excitement. Couples who neglect them often grow bored with each other. One thing that Dr. Bisagno pointed out was that doing kind things for others often leads to feelings of love and kindness towards that person. When we feel unloving, we should handle that by doing something loving. The feelings of love will always return after we have acted lovingly. Few people realize that treating someone like they are special will usually cause the person to become more special in their heart. This will also make the person feel more special and bring out the best in that person. Most people wait for the feeling to come before acting; however, often the feelings come only after the action has been taken [5].

Marriage is the most sacred union mentioned in the bible. Strong marriages result in strong families. Strong families result in strong communities. Strong communities result in a strong nation. When marriages fail, the community begins to fail and eventually the nation will fail. God has a divine order and wisdom that must be followed. Everything that we need to know about marriage and relationships is found in God's Word. We proudly and foolishly consult talk show hosts, the local psychologist or our best friend to get wisdom about marriage and relationships and then wonder why things are not working yet. God knows more than any of us about marriage and relationships because he created these things. We should consult the top expert about our relationships and use the top expert's manual called the Holy Bible for our guidance.

CHAPTER 12

Is Living Together
the Same as Marriage?-Just Asking

In our post-modern anything goes society, most people view living together—better known as shacking—as the same as marriage. I will never forget the Michael Baisden facebook question asking if shacking up is a good idea. It was amazing to see how many people responded that it is a good idea or that grown folks should be able to do whatever they want to do. Some of the responses included:

"Shacking is worth it. It is just like buying a car-you test drive it and kick the tires before you buy it." Wanda

"Definitely shack it up. Just because you love someone doesn't mean you can stand to live with them, especially if you are thinking about getting married." Clarissa

One lady even mentioned that shacking is better because it is less paperwork [1].

The statements by the bloggers were statements that I used to believe as well. I used to think that shacking was similar to marriage and that it was no big deal. Once I read the chapter of shacking up in John Bisagno's *Love is Something You Do* I was shocked and disturbed by how harmful this living arrangement is to both women and children. I really felt the need to share what I learned about shacking with the Baisden facebook community. I shared some of the statistics from Dr. Bisagno's book and that fell on deaf ears. Several others tried to point out the drawbacks about shacking as well; however, it was met with great resistance by those who felt that each person is entitled to create their own value system. The "create your own value system" answer could be summarized by a comment by a blogger named Jamie:

Do whatever makes you happy . . . I don't understand some of yall. Yall trying to act so chaste and holy. Yet still fornicating like the people you trying to condemn . . . just hypocritical. I am not a shacker, but I respect the fact that some people chose to do it. And I despise people who get off on trying to run other grown people's lives . . . Get one of your own and you wouldn't have to worry about who is living together or not . . . what works for some may not work for others.—Jamie

Many cheered Jamie for her chastisement of me and the other so-called "self-righteous hypocrites" who were against shacking. However, I came back at them with the following truth that silenced the pro-shacking crowd:

Jamie, we are our brother's keeper. If you see someone trying to jump off a cliff, you would try to save them, right. Right now we have a society with a lot of bad information. Some people have not heard the truth in years. We see the impact of this misinformation in the lives of our children. We live in a culture with the attitude "Do what you want to do". Before Rome fell, they had that attitude. Before Hitler came to power, Weimar Republic, Germany was filled with people with such an attitude. Great thinkers like C.S. Lewis in **The Abolition of Man** and Allan Bloom in **The Closing of the American Mind** put forth eloquent proofs that when a society embraces the doctrine of "I do my thing, while you do your thing", it is sure to fall or become a Totalitarian State. With freedom comes responsibility. If a citizenry cannot be morally responsible, at some point it will also cease to be free. The family is the basic institution of society. Strong families lead to strong communities and a strong nation. Weak families lead to easy occupation by men with evil motives. None of us are going to be happy with the results of this great social experiment that we are undertaking right now. I only wish to tell the truth in love. It is up to you as a grown person to accept or reject that truth . . . .

After the facebook shacking debate, I decided to research this topic and found some really interesting facts. Robert Sider, M.D. posted the following grim statistics on divorceforum. org:

- A woman is twice as likely to be assaulted by her live-in boyfriend versus a husband

- A British study showed that child abuse is 20 times more likely to occur in a cohabitation arrangement verses a marriage.

- A Canadian study showed that 1 in 5 women living with her boyfriend is assaulted each year.

Robert Sider concluded that much of the statistics on violence for women and children were due to cohabitation arrangements. [2] Some social workers say that the most dangerous living arrangement for a child is with a man that is not the biological Father. A writer for USA Today put it quite eloquently:

Many scholars and front-line caseworkers who monitor America's families see the abusive-boyfriend syndrome as part of a worrisome trend. These experts and observers note an ever-increasing share of America's children grow up in homes without both biological parents, and say the risk of child abuse is markedly higher in the non-traditional family structures. "This is the dark underbelly of cohabitation," said Brad Wilcox, a sociology professor at the University of Virginia. "Cohabitation has become quite common, and most people think, 'What's the harm?' The harm is we're increasing a pattern of relationships that's not good for children." [3]

The latest studies on cohabitation and income show some interesting findings. The median household income of those living together is significantly less than that for married couples for those without a college education-$56, 800 versus $46,540 [4]. For those with a college education, it is the same or slightly higher than the income for those married. This should not be a cause for celebration because cohabitation is a fundamentally unstable arrangement and many cohabitants are single again after ten years. I found a blog that gave a profound insight into the reason that living together does not equal marriage and tends to be an unstable way to live. According to the blog by Erin Roach of Baptist Press:

In comparing the longevity of marriage versus cohabiting, researchers found that about two-thirds of first marriages lasted 10 years or more, while only about one-fourth of men's and one-third of women's first cohabitations were estimated to last three years without either disrupting or transitioning to marriage. Albert Mohler Jr., in commentary on the subject March 2, said many young adults tend to believe they are wise to try living together before committing to marriage, but actually they are undermining the institution they hope to protect. [Mohler said], "They do not know that what they are actually doing is undoing marriage. They miss the central logic of marriage as an institution of permanence," Mohler, president of Southern Baptist Theological Seminary, said. "They miss the essential wisdom of marriage—that the commitment must come before the intimacy that the vows must come before the shared living, that the wisdom of marriage is its permanence before its experience. "Cohabitation weakens marriage—even a cohabiting couple's eventual marriage—because a temporary and transitory commitment always weakens a permanent commitment. Having lived together with the open possibility of parting, that possibility always remains, and never leaves," Mohler wrote at albertmohler.com. [5].

Mohler's insight that shacking is the experience of marriage without the permanence of marriage is profound. Shackers do not realize that the permanence of marriage is what makes it so special. It is nice to know that you have a life partner that will be by your side through thick and thin. It is wonderful to know that when you go to the hospital, there is someone camped out in the waiting room hoping and praying that you make it. It feels good to know that someone vowed to be by your side "in sickness and in health." It is nice to know that when you lose your job, your marriage partner vowed to be right there consoling you because they vowed to do this "for richer or for poorer." Marriage makes life's tough events like the loss of a parent easier to endure. It is comforting to know that there is someone by your side trying to make you feel better who wants the best for you. There is intimacy in marriage because two people have agreed to become one body. There is a feeling of freedom to express emotions because the other marriage partner agreed to be there in good times and bad. One feels that he or she can relax about being perfect and tell their partner about how they really feel because both parties made the vow, "Until death do us part."

When people live together they have one foot in the door and one foot out the door. A lot of people call "living together" a trial marriage partially because the relationship is always on trial. This lack of commitment creates both fear and anxiety. Each person in the arrangement is slightly fearful that the other person will leave at any time and this lack of stability causes anxiety instead of contentment. It is as if those who live together are constantly auditioning for marriage. This feeling of insecurity causes those who live together to be less inclined to watch out for the partner's health and well-being and less inclined to even be faithful. Since each person has it at the back of their mind that they are not really fully committed, cheating is a viable option. The lack of commitment also makes each party more guarded about sharing things. Why should you share your most intimate secrets with someone who may not be in your life within a few years?

We think that keeping our options open is beneficial to us without realizing that without commitment, there can be no real contentment. This was the main reason that I agreed to divorce my husband and became happier after the divorce. Towards the end of our marriage, my husband said that he wanted to test and see if we could make our marriage work. He gave me a list of demands and the moment I stepped out of line, he would start talking about divorce again. At that point he was already cheating and he was probably just looking for an excuse to leave. The months that my husband decided to turn our marriage into a trial marriage were truly the most miserable months of my entire life. I was constantly walking on egg shells, scared to say the wrong thing and afraid to just relax and be myself. I was doing the best I could but I was quickly getting burned out. I was so unhappy and felt so much anxiety about the future. About 3 days before actually beginning the divorce process I was so tired of working to make the marriage survive that I said to myself- "Lord anything beats this marriage, I am simply mentally and physically drained." That same night, my husband suggested that I quit my job and have a baby. Since I was scared to death of his lack of commitment towards me, I told him that I would think about it. Just a few days later, he showed me that I was right to hesitate about quitting my job. It was December 19, 2003 and I had just gotten off from work. I called my husband and asked what he wanted me to bring his son for Christmas. He said, "Don't buy him anything." I then asked, "What do you really want for Christmas?" He answered, "Don't buy me anything." I said, "Why are you saying these things?" He answered, "I don't love you anymore and I definitely want a divorce." I was mortified and felt so stupid for trying so hard those previous months. However, at the same time, the Holy Spirit kept telling me that this was for the best. I called my mom and cried over the phone for hours. After the good cry, I immediately began working on the divorce papers. I felt a peace for the first time in months. It was definitely time for the marriage to end because it had really been over for months anyway.

My marriage had become a marriage of works instead of a marriage based on grace. I was trying to work to earn my husband's love when my husband's love should have been the unconditional foundation for our marriage. The marriage had actually ended once my husband started cheating and decided to turn our relationship into a trial arrangement. A real marriage starts with commitment and the vow that we are going to make it work no matter what. My parents have been married for over 45 years and not every year was good. However, divorce was never an option for them and they managed to go through the ups and downs of life knowing that they needed to honor their commitment. People who see only darkness must realize that the light will come soon. They should just wait. There is no relationship so broken that God cannot repair it. The problem comes when both parties are not surrendered to God. If the husband hears from God and the wife hears from her husband and God, the bond should be unbreakable. The only thing that could break it is soul ties with another person. According to Jesus, the only excuse for dissolving a marriage is infidelity. Paul allows the additional reason of the unbelieving spouse leaving the home because the unbelieving spouse does not have the Spirit of God living in him.

Trust, intimacy, and love are impossible in a trial situation. A trial marriage is like a trial relationship with God. When I first got saved, I tried to earn my way to heaven. The harder I would try, the further I would get from the mark. After months of frustration, Jesus had to orchestrate a set of circumstances to show me that he saved me by grace and no effort on my part could do the job. A marriage should be based on grace in the same way that our relationship with Jesus Christ is based on grace. Marriage is a covenant that is for better or for worst, for richer or for poorer and lasts until one party dies. We deserve to have a man who loves us like Christ loves the church-so much that he would be willing to die for us. We are in a good marriage when we are in the habit of overlooking each other's faults while trying to bring out the best in each other. No one should feel like we are just shacking; we should feel like we are going to be there for each other no matter what happens. This is the relationship that we have with Jesus Christ and this is the way that we should expect for any future marriage to be.

We must commit first, and then positive experiences can flow out of that commitment. To get a better understanding of why experience before permanence is a bad idea, we can look at our own salvation with Christ. Did we get an intimate relationship with Jesus Christ before or after surrendering our life to him? It was afterwards. The surrender comes first, and then the benefits of the surrender emerge. As C.S. Lewis declared, we are "surprised by joy" after we made our commitment to Christ. We are the bride and Jesus is our groom. Imagine how Jesus would feel if each of us said, "Look, I am not too sure about this Christian thing. I will go to church from time to time. I will read the bible when I feel like it and I will pray whenever things go bad in my life. Just in case you don't come through, I will be open to trying the Hindu Gods or I will simply pray to my African Ancestors. If you don't give me what I want, then I am going to sin like crazy because you did not do what I told you to do." It is unfortunate that this is exactly how many Christian live before Christ. Many of us are just "shacking with Jesus" instead of surrendering our lives to him. He wants to share his secrets with us; but no wise man shares his secrets with someone who is uncommitted and just out for a good time. Jesus wants for us to know him and experience the peace and joy that only he can offer.

Many people shack with Jesus because they fear that Jesus is not going to accept their imperfections. However, Jesus promised that he would never leave or forsake us. Our physical husbands may put us away or die when we least expect it, but our Lord promises to be with us "until the end of time." Jesus is the perfect groom. He loves his bride so much that he was willing to die for her on the cross. Shacking with Jesus may give us temporary comfort, but it can never bring us the joy and peace that comes from being married to Christ. We are missing the comfort felt when we realize that we do not know what will happen tomorrow, but we do know the one who holds tomorrow in his hands and that is enough. We are missing the comfort of knowing the one who said that there would be trouble in the world but we can cheer up because he has overcome the world. When we shack with Jesus, we are missing the comfort of a husband willing to be with us through every trial and disappointment. We lukewarm Christians who shack with Christ think that we have found the best of both worlds, but in reality we are missing the most essential part. We are missing the comfort of an intimate relationship with the one who gave his life for us. We are missing the full knowledge that the things of this world are pale in comparison to the future that awaits us spending eternity with Christ, our true husband. Jesus is the perfect groom who invites all of us who are tired, weary and heavy laden to find rest in him because his yoke is easy and his burden is light.

If you have been shacking with Christ, you can enter the wonderful marriage relationship with him right now. All you have to do is repent and believe the following words with all your heart: "Lord, please forgive me for all of my sins. Thanks for dying on the cross to save me from my sins. Thanks for restoring my relationship with God, the Father. I surrender my entire life to you and I ask that you become the Lord of my life. Thank you for your free gift of eternal life. In the name of Jesus Christ, I pray Amen."

What does the bible say about relationships?

Qualities to Look for in a Good Mate

1. Good Character

"A wife of noble character is her husband's crown, but a disgraceful wife is decay to his bones." Proverbs 12:4, New International Version (NIV)

"There are six things that the Lord hates, seven that are detestable to him:

Haughty eyes (Proud)

A lying tongue (Dishonest)

Hands that shed innocent blood (Murders for gain)

A heart that devises wicked schemes (Conniving)

Feet that are quick to rush to evil (Always looking for trouble)

A false witness who pours out lies and a man who stirs up dissension among brothers (Someone who lies on others and causes fights).

Proverbs 6:16-19, NIV

"Who can find a virtuous woman? Her price is far above rubies. The heart of her husband [can] safely trust her, so that he [has] no need of spoil. She will do him good and not evil all the days of her life." Proverbs 31:10-12, King James Version (KJV)

2. Wise and God-fearing

"The fear of the Lord is the beginning of knowledge; but fools despise wisdom and instruction. My son, hear the instruction of thy father and forsake not the law of thy mother. For they shall be an ornament of grace unto thy head . . . if sinners entice thee, consent not."

Proverbs 1:7-10, KJV

"Happy is the man that [finds] wisdom and the man that [gets] understanding. For the merchandise of it is better than the merchandise of silver, and the gain [from it is better] than fine gold. [Wisdom] is better than rubies and all the things thou canst desire are not to be compared to her. Length of days is in her right hand; and in her left hand riches and honor. Her ways are ways of pleasantness and all her paths are peace."

(Proverbs 3: 13-17, KJV)

"Charm is deceptive and beauty is fleeting; but a woman who fears the Lord is to be praised."

(Proverbs 31:30, NIV)

"When pride comes, then comes disgrace, but with humility comes wisdom."

(Proverbs 11:2, NIV)

3. Peaceful

"Better to live on a corner of the roof than share a house with a quarrelsome wife."

(Proverbs 21:9, NIV)

"A quarrelsome wife is like a constant dripping." (Proverbs 19:13, NIV)

"Better a dry crust with peace and quiet than a house full of feasting with strife."

(Proverbs 17:1, NIV)

"He that covers an [offence seeks] love; but he that [repeats] a matter [separates] friends."

(Proverbs 17:9, KJV)

"Starting a quarrel is like breaching a dam; so drop the matter before a dispute breaks out."

(Proverbs 17:14, NIV)

4. Hard-working with Vision

"If a man is lazy, the rafters sag; if his hand is idle, the house leaks. (Ecclesiastes 10:18, NIV)

"Love not sleep, lest thou come to poverty" (Proverbs 20:13, KJV)

Four Main Rules When Dating

- **Let no man or pursuit of a man become an idol that takes the place of God as first place in your life.**

"I am the Lord thy God . . . [you shall] have no other gods before me . . . Thou shalt not bow down to [idols] nor serve them" (Exodus 20: 2-5, KJV).

"Thou shalt love the Lord thy God with all thy heart, and with all thy soul and with [thy entire] mind. This is the first and the great commandment. And the second is like unto it; [thou] shall love thy neighbor as thyself." (Matthew 22:37-39, KJV)

"Seek ye first the kingdom of God and his righteousness, and all of these things shall be added unto you." (Matthew 6:33, KJV)

"Delight [yourself] in the Lord and he shall give thee the desires of your heart. Commit thy way unto the Lord; trust in him and he shall bring it to pass." (Psalm 37:4-5, KJV)

"Christ is all and in all." (Colossians 3:11, KJV)

- **Treat others the way that you want to be treated-with kindness, mercy and unselfishness.**

"Fulfill my joy, be like-minded, having the same love, being of one accord, one mind. Let nothing be done through strife; but in lowliness of mind let each esteem others better than themselves. Look not every man on his own things, but also on the things of others."

(Philippians 2:2-4, KJV)

"I have become all things to all men, so that by all possible means I might save some."

(1 Corinthians 9:22, NIV)

"Put away lying, [let every man] speak truth with his neighbor: for we are members of one another. Be angry and sin not: [do] not let the sun go down upon your wrath: Neither give place to the devil. Let him that stole, steal no more: rather let him labor, working with his hands . . . Let no corrupt communication proceed out of your mouth, but [speak] that which is good to the use of edifying, that it may minister grace unto the hearers. And grieve not the Holy Spirit . . . Let all bitterness, and wrath, and anger and clamor, and evil speaking, be put away from you, with all malice: And be kind to one another, tenderhearted, forgiving one another, even as God for Christ's sake has forgiven you."

(Ephesians 4:25-32, KJV)

- **Do not get serious about a mate unless the mate is serious about God.**

  "Be not unequally yoked with unbelievers: for what fellowship hath righteousness with unrighteousness? And what communion hath light with darkness? And what [relationship] hath Christ with [Satan]? . . . And what agreement hath the temple of God with the temple of idols?"

  (2 Corinthians 6:14-16, KJV)

- **Avoid premarital sex.**

  "Do you not know that your bodies are members of Christ? Shall I then take away the members of Christ and make them the members of a prostitute? May it never be! Or do you not know that the one who joins himself to a prostitute is one body with her? For [God] says, 'The two shall become one flesh.'"

  (1 Corinthians 6:15-16, NASB)

  "Flee fornication. Every sin that a man [commits] is [outside of his] body. He that [fornicates sins] against his own body . . . your body is the temple of the Holy Ghost, which is in you, which [you] have of God, and [you] are not your own . . . . glorify God in your body and in your spirit, which are God's." (1 Corinthians 6:17-20, KJV)

"Therefore consider the members of your earthly body dead to immorality, impurity, passion, evil desire, and greed which amount to idolatry . . . for it is because of these things that the wrath of God will come . . . ." (Colossians 3:5-6, NASB)

"For this is the will of God, your sanctification; that is that you abstain from sexual immorality; that each of you know how to possess his own [body] . . . not in lustful passion . . ."

(1 Thessalonians 4:3-5, NASB)

"But I say unto you, that whosoever looketh on a woman to lust after her hath committed adultery with her already in his heart. And if thy right eye offend thee, pluck it out . . . it is [better] for one of thy [body parts] should perish, and not that the whole body should be cast into hell."

(Matthew 5: 28-29, KJV)

"But fornication and all uncleanliness . . . let it not once be named among you."

(Ephesians 5:3, KJV)

What are acceptable reasons to get married?

- **Marry to fulfill your destiny with a helper that offers companionship, wisdom and love.**

"And the Lord God said, 'It is not good that the man should be alone; I will make a help meet for him.' . . . And the Lord caused a deep sleep to fall upon Adam, and he slept: and took one of his ribs . . . And the rib [was used to make] a woman . . . And Adam said, 'This is now bone of bones, and flesh of my flesh: She shall be called Woman because she was taken out of Man.

"House and riches are the inheritance from fathers: and a prudent wife is from the Lord."

(Proverbs 19:14, KJV)

"Drink from the water of your own [well] never to be shared with others . . . May your fountain be blessed and may you rejoice in the wife of your youth. A loving doe, a graceful dear, may her breast satisfy you always, may you ever be captivated by her love. Why be captivated by an adulteress? Why embrace the bosom of another man's wife? For a man's ways are in full view of the Lord." (Proverbs 5: 15-21, NIV)

"All the believers were one in heart and mind. No one claimed that any of his possessions was his own, but they shared everything they had." (Acts 4:32, NIV)

"Like a lily among thorns is my darling [wife] among the maidens. Like an apple tree among the other trees of the forest is my [husband] among the young men. I delight to sit in his shade, and his fruit is sweet to my taste . . . His banner over me is love . . . for I am faint with love. His left arm is under my head, and his right arm embraces me." (Song of Songs 2: 2-6, NIV)

- **Marry in order to have sex and to avoid sexual sin.**

  "If a man seduces a virgin who is not pledged to be married and sleeps with her, he must pay the bride-price and she shall be his wife." (Exodus 22:16, NIV)

  "It is good for a man not to touch a woman. Nevertheless, to avoid fornication, let every man have his own wife and every woman have her own husband." (1 Corinthians 7:1-2, KJV)

  "I say to the unmarried and to the widows that it is good for them if they remain [single]. But if they do not have self-control, let them marry; for it is better to marry than to burn with passion." (1 Corinthians 7: 8-9, NASB)

- **Marry to provide a stable home for children.**

  "And God blessed them and said unto them be fruitful and multiply." (Genesis 1:28, KJV)

  "So I counsel the younger widows to marry, to have children, to manage their homes and give the enemy no opportunity for slander." (1 Timothy 5:14, NIV)

Rules for a Christian Marriage

- **Have a good sex life and have sex according to your spouse's needs, not just your own.**

"The husband should fulfill his marital duty to his wife and likewise, the wife to her husband. The wife's body does not belong to her alone, but also her husband. In the same way, the husband's body does not belong to him alone, but also to his wife. Do not deprive each other [sexually] except by mutual consent and for a time so that you may devote yourself to prayer."

(1 Corinthians 7:3-7, NIV)

- **Live together in a spirit of generosity and unselfishness.**

"All the believers were one in heart and mind. No one claimed that any of his possessions were his own, but they shared everything they had . . . and much grace was given them all." (Acts 4:32-33, NIV)

"No one should seek his own good, but the good of others." (1 Corinthians 10:24, NIV)

"Therefore shall a man leave his father and mother, and shall cleave unto his wife: and they shall be one flesh." (Genesis 2:24, KJV)

- **The man should love his wife as Christ loved the church and the woman should respect her husband as head of the household.**

"But I would have you know, that the head of every man is Christ; and the head of every woman is the man; and the head of Christ is God." (1 Corinthians 11:3 KJV)

"Wives submit yourselves to your own husbands, as unto the Lord. For the husband is the head of the wife even as Christ is the head of the Church: and he is the savior of the body. Therefore, as the Church is subject to Christ, the wives are subject to their own husbands in everything. Husbands love your own wives, even as Christ loved the Church and gave himself for it: That he might sanctify and cleanse it with the washing of water by the word . . . . So ought men to love their wives as their own bodies. He that loves his wife loves himself. For no man yet ever hated his own flesh, but [nourishes] and [cherishes] it, even as the Lord the church . . . We are members of his body, of his flesh, [and] of his bones. For this cause shall a man leave Father and Mother and shall be joined unto his wife, and they two shall be one flesh." (Ephesians 5: 22-31, KJV)

- **Love and forgive each other.**

"Beloved, if God so loved us, we ought also to love one another . . . If we love one another, God [dwells] in us and his love is perfected in us. (1 John 4:11-12, KJV)

"Put on . . . bowels of mercies, kindness, humbleness of mind, meekness, longsuffering; forbearing one another, if any man has a quarrel against any; even as Christ forgave you, so also do [you forgive others]. And above all of these, put on charity, which is the bond of perfectness. And let the peace of God rule in your hearts . . . and be thankful. Let the word of Christ dwell in you richly in all wisdom: teaching and admonishing one another in psalms and hymns and spiritual songs, singing with grace in your hearts to the Lord. And whatsoever [you] do in word or deed, do all in the name of the Lord Jesus, giving thanks to God and the Father by him.

(Colossians 3: 12-17, KJV)

"Thou shall love thy neighbor as thyself." (Matthew 22: 39, KJV)

"Love is patient. Love is kind. It does not envy, it does not boast, it is not proud. It is not rude, it is not self-seeking, it is not easily angered, and it keeps no record of wrongs. Love does not delight in evil, but rejoices in the truth. It always protects, always trusts, always hopes, and always perseveres. Love never fails. (1 Corinthians 13:4-8)

The Only Valid Reasons to Divorce

- **Divorce is allowed when the non-believing spouse leaves or abandons the home.**

  "If the unbelieving spouse leaves, let him do so. A believing man or woman is not bound in such circumstances." (1 Corinthians 7:15, NIV)

- **Divorce is allowed when adultery has occurred. Since the person committing adultery has joined his body to another during the marriage, the marriage bond broke.**

  "It has been said that anyone who divorces his wife shall give her a certificate of divorce. But I tell you that anyone who divorces his wife, except for marital unfaithfulness, causes her to be an adulterous and anyone who marries the divorced woman commits adultery." (Matthew 5:31-32, NIV)

Raising Children

"Children obey your parents in all things: for this is well-pleasing unto the Lord. Fathers provoke not your children to anger, lest they be discouraged." (Colossians 3: 20-21, KJV)

"Children obey your parents in the Lord, for this is right. 'Honor your Father and Mother' is the first commandment with a promise-that it may go well with you and you may enjoy a long life on earth. Fathers do not exasperate your children; instead bring them up in the training and instruction of the Lord." (Ephesians 6:1-4, NIV)

"Discipline your son, for in that there is hope; do not be a willing party to his death." (Proverbs 19:18, NIV)

""Folly is in the heart of a child, but the rod of discipline will drive it far from him." (Proverbs 22:15, NIV

NOTES

Chapter 1: Learning to Sit Where Others Sit

1. George Barna, foreword, **Rechurched** by Steven Mansfield, (Ventura California, Tyndale House Publishers, Barna Books, 2010) pgs. xii-xiii

2. Thom S. Rainer, **The Unchurched Next Door**, (Grand Rapids, Michigan Zondervan, 2003) pg. 166

3. Rainer, **The Unchurched Next Door**, pg. 167

4. C.S. Lewis, **Mere Christianity**, (New York, New York, Touchstone, Simon and Schuster ed.,1996 original by McMillan, 1943) p. 95

Chapter 2: Moving from Pride to Humility

1. C.S. Lewis, **Mere Christianity**,S. Lewis, **Mere Christianity**, (New York, New York, Touchstone, Simon and Schuster ed.,1996 original was Macmillan in 1943) pg. 109-110

2. Dr. John Gray, **Mars and Venus on a Date**, (New York, New York, Perennial Currents, 1997, 2005) pg.

3. C.S. Lewis, **Mere Christianity**, pg. 114

4. Amy Lee Ball, "*Groundbreaking Research on Self-Esteem*" The Oprah Magazine, January 2008

5. Joseph Cotto, "*Interview with Dr. Twenge: Is Generation Y More Narcissistic than Earlier Generations*", The Washington Times Communities, Sunday September 16, 2012

6. Anton LaVey, *The Satanic Bible*, (New York, New York, Avon Books, 1972), pg. 94

7. Anton LaVey, *The Satanic Bible*, pg. 34

8. Walshe, *Conversations with God*, Book 1, pg. 124, 129

9. Alan Bloom, *The Closing of the American Mind*, Simon and Shuster, a Touchstone Book, New York, New York, 1987

10. Duke Clarke, Press Release WEB, February 16, 2006 for "*The Way of Prosperity: The 7 Stages of the Prosperous Mind*" article titled "Christian Minister's New Book Says that God Wants You to be Selfish and Wealthy" at http://www.prweb.com/releases/2006/02/prweb344717.htm

11. Anton LaVey, *Satanic Bible*, pgs. 47-48

Chapter 3: Sex My Way or God's Way? Which One Works?

1. Paul Kurtz, *Humanist Manifesto I and II*, (Prometheus Books, 1973) pg. 3-13

2. Anton LaVey, *Satanic Bible*, pg. 69

3. Dr. John Bisagno, *Love is Something You Do*,(Brenham, TX, Lucid Books, 2010) pgs.54—55

4. Review by Richard Niolon, PhD of *The Case for Marriage: Why Married People are Happier, Healthier, and Better Off Financially*, by Linda Waite and Maggie Gallagher on PsychePage (psychepage.com) October 23, 2010

5. Karrine Steffans, *The Vixen Manual Corinthian Order*, (New York, New York, Grand Central Publishers, 2009), pg. 15-16

6. Amplified Bible,(Grand Rapids, Mi., Zondervan Publishers, 1987) p. 746

7. C.S. Lewis, *Mere Christianity*, pg. 94

8. Paul Kurtz, *The Humanist Manifestos I and II* (Prometheus Books, 1973) pgs. 3-13

9. Anton LaVey, *The Satanic Bible*, pg. 96

10. Anton LaVey, *The Satanic Bible*, pg. 33

11. LaVey, *The Satanic Bible*, pgs. 50-53

12. Aleister Crowley, *The Book of the Law*, 1904 (Vondel Park Audio Book, 2003)

Chapter 4: Dating in the Age of Bad Information

1. Aleister Crowley, *The Book of the Law*, 1904 (Vondel Park Audio Book, 2003)

2. Pastor Terrence Johnson, "Whose Fries are These?" June 27, 2010, higherd.net

3. David Kinnaman and Gabe Lyons, *UnChristian*, pg. 48

4. David Kinnaman and Gabe Lyons, *UnChristian*, pg. 53

5. C.S. Lewis, *The Screwtape Letters*, (New York, New York, Harper Collins Books, 1987) pg.208

6. Timothy Keller, *Counterfeit Gods*, (New York, New York, Penguin Group, 2009) p 31

7. Donna Freitas, *Sex and the Soul* (Oxford University Press, 2008) pg. 155

8. Anton LaVey, *The Satanic Bible*, pg. 53

Chapter 5: Facing the Problem-The Christian Dating Hall of Shame

1. Jennifer Riley, "*Survey: Less than 1% of Young Adults Hold Biblical Worldview*" Christian Post, March 10, 2009

2. Michael Remez and others, "*Many Americans Mix Multiple Faiths*", PEW Research Center. December 9, 2009

Chapter 6: A Deeper Understanding of the Christian Dating Myths

1. Elysse Barrett, "Five Reasons My Generation is Not Getting Married and What Can Be Done about It"., American Vision, June 23, 2010

2. Dr. John Gray, **Mars and Venus on a Date**, (New York, New York, Perennial Currents, 1997, 2005), pgs. 305-307

3. Dr. Henry Cloud, *How to Get a Date Worth Keeping*, (Grand Rapids, Michigan, Zondervan, 2005) pg. 15-17

4. Jenna Turton, "Relationships Part One: What Happens When We Kissed Dating Goodbye", examiner.com, December 10, 2010

5. Kathy Lee Grossman, "Young adults aren't sticking with the church" *USA Today*, based on research by LifeWay August 7, 2007

6. Jimmy DeYoung, "Survey: Less than 10% of all Born-Again Christians Look at the World with a Biblical Worldview", *Standing for God*, www.standingforgod.com, August 14, 2010

7. Cathy Lynn Grossman, "Survey: 72% of millennial 'more spiritual than religious'", *USA Today*, October 14, 2010

8. Audrey Barrick, "Survey: Most Young People are Lost Despite Christian Label", April 27, 2010, Christianpost.com wisegeek.com "How has the average age of marriage changed over time?

Chapter 7: The Danger of Making Men Our Idols

1. C.S. Lewis, *Mere Christianity*,(New York, New York, Simon and Schuster, Touchstone 1996, *original by McMillan in 1943*), pg. 111

2. Tim LaHaye and Ed Hindson, *Seduction of the Heart*, (Colorado Springs, Colorado W Publishing Group, 2001) pg. 83

Chapter 8: Finding Success Dating God's Way

1. Deborrah Cooper, survivingdating.com "The Black Church: How Black Churches Keep African-American Women Single and Lonely" June 14, 2010

2. C.S. Lewis, *Mere Christianity*, pg. 178

Chapter 9: Picking the Right Person

1. Steve Harvey, *Act Like a Lady, Think Like a Man*, (New York, New York, Harper Collins Publishers, 2009) pgs. 21-25, 31

Chapter 10: Three Secrets for Being the Best Catch When Men go Fishing

1. C.D. Mohatta Article Source: http://EzineArticles.com/202497, "Quiz for men: Do You Know What Women Prefer—looks or money?" May 21, 2006

2. Michael Baisden, What are men's Deal breakers?, Baisden Live on Facebook, July 2011

3. Darryl James, "The Bridge, Independent Women", *Black in LA*, http://www.blacknla.com/news/Articles/DJIndependent.asp

4. Miss understood, Yahoo Associated Content Contributor, July 10, 2007, "Black Skin + Independent Woman =No Husband" http://www.associatedcontent.com/article/296183/black_skin_independent_woman_no_husband.html?cat=41 eHarmony Staff, "5 Dating Dealbreakers for Men" eHarmony Advice http://advice.eharmony.com/dating/date-tips/5-dating-deal-breakers-for-men?view=article/5-dating-deal-breakers-for-men.html

Chapter 11: Marriage-The Building Block of Society

1. Paula Whidden, www.faithfulchoices.com, "Outrageous Statistics on Christian Marriage"

2. Gregg Matte, I Am Changes Who I Am, Regal Publishers, Ventura, CA 2012, pg. 98

3. C.S. Lewis, *Mere Christianity*,(New York, New York, Simon and Schuster, Touchstone 1996, *original by McMillan in 1943*) pg. 108

4. Dr. John Bisagno, "Marriage Deception" from the Isaac Series, Houston First Baptist Church, April 25, 2010

5. Dr. John Bisagno, *Love is Something that You Do*, (Brenham, TX Lucid Books, 2010) pgs. 17-24.

Chapter 12: Is Living Together the Same as Marriage?-Just Asking

1. http//www.facebook.com/#!michaelbaisdenlive Question: "To shack or not to shack? Why buy the cow when you can get the milk free?" July 13, 2011 1:48pm Tweetdeck

2. Robert Sider, MD, "Living Together Risky for Young Women and Children", Grand Rapids Press. January 28, 1999, http://www.divorcereform.org/mel/adomesticviolence.html

3. David Crary, Associated Press, "Abuse more a risk in nontraditional families" *USA Today,* November 17, 2007

4. Richard Fry and D'Vera Cohn, "Living Together: The Economics of Cohabitation" PEW Research Center Publications, Washington, DC June 27, 2011

5. Erin Roach, Cohabiting Normative but Harmful, crosswalk.com, Saturday April 30, 2011, Original Baptist Press, posted March 13, 2010

Bibles Used for the Book

KEY INSIGHTS JOURNAL

Date: _____

Speaker: _____

Insights:

_____
_____
_____
_____
_____
_____
_____
_____
_____
_____

How can I apply what I have learned?

_____
_____
_____
_____
_____

Scriptures Concerning Insight:

_____
_____
_____
_____
_____

LESSONS LEARNED JOURNAL

Problem/Mistake	Lesson Learned

BOOKMARKS TO REMIND US OF THE TRUTH

We are precious daughters of the Most High King. He is King of Kings and Lord of Lords. He can do all things. He can fix all problems. He can change any situation. Our Heavenly Father loves us.

But seek ye first the kingdom of God and his righteousness; and all these things shall be added unto you.

Matthew 6:33, KJV

We are mighty men of honor and integrity. We are sons of the Most High King. Jesus is the King of Kings and Lord of Lords. As we seek his wisdom and direction, we receive the love and strength to be great leaders of our families and our communities.

And he hath on his vesture a name written, KING OF KINGS, AND LORD OF LORDS.

Revelation 18:16, KJV